Lecture Notes in Computer Science 4821

Commenced Publication in 1973
Founding and Former Series Editors:
Gerhard Goos, Juris Hartmanis, and Jan van Leeuwen

Editorial Board

Jens Bennedsen   Michael E. Caspersen
Michael Kölling (Eds.)

Reflections on the Teaching of Programming

Methods and Implementations

 Springer

Volume Editors

Jens Bennedsen
IT University West
Fuglsangs Allé 20, 8210 Aarhus V, Denmark
E-mail: jbb@it-vest.dk

Michael E. Caspersen
University of Aarhus, Department of Computer Science
Aabogade 34, 8200 Aarhus N, Denmark
E-mail: mec@daimi.au.dk

Michael Kölling
University of Kent, Computing Laboratory
Canterbury, Kent CT2 7NF, UK
E-mail: mik@kent.ac.uk

Library of Congress Control Number: 2008925133

CR Subject Classification (1998): K.3, K.4, D.2, J.1

LNCS Sublibrary: SL 2 – Programming and Software Engineering

ISSN   0302-9743
ISBN   3-540-77933-7 Springer Berlin Heidelberg New York
ISBN   978-3-540-77933-9 Springer Berlin Heidelberg New York

Springer is a part of Springer Science+Business Media

springer.com

© Springer-Verlag Berlin Heidelberg 2008

Typesetting: Camera-ready by author, data conversion by Scientific Publishing Services, Chennai, India
Printed on acid-free paper   SPIN: 12224616   06/3180   5 4 3 2 1 0

Foreword

For 50 years, we have been teaching programming. In that time, we have seen momentous changes. From teaching a first course using an assembly language or Fortran I to using sophisticated functional and OO programming languages. From computers touched only by professional operators to computers that children play with. From input on paper tape and punch cards, with hour-long waits for output from computer runs, to instant keyboard input and instant compilation and execution. From debugging programs using pages-long octal dumps of memory to sophisticated debugging systems embedded in IDEs. From small, toy assignments to ones that inspire because of the ability to include GUIs and other supporting software. From little knowledge or few theories of the programming process to structured programming, stepwise refinement, formal development methodologies based on theories of correctness, and software engineering principles.

And yet, teaching programming still seems to be a black art. There is no consensus on what the programming process is, much less on how it should be taught. We do not do well on teaching testing and debugging. We have debates not only on whether to teach OO first but on whether it *can* be taught first. This muddled situation manifests itself in several ways. Retention is often a problem. Our colleagues in other disciplines expect students to be able to program almost anything after a course or two, and many complain that this does not happen. In some sense, we are still floundering, just as we were 50 years ago.

Part of the problem may be that we are not sure what we are teaching. Are we simply providing knowledge, or are we attempting to impart a skill? Many introductory texts are oriented at teaching *programs* rather than *programming*— they contain little material on the programming process and on problem solving. And, judging from introductory texts, there is little consensus on how and when to specify program parts, how to document variables, how to teach algorithmic development, etc.

Another part of the problem may be that programming is indeed a difficult mixture of art and science—difficult to do and more difficult to teach. Yet another part of the problem may be that we have not discovered enough about programming and about teaching it. We need more research, experimentation, assessment, discussion, and debate.

In this context, this book, *Reflections on the Teaching of Programming*, is a welcome—and much needed—addition to our knowledge of programming and its teaching. Written by Scandinavian researchers and practitioners in computer science education, this book brings together a nice collection of articles on programming education, providing food for thought for anyone involved in the field, with articles that are, for the most part, based on proven implementation and real experience.

Learn about pedagogical experiments in using online tutorials, apprentice-based learning, the programming process, and problem-based learning. Delve into some issues of teaching OO. Look at software engineering issues in later courses. And read two chapters that deal with how we assess the work of students—a topic that has just begun to be explored.

You may not like, agree with, or believe everything you read—if you did, the book would be too "safe" and not provocative enough. But the book is clearly written by professionals who have thought deeply about and care about teaching programming, and we can all learn from it.

Perhaps, even, this book will be a catalyst for a renewed effort by our field to debate and do research on the teaching of programming, with teachers and researchers and textbook authors working together. Perhaps it will inspire us to incorporate research on pedagogy into our work, to learn how to assess our own teaching methods, and to think more deeply about the skill of programming and how it can be taught. Goodness knows, we need all this.

So, members of the SPoP network—the Scandinavian Pedagogy of Programming Network—thanks for developing this wonderful book. I have benefited greatly from reading it in draft form, and now the computing community will get the chance to benefit too.

February 2008   David Gries

Preface

The book you are holding is the result of the cooperation of a number of computing educators passionate about programming and teaching and is aimed at programming education practitioners in secondary and tertiary education and at computing education researchers.

The book is written by a group of primarily Scandinavian researchers and educators with special interest and experience in programming education. There are contributions from 24 authors about practical experience gathered in the process of teaching programming —for most of the authors for the past 15–20 years.

The reports are practically oriented. While several experiences described are associated with computing education research work, the emphasis here is on practical advice and concrete suggestions. It is expected that readers can get ideas for the teaching of programming that are directly applicable to the implementation of their own programming courses.

Care has been taken to select work for inclusion in this book that is not speculative, but based on proven implementation and real experience. The topics span a wide range of problems and solutions associated with the teaching of programming.

Part I consists of five chapters addressing issues related to introductory programming courses. The primary issues covered in this part are exposition of the programming process, apprentice-based learning, functional programming first, problem-based learning, and the use of on-line tutorials.

Part II consists of four chapters that specifically address issues related to introductory courses on object-oriented programming —the currently most prevailing approach to introductory programming. The primary issues covered are transitioning to object-oriented programming and Java, the use of the BlueJ environment to introduce programming, the use of model-driven programming as opposed to the prevailing language-driven approach, and the particular challenge of how to organize the first couple of weeks of an introductory course.

Part III consists of three chapters that address the more general challenge of teaching software engineering. The primary issues covered in this part are testing, extreme programming, and frameworks. These are all issues that are typically covered in later courses.

Part IV, the last part of the book, consists of two chapters addressing innovative approaches to feedback and assessment. The primary issues covered are active learning, technology-based individual feedback, and mini project programming exams.

It is expected that the topic areas covered will be of interest to a wide range of programming educators.

The authors have substantial experience in teaching programming, as well as a substantial body of publications in the computer science education literature.

The authors are members of the *Scandinavian Pedagogy of Programming Network*, and bring together a diverse body of experiences from the Nordic European countries. The 14 chapters of the book broadly describe experiences from their varying backgrounds, but are carefully written and edited to present coherent units, not just individual, independent papers. Although the experiences described were gathered largely in Scandinavian countries, the book should be of equal interest to programming educators throughout the world.

February 2008   Jens Bennedsen
                                                                     Michael E. Caspersen
                                                                        Michael Kölling

Table of Contents

III   Teaching Software Engineering Issues

IV   Assessment

V   Appendix

Part I

Issues in Introductory Programming Courses

Introduction to Part I
Issues in Introductory Programming Courses

Learning to program is notoriously difficult. Since the early 1970s, teaching programming to novices has been considered a big challenge and —according to the number of people attending conferences on programming— it still seems to be [Dijkstra, 1969; Gries, 1974; McCracken et al., 2001; Robins et al., 2003; Soloway and Spohrer, 1988; Wegner et al.,1996]. Indeed, it is considered one of seven grand challenges in computing education [Mcgettrick et al., 2005]. Teaching introductory programming at university level has been the basis for many lively discussions among computer science teachers [Astrachan et al., 2005; Bailie et al., 2003; Bruce, 2005; SIGCSE-members, 2005], and for a substantial number of articles (e.g., searching "CS1" at ACM's digital library gives 1402 hits and searching "introductory programming" gives 62,654 —[search done December 20, 2007]). More official approaches to the design of computing curricula have also been taken —the most well know and influential being the series of curricula recommendations made by the ACM (American Association for the Computing Machinery) and IEEE (Institute of Electrical and Electronics Engineers, Inc).

Today Information Technology (IT) is embedded in everything. IT has a dominant position in the economy of the world. Therefore, the declining number of students enrolling in computer science programmes has become an issue in the political debate [Denning, 2004]. This problem is made worse by the relatively low retention rate within computer science education [Kumar, 2003]. These two problems stress the importance of describing and using good practice when tackling the challenges and pitfalls in computer science education.

One of the first courses students encounter when learning computer science or related fields (e.g., multimedia and information science) is an introductory programming course. CC2001 conclude that "the programming-first model is likely to remain dominant for the foreseeable future" [Engel and Roberts, 2001, p.24]. This gives an extra incitement to focus on the problems related to introductory programming courses commonly known as CS1 courses.

This chapter has exactly this focus. It addresses typical problems and challenges in teaching introductory programming at the university level.

Programming is a process and therefore it is important that the students are exposed to the different activities in programming and their interconnections. This is the message of Bennedsen and Caspersen in *Exposing the Programming Process*. They discuss several ways of showing the programming process to students, including process recordings. Process recordings are easy-to-create videos capturing the on-screen interactions of an expert programmer while she thinks aloud to explain what she is doing. The authors describe several different categories of process recordings they have created and how they have been used in a course context.

Apprenticeship learning has become more popular in the last 10 to 20 years. In their pioneering work, [Lave and Wenger, 1991] described how different people in

J. Bennedsen et al. (Eds.): Teaching of Programming, LNCS 4821, pp. 3–5, 2008.

different professions learn by observing and studying a master of the profession. In *Apprentice-based Learning via Integrated Lectures and Assignments*, Kölling and Barnes discuss how this pedagogical approach can be used in an introductory programming course. They find that the first activity a student must perform is reading code developed by experts in order to gain insight into its structure and quality. Following reading, the students should modify the code they have studied. The rationale for this is twofold. First, the students have a starting point, thus, circumventing the traditional "not knowing where to start" problem. Secondly, their approach focuses on software engineering principles such as refactoring. Lastly, the students should create something of their own, typically another instantiation of the same problem domain.

Kölling and Barnes suggest that the lectures should change from presenting concepts and ideas to showing an expert in action. In this way, this chapter can be seen as a live example of the ideas presented by Bennedsen and Caspersen in *Exposing the Programming Process*.

Most introductory programming courses are within the object-oriented paradigm. There are other paradigms. For instance, Hansen and Kristensen describe in *Experiences with Functional Programming in an Introductory Curriculum* how the functional paradigm can be taught in the first programming course. They argue that it is important that the students learn general problem solving skills. By using a strongly-typed functional programming language like SML, they describe how students create models of the domain of the application.

Hansen and Kristensen discuss pros and cons of starting with a functional language as opposed to an object-oriented language. They report on their experience with teaching object-orientation on top of a functional programming course and the other way around. Their conclusions are not definite, but they find that students with a background in functional programming find it easier to learn object-orientation afterwards than it is for students with an object-oriented background to learn functional programming.

In medicine, one successful teaching strategy is the use of problem-based, learning cases. Such a case is a description of a real-world problem (e.g., the symptoms of a person). The students start by creating a shared understanding of the case and a definition of their learning resources and goals. This is followed by an independent self-study period. After some time, the students meet again in order to close the case by discussing their understanding. In *Learning Programming with the PBL Method —Experiences on PBL Cases and Tutoring*, Nuutila, Törmä, Kinnunen and Malmi discuss how this pedagogical approach can be used in introductory programming. They give several examples of problem-based learning cases they have used in teaching programming and evaluate these. They discuss the differences between learning medicine and programming and, based on these, identify necessary characteristics of good cases in the field of programming.

In *Using On-line Tutorials in Introductory IT Courses*, Thomsen describes an implementation of a course introducing IT applications and a little programming (a course that are traditionally termed CS0). He describes the transition from a traditional lecture-based course to a course where the students are more responsible for their own learning. The materials used for this transformation are freely available on-line tutorials like Sun's Java tutorial. Thomsen reports on the students' views on the course and discusses reasons why the change has resulted in an increase in the number of students actively following the course.

Jens Bennedsen

Exposing the Programming Process*

Jens Bennedsen[1] and Michael E. Caspersen[2]

[1] IT University West, Denmark
jbb@it-vest.dk
[2] Department of Computer Science, University of Aarhus, Denmark
mec@daimi.au.dk

Abstract. One of the most important goals of an introductory programming course is that the students learn a systematic approach to the
development of computer programs. Revealing the programming process
is an important part of this. However, textbooks do not address the issue —probably because the textbook medium is static and, therefore, ill-
suited to expose the process of programming. We have found that process
recordings in the form of captured, narrated programming sessions are a
simple, cheap, and efficient way of providing the revelation. We identify
seven different elements of the programming process for which process
recordings are a valuable communication media in order to enhance
the learning process. Student feedback indicates both high learning outcome and superior learning potential compared to traditional classroom
teaching.

1 Introduction

An important goal of an introductory programming course is that the students
learn a systematic approach to the development of computer programs. Revealing the programming process is an important part of this, and we have found
that process recordings in the form of screen-captured, narrated programming
sessions are a simple, cheap, and efficient way to provide the revelation. We
hereby expand the applied apprenticeship approach as advocated in the works
of [Astrachan and Reed, 1995] and [Linn and Clancy, 1992].

Revealing the programming process to beginning students is important, but
traditional *static* teaching materials such as textbooks, lecture notes, blackboards or slide presentations, etc., are insufficient for that purpose. They are
useful for the presentation of a product (e.g., a finished program), but not for the
presentation of the *dynamic* process used to create that product. Besides being
insufficient for the presentation of a development process, the use of traditional
materials has another drawback. Typically, they are used for the presentation
of an *ideal* solution that is the result of a non-linear development process. Like

---

* This chapter is based on Bennedsen, J. and Caspersen, M. E. 2005. Revealing the
programming process. In *Proceedings of the 36th SIGCSE Technical Symposium on
Computer Science Education*, St. Louis, Missouri, USA, February 23-27, 2005, pp.
186-190.

J. Bennedsen et al. (Eds.): Teaching of Programming, LNCS 4821, pp. 6–16, 2008.
© Springer-Verlag Berlin Heidelberg 2008

others [Soloway, 1986; Spohrer and Soloway, 1986a,b], we consider this to be problematic. The presentation of the product independently of the development process will inevitably leave the students with the false impression that there *is* a linear and direct "royal road" from problem to solution. This is very far from the truth, but the problem for novices is that when they see their teacher present clean and simple solutions, they think they themselves should be able to develop solutions in a similar way. When they realize they cannot do so, they blame themselves and feel incompetent. Consequently, they will lose self-confidence and, in the worst case, their motivation for learning to program.

Several tools for visualizing programs exist such as Jeliot [Levy et al., 2003] and Alice [Cooper et al., 2000]. These tools focus on visualizing the execution of programs, not the development of programs.

Besides teaching the students about tools and techniques for the development of programs (e.g., a programming language, an integrated development environment also known as IDE or programming techniques), we must also teach them about the development process. This can include the task of using these tools and techniques to develop the solution in a systematic, incremental and typically non-linear way. An important part of this is to expound and to demonstrate that

- many small steps are better than a few large ones
- the result of every little step should be tested
- prior decisions may need to be undone and code refactored
- making errors is common also for experienced programmers
- compiler errors can be misleading/erroneous
- online documentation for class libraries provide valuable information, and
- there is a systematic, however non-linear, way of developing a solution for the problem at hand.

We cannot rely on the students to learn all of this by themselves, but by using an apprenticeship approach we can show them how to do it. For this purpose, we use process recordings.

The chapter is structured as follows: section 2 is a brief introduction to the notion of process recordings. In section 3, we discuss the need for exposition of the programming process (e.g., through process recordings) and why textbooks are ill-suited for this purpose. Section 4 is a more detailed description of process recordings where we identify seven different categories of recordings. In section 5, we discuss the use of process recordings in a course context. Section 6 is a brief discussion of related work, and the conclusions are drawn in section 7.

2   Process Recordings — A Brief Introduction

Written material in general and textbooks in particular are not a suitable medium through which to convey processes. We have used process recordings and captured and narrated programming sessions to do that. The creation of a process recording is easy, fast, and cheap, and does not require special equipment besides a standard computer.

The term *process recording* refers to a screen capture of an expert programmer (e.g. the teacher) solving a concrete programming problem and thinking aloud as she moves along. A process recording can be produced by using a standard computer —there is no need for a special studio or other expensive equipment. The software for capturing is free, and depending on how advanced one needs the post production facilities to be, that software is either free or very cheap. We have used Windows Media Encoder and Windows Media File Editor which are both freeware programs.

We have found that 15 to 20 minutes is an appropriate duration of a process recording, although for some problems, the duration can be longer. For convenience, we offer an index (a topic → time mapping) to help retrieve sections of special interest. The index of each recording is stored in a database allowing the students to search for specific material at a later stage. Figure 1 shows a snapshot of a playback of a process recording.

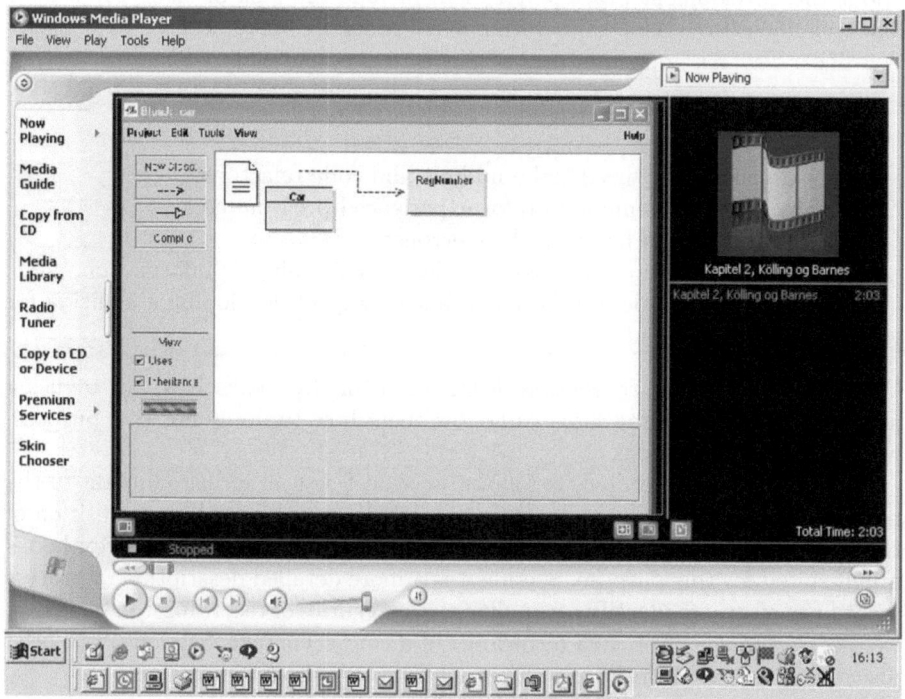

Fig. 1. Playback of process recording

2.1 The Production Process

Most process recordings can be produced without too much preparation. It is our experience that a detailed manuscript is superfluous. Too detailed a manuscript tends to make the process recording less authentic, and in the worst case, plain boring. For a distance education introductory programming courses we have created approximately 60 process recordings. It is our experience that we use one hour to prepare a 30-minute recording and another 20 minutes for post-production.

The technical setup is rather simple. The lecturer sits in front of his or her computer with a microphone. She starts by introducing the problem and after that, talks aloud about the problems encountered and the possible solutions to these problems. Hereby, she makes the programming process explicit —what are the problems, what are the solutions, what are the alternatives...

To increase the motivation for the students, we have used some of their solutions as a starting point. One needs to be careful not to belittle the solution but to show how different techniques can improve an already working solution in order to make it more readable, shorter, and more reusable or whatever the focus is.

To increase usability we make it possible for students to navigate within the process recording. The addition of the topic → time mapping has added a new usage of the material because the students can search the material afterwards and use it as yet another part of their learning material repository. In this way, the value of the lectures has expanded from something that is only useful if you are present, to a material that can be used repeatedly over time.

3   Teaching the Process of Programming

The concern for teaching process and problem solving is not new. For example, [Gries, 1974] wrote:

> Let me make an analogy to make my point clear. Suppose you attend a course in cabinet making. The instructor briefly shows you a saw, a plane, a hammer, and a few other tools, letting you use each one for a few minutes. He next shows you a beautifully-finished cabinet. Finally, he tells you to design and build your own cabinet and bring him the finished product in a few weeks. You would think he was crazy!

Clearly, cabinet making cannot be taught simply by teaching the tools of the trade and by demonstrating finished products. The same applies to teaching programming! Nevertheless, this seems to be what was being attempted thirty years ago when Gries wrote the above analogy, and it seems largely to be the case today.

[du Boulay, 1989] identifies *pragmatics* —the skills of planning, developing, testing, debugging and so on— as an important domain to master. The latter is concerned with skills related to the programming process. However, only few of these are addressed in traditional textbooks on introductory programming.

[Caspersen and Kölling, 2006] describe in detail how a programming process for novices could be described. They focus on five steps:

1. Create the class (with method stubs)

2. Create tests

3. Alternative representations

4. Instance fields

5. Method implementation

6. Method implementation rules (pp. 893-894)

Their focus is on how newcomers can come from a specification of a class (expressed as a UML class diagram) to an implementation fulfilling the specification. In chapter 9, (*Model-driven Programming*) Bennedsen and Caspersen describe a process for implementing a UML class diagram with more classes; focus is particularly on the systematic implementation of relations between classes (e.g. associations).

3.1 Textbooks Neglect the Issue

In 2003, Kölling presented a survey of 39 major-selling textbooks on introductory programming [Kölling, 2003]. The overall conclusion of the survey was that all books are structured according to the language constructs of the programming language, and not by the programming techniques that we (should) teach our students. This is consistent with the findings by [Robins et al., 2003] which state *Typical introductory programming textbooks devote most of their content to presenting knowledge about a particular language* (p. 141). The prevailing textbook approach will help the students to understand the programming language and the structure of programs, but it does not show the student how to program. In short, it does not reveal the programming process.

We know what is needed, so why has the topic not found its way into textbooks on introductory programming? The best answer is that the static textbook medium is unsuitable for this kind of dynamic descriptions.

3.2 New Technology Allows for Changes

Earlier it has been difficult to present actual programming to students. When programs, in the form of finished solutions, were presented to students it was in the form of writings on the blackboard or copies of finished programs (or program fragments) on transparencies for projection.

Programming on a blackboard has the advantage that it is possible to create programs in dialogue with the students at a pace that the students can follow. Also, the teacher and the students can interact during the development of the program. The obvious drawback is that only small programs can be presented, and neither are we able to run and to modify the programs nor be able to demonstrate professional use of the development tool(s) and programming techniques.

Finished programs on transparencies provide a way of presenting larger and more complex programs to the students that we would never consider writing on a blackboard. This approach has the drawback that teachers tend to progress too fast and to exclude the students from taking part in the development.

Thus, the emergence of new technology has made it possible in a simple and straightforward manner to present live programming to students. Live programming can be presented in two different ways: live programming by using a computer and a projector and process recordings showing an expert at work.

Live programming in the lecture theatre by using computer and projector is like a combination of using blackboard and slides. But, it also has the important, additional ability to run and to test the program and to use the programming tools (e.g., IDE, online documentation, diagramming tools). This is much closer to the actual programming process than the first two approaches. However, there are still drawbacks that include limited time in the class room, which restricts the complexity of the examples that are presented. Also, the presentation vanishes as it takes place and nothing is saved afterwards.

Process recordings showing the programming process of an expert are similar to live programming, but without its limitations. In process recordings, you can take the time needed to present as complex an example as you wish, and the presentation can be reviewed over and over as many times as a student needs it.

The first three approaches have in common that they are synchronous, one time events. There is no possibility for the student to go back and review (a step in) the development process if there were something that he or she did not understand. This opportunity is exactly what is added by using process recordings.

4   A Categorization of Process Elements

In this section, we present a more detailed description of the process elements that are exposed through process recordings, and we identify seven different categories that we have found useful in CS1.

A typical programming process encompasses the following process elements:

- Use of an IDE
- Incremental development
- Testing
- Refactoring
- Error handling
- Use of online documentation
- Model-based programming

All are unsuitable for textual descriptions, but important for the student to master. For each process element, we will discuss how to address it in an introductory programming course and how process recordings can be used to reveal its core aspects.

Use of an IDE. We use a simple IDE [Kölling, 1999]. However, a short recording demonstrating the use of special facilities in the IDE makes it still easier for the students to start using it.

Incremental development. Students often try to create a complete solution to a problem before testing it. However, this is not the behaviour that we want the students to exhibit. Instead, we want them to create the solution in an incremental way by taking small steps where they alternate between implementing and testing. Following this advice makes it much easier to find and to correct errors and it simplifies the whole programming activity. This topic is very difficult to communicate in a book. With a process recording, it is simple and straightforward to demonstrate how to behave.

Testing. We promote two simple techniques for testing: interactive testing through the IDE (BlueJ) or the creation of a special class with test methods. The process aspect of the former technique is covered under "Use of the IDE" above (see also [Rosenberg and Kölling, 1997]). A textbook is useful for describing principles and techniques for testing, but the method of integrating testing in the development process is best demonstrated by showing a live programming process.

Refactoring. When the students read a textbook they easily get the impression that programmers never make mistakes, that programmers always create perfect, working solutions in take one, and that programmers, therefore, never have to correct and to improve their programs. [Fowler and Beck, 1999] state that an experienced programmer should expect to use approximately 50% of his or her time refactoring code. If this is the case for an experienced programmer, a novice programmer should expect to use significantly more time refactoring and correcting code. Clearly, students cannot expect to create perfect solutions in their first attempt; it is therefore important not to give them the impression that they should.

We have found it difficult to motivate the need for refactoring to students. The goal of refactoring is to create better programs in the sense of exhibiting lower coupling and higher cohesion. The students, however, do not know when it is advantageous to refactor a program. Instead, they consider the job done when the program can compile and run. However, showing them the refactoring techniques "live" gives them a much better understanding of the techniques and an appreciation of the necessity for refactoring. In order to optimise motivation, we often start out with a students program, showing how refactoring can make that program more readable, and how lower coupling and higher cohesion can be obtained through successive applications of simple standard techniques.

Error handling. In order to make the students feel more comfortable, it is important to show them that every programmer makes errors and that error handling is a part of the process. It is important to show the students how errors are handled. In particular, it is important to demonstrate to the students that the output from the compiler does not always indicate the real error and that there are different types of errors. The process recordings help by being explicit and by dealing systematically with each kind of error.

Online documentation. Modern programming languages are accompanied by large class libraries, which the students need to use. The documentation for Java is available online, and the students have to be acquainted with the documentation and how to use it in order to write programs. When the students write code, we force them to write Javadoc too. In order to teach them how to write and to generate the documentation, we show them how to do this as an integrated part of the development process by using live programming and process recordings.

Model-based programming. We teach a model-driven, objects-first approach as described in *Model-Driven Programming* by Bennedsen and Caspersen. In order to do so, the students need to use more than the traditional programming tools. They also need to use a tool for describing the class models. The students also need to understand the interaction between the IDE and the modelling tool as well as the relation between model and code. To reinforce the importance of modelling as an integrated part of program development, it is vital to show the students the relevant tools.

5 Process Recordings in a Course Context

In this section, we will describe how the process recording materials are used in an introductory object-oriented programming course.

5.1 Categories of Process Recordings

We have created the following five different types of process recordings: introduction to assignments, solutions to the assignments, documentation of synchronous activities (lectures and online meetings), alternative teaching materials, and tool support.

Introduction to assignments. Many students struggle with getting started with an assignment and have questions like the following: what is the problem, how shall I start, what exactly is it that I have to do? Many such questions can efficiently be addressed in a process recording where fragments or the structure of a solution can be presented.

Solutions to assignments. This includes the presentation of a solution to a programming assignment along with aspects of the development process.

Documentation of synchronous activities. By capturing live programming as it takes place, the students will also have the opportunity to review (parts of) the process at a later stage.

Alternative teaching materials. For the core topics in the text, we create small programming problems to illustrate the use and the applicability of the topic. This provides diversity in the course material by supporting different styles of learning.

Tool support. We have created different kinds of process recordings for tool support. Like [Alford, 2003], we have found that, instead of creating written descriptions and manuals for these tasks, it is much easier for us as well as the students if we create a process recording that shows students how to *do* things. It is more effective to explain what one is doing on the screen while capturing it.

5.2   Student Feedback

Recently, we taught two introductory programming courses based on distance education with respectively 35 and 20 students (a detailed description of the design of this course can be found in [Bennedsen and Caspersen, 2003]. For these courses, we made extensive use of process recordings. All of these materials are stored on a web-server and the students can access them whenever they want and from where they want.

We have evaluated the use of process recordings in our introductory programming course. The evaluation was done quantitatively by using a questionnaire as well as qualitatively by interviewing a number of students about their attitude towards the material. From the questionnaire we can see that more than 2/3 of the students have seen more than 50% of the process recordings.

The distribution of hits for the different types of process recordings is as follows: introduction to assignments: 28%, solutions to assignments: 19%, documentation of synchronous activities: 9%, alternative teaching materials: 21%, and tool support: 23%. The interesting thing is that the possibility of reviewing the synchronous activities has by far the smallest hit rate. This indicates the web casting of lectures, which is a widespread use of process recordings [Berkeley, 2007,MIT, 2006], is viewed by the students as the least useful of the five categories.

The students have self-evaluated the learning outcome of the process recordings. The result of the evaluation is as follows: None: 21%, Small: 0%, Ordinary: 21%, High: 14%, and Very high: 44%. 58% has indicated a high or very high learning outcome which is very encouraging. In post-course interviews, the students generally confirmed these findings.

6   Related and Future Work

Streaming video has become more and more popular and common [Ma et al., 1996; Smith et al., 1999]. Compression techniques have been standardized and improved. Also, bandwidth is increasing (also in private homes) making it realistic to use videos in an educational setting.

Web casts of lectures is used by many universities including prominent ones like Berkeley and MIT [Berkeley, 2007; MIT, 2006] While such videos may be valuable to students who are not able to attend the lecture or would like to have (parts of) it repeated, they do not significantly add new value to the teaching material.

The use of process recordings in teaching is not new [Smith et al., 1999]. Process recordings are used extensively in [Gries et al., 2002], but their use is somewhat different from ours. All process recordings are very short and focused on explaining a single aspect of the programming language or programming. However, the process recordings are "perfect", and they do not show that it is common to make errors (and how to correct them). Also, the process recordings do not show the integrated use of the different tools like IDE or online documentation, etc. The process recordings in [Gries et al., 2002] can be characterized as alternative teaching materials according to our categorization in the previous section.

Others use a much richer form of multimedia than plain video. One example is the learning objects discussed in [Boyle, 2003]. The same differences as described above apply here as well along with the fact that the production cost for creating these learning objects is extremely high.

Much more needs to be done in this area. The overall, long-term objective of programming education is that students learn strategies, principles, and techniques to support the process of inventing suitable solution structures for a given programming problem. One possible approach to advance our knowledge is to identify, to analyze, and to categorize existing methodological and systematic approaches to the practice of programming and programming education. This includes the classical programming methodology of the Dijkstra-Gries school, design by contract, elementary patterns, the existing but scarce literature on the practice of programming, and a study of the practice of masters. Furthermore, it is necessary to identify, to categorize, and to operationalize strategies, principles, and techniques for object-oriented programming. Similarly, it would be worth indicating how these can be made available to novices as well as more experienced programmers through education. Finally, the insight from this work should form the basis of a formulation of requirements for programming environments and languages for programming education.

7   Conclusions

The idea of revealing the programming process is not new as can be seen in the following quote:

> *Anyone with a reasonable intelligence and some grasp of basic logical and mathematical concepts can learn to program; what is required is a way to demystify the programming process and help students to understand it, analyse their work, and most importantly, gain the confidence in themselves that will allow them to learn the skills they need to become proficient.*

This quotation is almost twenty years old [Gantenbein, 1989], but nevertheless, the issue still has not found its way into programming textbooks.

Revealing the programming process is an important part of an introductory programming course that is not covered by traditional teaching materials such as textbooks, lecture notes, blackboards, slide presentations, etc. This is just as good since these materials are insufficient and ill-suited for the purpose.

We suggest that process recordings in the form of screen-captured, narrated programming sessions is a simple, cheap, and efficient way of providing a revelation of the programming process. Furthermore, we have identified seven elements included in the programming process. For each of these, we have discussed how to address it in an introductory programming course and how process recordings can be used to reveal its core aspects.

From our evaluation of the approach we know that the students use and appreciate the process recordings, and that some students even find the material superior to traditional face-to-face teaching. The creation of video-mediated materials has proven to be easy and cheap as opposed to other approaches to create learning objects.

The advance of new technology in the form of digital media has made it possible to easily create learning material to reveal process elements that in the past only have been addressed implicitly. The students welcome the new material, which has great impact on the students' understanding of the programming process and their performance in practical programming. With new technology, in this case computers and video capturing tools, it becomes possible to store information that represents dynamic behaviour. This is something that is virtually impossible to describe and to represent by using traditional tools and materials such as blackboards and books. We are looking forward to further pursuing this new opportunity.

Apprentice-Based Learning Via Integrated Lectures and Assignments*

Michael Kölling and David J. Barnes

The Computing Laboratory, The University of Kent, Canterbury, Kent CT2 7NF,
United Kingdom
{m.kolling,d.j.barnes}@kent.ac.uk

Abstract. Various methods have been proposed in the past to improve student learning by introducing new styles of working with assignments. These include problem-based learning, the use of case studies and apprenticeship. In most courses, however, these proposals have not resulted in a widespread, significant change of teaching methods. Most institutions still use a traditional lecture/lab class approach with a strong separation of tasks between them.

In this chapter, we propose an approach to teaching introductory programming in Java that integrates assignments and lectures, using elements of all three approaches mentioned above. In addition, we show how the BlueJ interactive programming environment can be used to provide the type of support that has hitherto hindered the widespread take-up of these approaches. We arrive at a teaching method that is motivating, effective and relatively easy to put into practice.

1   Introduction

Most introductory computing courses follow a roughly similar organizational structure: a sequence of weekly lectures is complemented by laboratory classes. The lectures are used to introduce new programming language material to the students, and the lab classes reinforce the material by requiring the students to work through and to discuss small exercises and somewhat larger assignments. One might reasonably expect a change of introductory programming language, or the use of a new programming paradigm to provide an opportunity to review the method of delivery as well. However, this pattern has changed little over the last three decades, and remains the predominant one in many institutions. One reason is that new teachers tend to model their practices on those that they experienced as students. In addition, introductory programming textbooks have also changed little over the years and (often unconsciously) reinforce the delivery style through a pattern of successive introduction of language features followed by small-scale exercises that use those features.

---

* This chapter is an extension of Michael Kölling and David J Barnes, 2004. Enhancing Apprentice-Based Learning of Java. In *Proceedings of the Thirty-Fifth SIGCSE Technical Symposium on Computer Science Education*, Norfolk, Virginia, USA, March 3-7, 2004, pp. 286-290.

J. Bennedsen et al. (Eds.): Teaching of Programming, LNCS 4821, pp. 17–29, 2008.

For teachers and students alike, appropriate practical work is the key to the success of the teaching and learning process. Small-scale exercises that focus on programming language details offer little scope for creativity on the part of students, and are unlikely to create a sense of ownership. In contrast, learner-centred tasks [Norman and Spohrer, 1996] that capture the interest of students are more likely to generate a sense of excitement and to motivate further investigation. If programming projects are offered that have interesting goals and are rather more than purely syntactic exercises, the results have the potential to be enlightening and rewarding for both students and teachers. A coincidental, yet worthwhile, side-effect is that they offer few opportunities for plagiarism.

However, several problems exist in providing sufficiently motivational assignments:

- In an introductory programming course, it is not easy to see how students can work on problems large enough to be truly interesting early in the course, as they have little experience with software development.
- It is often hard to create an obvious connection between the lecture and the assignment. Both often exist as fairly separate activities, making it harder to create interest in and motivation for the lectures.
- Students taking an introductory course often have a broad range of experience that needs to be accommodated.
- Assignments of a significant size require environment support to be manageable by novice students. However, programming environments are often overly complex, incomplete in their language support, or do not provide good support for the teaching and learning processes, thus hindering active assignment work early in the course.

In this chapter, which extends the discussion in [Kölling and Barnes, 2004], we consider a technique that can be used to integrate assignments and lectures more tightly. This serves better to motivate lecture content, results in the ability to carry out more interesting assignments and allows inclusion of important software engineering concepts into an introductory course.

All of the techniques described here have been tested for several years in CS1 level university courses in Denmark and in England. Courses have ranged between 7.5 and 15 ECTS points, with student numbers up to about 200. Course durations have been between one and two semesters (12-24 weeks) with typically two, one-hour lectures and a single, one-hour class per week.

2   Previous Work

In the 1990s, several related tracks were followed in an attempt to find more effective ways of motivating and presenting material on introductory programming courses. Seminal among these attempts was the work of [Linn and Clancy, 1992], who made a strong argument for the use of case studies to support program design. Particularly effective in their study was the use of expert commentary to accompany a design.

Also significant was the work of Astrachan and Reed [Astrachan and Reed, 1995; Astrachan et al., 1997] whose 'applied apprenticeship approach' encouraged students to read, study, modify and extend programs written by experienced programmers. One of the principles of the apprentice-based approach is that particular *applications* are the motivation for introducing new programming constructs or data structures, rather than studying language constructs as an end in themselves. This is significantly different from the typical language-feature driven approach. Providing a credible context for features, structures and algorithms makes it more likely that students learn language-independent skills in addition to a particular programming language.

A similar problem-driven motivation can be found in the use of problem-based learning environments [Kay et al., 2000b; Ellis et al., 1998]. This approach also often features group work.

Modern students —and hence, necessarily, the introductory programming courses they take— are dependent upon the availability of suitable companion textbooks to support them. Progress in this area has been slow. Despite the insights of the early 1990s offered by Astrachan et. al., most modern, introductory programming text books still tend to exhibit mainly traditional characteristics of language-construct driven chapters and small example problems. Why is this? One reason may be the arrival on the scene of Java in the late 1990s.

Java appeared to be very attractive when compared with many of the alternative procedural and object-oriented programming languages of the time such as Pascal, C and C++. Increasingly, Java became the most common language chosen for introductory programming courses [Reges, 2000]. A strong influence here was that the easy availability of GUI-based examples was seen as one of the main means to motivate students, particularly via the synergy that Java offered with the emerging World Wide Web through applets. Unfortunately, while these may well have motivational potential, there remains the question of whether these features alone offer enough to deliver the broader educational requirements of an introductory programming course. For instance, just because a course is interesting and motivational doesn't necessarily guarantee that its teaching and learning objectives are met.

An unfortunate consequence of Java's arrival was that an educational community consisting of relatively stable language usage and emergent thinking about appropriate pedagogy was disrupted, and a partially revitalised textbook market largely reverted to the familiar pattern of syntax-driven instruction and assessment.

It would appear, therefore, that there is a good case for revisiting and extending this earlier work in order to make the case for a high quality introduction to object-oriented programming that is pedagogically driven.

3   Problems with Assignments

In most courses, assignments are not set weekly, whereas lectures are held at least once a week. Therefore, assignments tend to be somewhat removed from the lectures in both organization and content. Usually, a lecture introduces new programming constructs or techniques and, some time later, an assignment is given to practice the application of these techniques. The larger (and with it, the more interesting) the assignment is, the more removed it would tend to be from the lecture content, since it would include material covering a longer period of time. Particularly in the early stages of a programming course, such a separation limits students' engagement with the practical task of programming and may be unhelpful.

Another problem with early programming assignments is that it is hard to get students to do things well. While students are struggling with getting their program to do something at all, they often have little time left for thinking about non-functional aspects, such as structural software quality. The solution in many courses is to leave software quality aspects, such as maintainability, coupling and cohesion, to later courses, and to concentrate on getting something running first. This is unfortunate and we would like to incorporate critical assessment and evaluation of existing code into the curriculum very early on, because we believe this is a fundamental part of programming activity.

4   Our Goals

Our goals are twofold:

- Firstly, we want to use an approach that is more problem-driven than the traditional style. The problem-driven approach starts by presenting a practical programming problem, and then examines a range of possible solutions. In the course of this discussion, new programming constructs or techniques are often introduced. This approach both ties the assignment and the lecture close together, and provides a motivation for the introduction of new lecture material. In fact, the role of lecture and assignment is reversed: it is not the lecture content that drives the assignment, but the assignment problems that drive the lectures. This is a significant change because the curriculum is no longer driven by the features of a particular programming language, but by the problems we wish to solve.
- Secondly, we want to achieve the inclusion of modern software engineering tasks into the computing curriculum early on. Traditionally, early computing assignments often use a blank screen approach: students start with nothing more than a problem specification. They then start designing and coding a new application from scratch. The essential assignment task is to write code. This style does not reflect realities in the contemporary computing industry where tasks such as reading and understanding of existing code, maintaining and refactoring, adaptation and extension are far more common than the development of new applications. We would like to emphasize that critical code reading and maintenance are essential skills for any programmer let loose on the world today.

Thus, this proposal affects both the form and the content of the material used in lectures and assignments. While our discussion of previous work shows that neither of these goals is new in itself, experience shows that the implementation of them has been slow. In part, this is because it has often remained difficult to put these ideas into practice. [Linn and Clancy, 1992] noted, for instance, that students often found lengthy expert commentaries difficult to read, while the familiar syntactic hurdle of Java's `main` method almost forces an early focus on syntax that may be hard to break away from.

Although we have suggested the widespread adoption of Java has had a possibly negative influence, it does actually also have a positive effect in this area. Java libraries and tools are now available that may help in supporting these approaches and make it worthwhile to revisit these issues. In the remainder of this chapter we present a very practical, easily realizable example of how these goals can be achieved. We aim to do this on two levels: firstly, by presenting one concrete example, and secondly, by presenting abstract guidelines for the development of such teaching units in general.

5 A Concrete Example

5.1 Exploration

The example we discuss here to illustrate our approach is called *The World of Zuul* [Barnes and Kölling, 2006], which is a game-based example. We typically use this application towards the end of the first semester of an introductory course. By this point in the course students have encountered all of the fundamentals of object-based programming, short of inheritance.

When introduced to the students, the application has already reached a coherent stage of development. It compiles and displays recognisable runtime behaviour. The first student activity is to explore and to describe the application. The exploration takes place within the BlueJ environment (Fig. 1) [BlueJ, 2007; Kölling et al., 2003]. The UML-like visualisation that occupies the majority of the environment view gives a clear external view of the overall application structure, and later serves to reinforce the discussion of coupling between classes.

BlueJ overcomes the problems usually associated with the use of many other programming environments because:

- Unlike professional programming environments, it is designed for use by novice programmers.
- In spite of its target audience being novice programmers, BlueJ supports the full implementation of the Java language and not just a subset.
- Most important of all is that it is specifically designed to support the teaching and learning of key object-oriented concepts.

Exploration of key object-oriented concepts is supported in a number of ways by the features provided by BlueJ. For instance, an instance of any class shown in the class diagram can be created independent of running the whole application. This results in a visualisation of an object being placed on an *object bench* — the area below the diagram. Instances appearing here serve to reinforce the

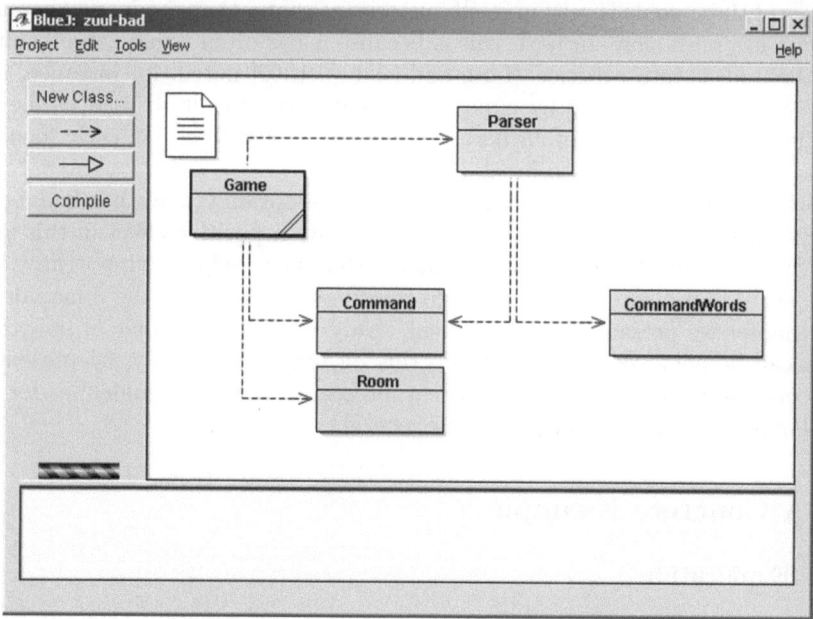

Fig. 1. The World of Zuul project within BlueJ

distinctions between class and objects. Furthermore, multiple instances of the same class are possible and have an independent existence. Objects on the object bench can be interacted with directly; for instance, methods may be called on them and their state inspected (Fig. 2). Source-code may be viewed via the class diagram.

The exploration within BlueJ includes a discussion of both the application's functional aspects (*What does the program do?*) and aspects of its implementation (*What is the role of each class in the application?*). Students quickly find out that the application implements a framework for a text-based adventure game [Adams, 2002] that allows the player to enter text commands and to move around between a small number of locations, by using commands such as *go east* (Fig. 3). Exploration of the implementation is done as a group activity, in which students examine the classes' source code and explain each class in turn to other group members. The classes are well-commented, so that most of the important information is easily accessible without the need to understand all details of the code.

5.2   The First Tasks

It is clear to the students from their exploration that the game framework in its current form is rather limited in its functionality, and that it needs to be extended to turn it into something more interesting.

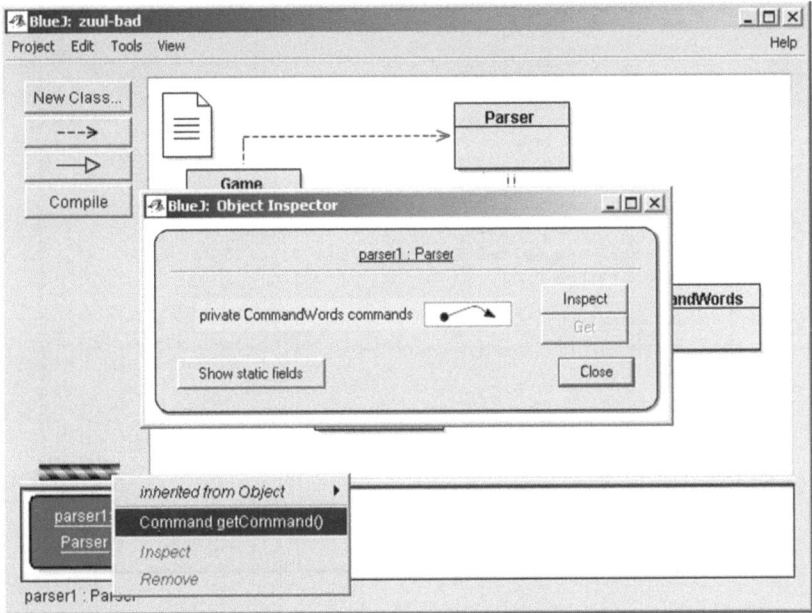

Fig. 2. Direct object manipulation and inspection

The next thing the students do is to invent an alternative game scenario. This can be done using a large variety of interactive or group activities, in which students are able to develop and to discuss ideas. It then finishes with every student selecting and describing a game plan. The explorations do not need to be constrained by implementation considerations. Topics can be anything such as blood cells travelling through the human body, "you are lost in the shopping mall" themes, or the typical dungeon and dragon style scenarios.

Next, a number of small improvements to the given application are discussed. These are the addition of new movement directions (*up* and *down*), introduction of items in rooms (initially only one item per room) and appropriate new commands, such as 'take' and 'drop'.

5.3 Discussion

These first small tasks are discussed in detail, apprentice-style, in a lecture, including interactive development of an improved solution from the original limited version. Even without the students having written a single line of code, it is clear that a number of important topics have been explored and practiced, such as code reading, exploring class interfaces, and abstracting from the details of a particular game to its general characteristics.

Discussion of the necessary changes to the source code to attempt the first extension fits the model of learning from experts [Astrachan and Reed, 1995; Linn and Clancy, 1992]. But, there is an important difference involving the quality of

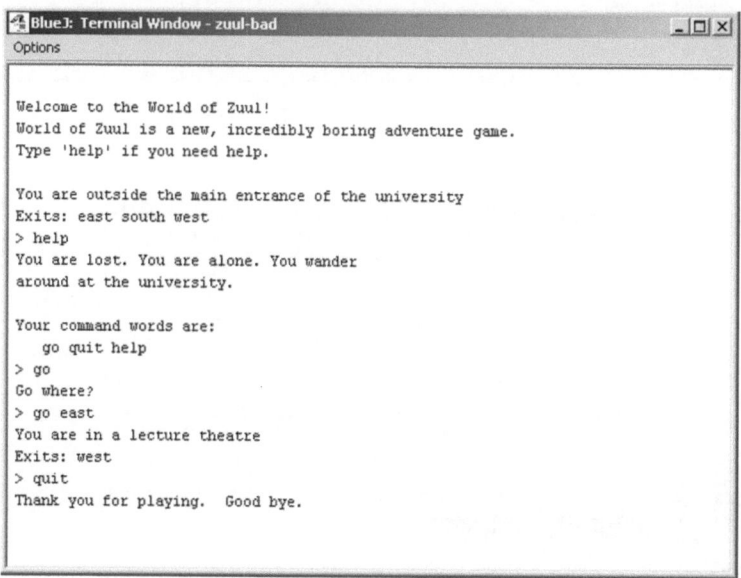

```
BlueJ: Terminal Window - zuul-bad                              _ □ ×
Options

Welcome to the World of Zuul!
World of Zuul is a new, incredibly boring adventure game.
Type 'help' if you need help.

You are outside the main entrance of the university
Exits: east south west
> help
You are lost. You are alone. You wander
around at the university.

Your command words are:
   go quit help
> go
Go where?
> go east
You are in a lecture theatre
Exits: west
> quit
Thank you for playing.   Good bye.
```

Fig. 3. The user interface and exploration of the Zuul game

the artefact being presented. Discussion quickly focuses on code quality and it becomes obvious that the given code makes the proposed extensions quite hard to implement, because it is badly structured. This gives us the opportunity to discuss aspects of code that make maintenance easy or difficult.

We discover cases of code duplication, broken encapsulation and bad distribution of responsibilities, and we see how these make our life harder. Developing an ability to evaluate code critically is key here. This gives us the further opportunity to discuss the fact that the functional view of an application does not tell us about the quality of the underlying code (the program 'worked', after all). Students often struggle with the idea that they received a low mark because their program appeared to do all that was required of them, but it was badly implemented.

From what we have, and where we want to get to, we can illustrate the process of refactoring —improving quality without increasing functionality. This is a process students rarely engage in, usually because of time constraints —a not dissimilar experience of programmers in 'the real world'! Closely associated with the task of refactoring is the need to establish that changes to the source code have not broken anything. Any course that seeks to embrace key software engineering concepts and techniques [Jackson et al., 1997] must include testing as an integral part. BlueJ supports JUnit-style unit testing [JUnit, 2007] through interactive recording and replay of test cases and establishment of test fixtures [Patterson et al., 2003]. Use of these features during both the sort of refactoring activities we are discussing here, and during work on the extensions, reinforces the message that testing is an activity that is naturally concurrent with development rather than an afterthought.

The refactoring process allows us to evaluate the code in terms of concepts such as coupling and cohesion, and goals such as localization of change. We improve the underlying design first by refactoring relevant bits of code, and then we find that making our intended extensions has become much easier than it would have been previously. The first task (adding up and down movement) is solved completely via a practical demonstration in the lecture, with extensive discussion about considerations of code quality while making modifications to the given source.

5.4 Exercises

The second task (adding items to the game scenario) is done as a series of exercises. The problem and some aspects of a solution are discussed, and then students are expected to implement the detailed solution on their own.

The discussion contains a hint to the solution, and asks relevant questions to make students consider important aspects. An example would be, 'We have discussed responsibility-driven design —which class should be responsible for printing out the details of the items present in a room? Why?'

The exercises are organised in a sequence of manageable steps of increasing complexity. Adding items to rooms, for example, is initially done by supporting at most a single item being placed in each room, and then extended in a separate exercise to allow rooms to hold an arbitrary number of items. Correspondingly, the player can initially pick up and carry a single item, which is later extended to multiple items. The number of items carried can later be limited by a maximum possible weight that a player can carry, for instance, or by the incompatibility between items (e.g., The player may not carry both matches and a flammable potion at the same time).

5.5 Assignment

The exercises then lead into a larger assignment. In this assignment phase, students implement their own game scenario including their own ideas for making the game interesting. Typical elements students implement include forms of time limits, magic transporter rooms, trap doors, locks, talking characters, moving characters and more.

At this stage, students receive less help and guidance in developing their solutions than during the exercise phase. They are expected to develop solutions on their own, with the possibility of asking a tutor for support. During this phase, tutors frequently discuss the quality of students' solutions under maintainability and extendibility aspects with the students. It is made clear that code quality, reviewed under the aspects discussed in the lecture, will be a major component in the marking scheme for the assignment.

6 The Three Steps

The previous section described a specific example of an assignment following our approach. In this section, we discuss the ideas behind this structure in a more general form. On the first level, the assignment approach can be divided into three steps: Observation, Application and Design. We discuss each of these in detail below. It is worth noting that the order of these activities is exactly reversed compared to the classical, clean slate style of assignments. There, students typically have to start with design, followed by application, before they observe behaviour.

6.1   Step 1: Observation

In this step, the instructor actively demonstrates a software engineering task in the lecture. This part is modelled on the apprentice approach in which students observe the instructor performing a relevant task and listen to the instructor's commentary, while having the opportunity to interrupt and to ask questions.

Aspects of this phase are typically the analysis of given code and the discovery of problems and ideas for solutions. It gives an opportunity to reflect on existing code and to evaluate critically before making changes.

Typically, the problems discovered during the evaluation of the code lead to a motivation for new course material, which can then be introduced and discussed. Students then observe the application of the new material in a well-chosen example, with the opportunity to discuss alternatives.

An important element of this stage is that the instructor's activities must not be rushed and full of short-cuts. For instance, code should be commented as it is written, appropriate identifiers should be used, and appropriate testing conducted. If coding errors are made then this can be treated as a positive aspect because it is a natural part of coding, and helps to demystify the nature of the programming process. Students witness how the process is done by an expert, but also for as a piece of professional practice.

6.2   Step 2: Application

The educational goal of the second step is the application of new material under guidance. Teachers discuss selected problems chosen to display similar challenges to those demonstrated in step one and give hints to solutions. Problems are chosen so that variations of the material from step one are applicable for the solution. Students are expected to mirror the critical analysis and evaluation activities of their teacher and to reason actively about the given code as well as to argue about intended solutions. This phase usually spans an arbitrary mix of lecture and lab classes, and alternates repeatedly between active coding activities and reflective discussion.

6.3   Step 3: Design

In the third step, students design their own tasks as extensions of the project at hand. It is a free programming assignment that allows students to apply all the techniques they are familiar with at that stage. Typically, students are given a minimum of guidance on expected tasks, simply to communicate the required amount of work for evaulation purposes. At this stage, this only includes the description of sample tasks, not usually pointers to solutions.

One of the advantages of doing an assignment task in this context is that students are familiar with the framework they are expected to extend. Since steps one and two have served to familiarize the student with a given application, larger, more complex and more interesting applications can be used. Extension tasks proposed by students are typically reviewed and guided by a tutor to ensure their usefulness in applying interesting course material, and their suitability in workload and level of difficulty.

7   Important Aspects of This Approach

7.1   Problem Driven

The introduction of new material is driven by a concrete problem. The motivation for the introduction of new concepts comes from a concrete task at hand. This can easily be combined with additional problem-based learning approaches, such as student-controlled discovery of new material. Instead of presenting all new constructs in a lecture, students can be guided towards resources that enable them to discover new material as part of a student activity.

7.2   Apprentice Approach

Our approach is an extension of the apprentice approach. Students start by studying expert-written code that includes both well-written code and code to be critically evaluated and improved under expert guidance. In our introductory course, we rarely (if ever) expect students to start with a blank canvas and to create a program from scratch. Hence, the starting point for our demonstrations is an existing application. An important part of students' learning comes from witnessing an expert in action and hopefully imitating some of the activities considered good practice within their own work. This activity should be facilitated by a Java environment that supports incremental development and testing. One of the important additions to the original apprentice approach as described in [Astrachan and Reed, 1995] is that students can also observe the *process* of the expert's work, in addition to the created artefact.

7.3   Open/Closed

It is important to have characteristics of both open and closed assignments. The task should be well enough described so that weaker or less enthusiastic students have clear guidance as to what is expected of them, and how much they have to accomplish to receive a satisfactory mark in the assessment. On the other hand, the task should be open enough so that students can incorporate their own ideas and progress much further than the minimum required pass level. It is common in computing classes that student groups display a wide variety of skills, and thus, making the task challenging and interesting for even the best students is an important goal. This encourages both creativity and innovation.

7.4   Ownership

Whenever possible, the problem should be set in such a way that the student can take ownership of the task. In the *Zuul* example, this is achieved by letting students invent and design their own game scenarios and individual extension tasks. This, in turn, is the result of their abstracting from a particular example to the general principles it embodies, and on to a further instantiation. From that moment on, when students work on the implementation of the task, they don't view it so much as work on a problem outside their control, but as implementing *their* game.

7.5   Student Controlled

Another related (but distinct) issue is the ability of a student to take control over significant parts of the task. Game-based assignments have been discussed in the past in the context of gender bias [Inkpen et al., 1994]. Studies have found that female students are often interested in different kinds of computer games than male students, and that games without any social component or relevance are less likely to engage female students.

While *The World of Zuul* is clearly a game-based example, we have not observed the described gender effect in its use. (While we have not carried out a formal investigation, we have consciously monitored this aspect and held informal talks with students about it.) We speculate that the reason for this is that students can individually decide the context of their tasks by inventing their own scenarios. Giving students this degree of control might lead to higher acceptance of the relevance of the task.

8   Conclusion

Despite the evident educational and motivational value of problem-based approaches to introductory computer science, the traditional delivery style involving separation of lecture material and lab material continues to dominate in many places.

In this chapter we have described a concrete example of a more integrated approach that can be used in introductory programming courses. It includes problem-driven aspects, but is easier to realise than a complete problem-based learning model.

In addition, we have provided guidelines to assist others to apply this approach to their own material. This approach fosters a concept-driven approach to delivery of new material, and encourages ownership of these concepts by the students. It has been used by the authors for several years at the University of Southern Denmark in Odense and at the University of Kent in Canterbury, England. Experiences are overwhelmingly positive, including student feedback, pass rates and teacher satisfaction.

Further ideas for application of this approach within the context of an object-first programming course can be found in [Barnes and Kölling, 2006] where, for instance, study of a multimedia database motivates the introduction of inheritance features, and a predator-prey simulation leads to discussion of abstract classes and interfaces. It is worth pointing out that the approach is general enough to be applicable in an even broader context than simply introductory, object-oriented Java teaching.

Experiences with Functional Programming in an Introductory Curriculum

Michael R. Hansen and Jens Thyge Kristensen

Informatics and Mathematical Modelling
Technical University of Denmark
Richard Petersens Plads, Bldg. 322
DK-2800 Kgs. Lyngby, Denmark
{mrh,jtk}@imm.dtu.dk

Abstract. We present the rationale behind a first semester course on functional programming. We describe the design of the course, emphasizing programming as a modelling discipline, as well as the curriculum it was a part of. In particular, we discuss our experiences concerning the transition from functional programming to object-oriented programming. We also discuss and compare this functional-first approach to the objects-first approach of our recently introduced curriculum.

1   Introduction

Teaching programming to university freshmen is a challenging task, because there may be a conflict between what students expect from the course and the long term goals of the teachers:

1. The students want to solve interesting problems by using a computer.
2. The teachers think of programming as an intellectual activity in order to create a solid foundation for further education in computer science.

The challenge is to find a balance between the expectations of the students and the long term goals of the course.

The first point can be satisfied in an environment where students can express their solution to problems without bothering about low-level details. In a traditional first course (e.g., based on Java) this can be achieved by supplying the students with a collection of libraries and a development environment. Without these facilities the danger is that the language learning phase may be tedious and boring. An advantage with this approach is that students from the start learn to make their software solutions by extension of given components as this is a typical case for many real projects. A disadvantage is that it is not obvious for students how to construct programs from scratch.

An alternative is to start with a high-level, declarative programming language, based on Haskell or SML, for example. An advantage of doing so is that the distance between a variety of problems and their (functional) solutions are so short that students can construct understandable programs from scratch by using a

J. Bennedsen et al. (Eds.): Teaching of Programming, LNCS 4821, pp. 30–46, 2008.
© Springer-Verlag Berlin Heidelberg 2008

few, well-understood language constructs and basic principles. Another advantage with this approach is that students from the start learn to write working, stand-alone programs. Some students consider it a disadvantage that functional languages are seldom used in the industry.

In this chapter, we will discuss the rationale behind and our experience, covering about a ten year period, with an approach to a programming curriculum [Hansen and Rischel, 1999; Hansen et al., 1999; Kristensen et al., 2001]. This approach is called *functional first* in the ACM 2001 Computer Science curriculum [Engel and Roberts, 2001]. In an over-simplified setting, the first programming language taught is a functional language, like SML [Milner et al., 1997], Haskell [Thompson, 1996] or Scheme [Abelson et al., 1985], and the second taught is an object-oriented language, like Java, C++ or C#. Our first course was based on SML and the next on Java. We shall also compare this experience with the far less experience we have with an *objects-first* approach.

1.1   A Functional-First Approach

Some advantages of approaches starting with functional languages, like SML, are given now. First, computationally non-trivial problems can be solved by students *the first day*. A short introduction to recursion and natural numbers suffices to make students capable of solving problems like prime number testing, computation of binomial coefficients, etc. Students are later on asked to solve exercises without a mathematical origin as soon as structured values are introduced (after a few lectures).

Secondly, there is a rich and orthogonal set of structured values. This orthogonality is important from a teaching point of view, as the different topics can be introduced independently of most other topics. For example, it is possible within a few lectures to introduce the concept of lists, algorithms following the structure of lists, and applications using lists, without bothering about other topics concerning the programming language. As lists and tuples, for example, are useful and quite sufficient in many applications, the orthogonality aspect supports a natural interleaving of the language learning aspect and the problem-solving parts of the course.

As a third point, the functional paradigm supports a programming and problem-solving style, where monolithic programs are avoided by use of a functional decomposition of the problem. Furthermore, it is easy to get a natural progression in the problem-solving techniques exercised, ranging from algorithms following the structure of the composite values, to more powerful techniques such as divide and conquer.

As the fourth point, functional languages have very simple operational semantics, and using concepts like step by step evaluation and environment (or substitution) only, the students learn how to perform the computation steps of the programs. More fundamentally, students are acquainted with the attitude that programs are entities that must be comprehensible, in the sense that they can understand, communicate, and reason about programs.

Our preference for the functional-first approach is based on the following assumptions and attitudes to programming:

- It is important that students learn that a program should be a well-under-stood comprehensible entity. This attitude is best developed using a language with a simple semantics, like a functional language. We also require that students can write computationally interesting programs from scratch, so that they are in command of every piece of the produced code.
- It is important that students learn that fundamental concepts of a problem should be reflected as directly as possible in the corresponding program. This is best achieved using a high-level programming language with a rich type system supporting a collection of composite types like tuples, lists, tree, etc.
- Basic problem-solving skills, like functional decomposition and divide-and-conquer, are best taught in a functional setting where they fit in naturally.

There are, of course, many arguments for starting with an object-oriented language as well. For example:

- some students favour a start using a fashionable industry language, as it seems that what they learn is immediately applicable,
- it is possible to teach graphical user interfaces, and students often appreciate this topic, and
- a wide range of programming paradigms (e.g., imperative, object-oriented and parallel programming), may be studied by using the same language.

But, we advocate for an approach where students master a collection for data types and their applications, and a collection of general problem-solving techniques before they are introduced to object-oriented programming.

1.2   Description of the Programming Curriculum

In a period of about 8 to 10 years, the informatics students at the Technical University of Denmark followed the approach *functional first* in the ACM 2001 Computer Science curriculum [Engel and Roberts, 2001]. The number of students in the curriculum ranged from 50 to 120 students each year in that period. The sequence of courses was:

- Functional programming and program design (approx. 7.5 ECTS) using SML.
- Imperative and object-oriented programming (5 ECTS) using Java.
- Algorithms and data structures (5 ECTS).
- Software engineering project course (7.5 ECTS).

We give further details for the first two courses as we focus on them from now on.

The course on functional programming was a first semester course given in the fall semester (14 weeks). In a typical week there were three lectures (70 minutes each) and two exercise classes (2 hours each), where each exercise class had a class room part and a lab part. The students were evaluated on the basis of

- a small collection of mandatory assignments,
- a mandatory project comprising program documentation, and
- a written examination (4 hours).

The course on imperative and object-oriented programming was given in a three week period immediately following the fall semester. The first 1.5 weeks (full time) constituted the language learning part of the course. A typical day in this period had about 2.5 hours of lecturing and 4 hours of exercise classes and labs. In the final 1.5 weeks (full time), a programming project with associated documentation was carried out. The students were evaluated on the basis of a report.

1.3 Learning Goals

The learning goals of the above programming curriculum were:

- Students must learn lasting concepts such as the classical data types (e.g., lists, trees, sets, tables), a wide range of applications of the data types, and selected classical algorithms.
- Students must learn that programs are intellectual entities, which must be understandable, can be assessed and discussed. When solving problems, the important concepts of the problems must be reflected in the programs.
- Students must learn how to comprehend and to solve non-trivial problems, and they should be able to produce a succinct documentation of their solution.
- Students must learn different programming paradigms so that they can learn new programming languages by themselves.

1.4 Overview of Rest of the Chapter

The remaining parts of the chapter are structured as follows. In Section 2 we give the rationale behind our approach to the first course on functional programming. Section 3 contains an example of programming as a modelling activity as taught in the first course. In Section 4, Java as a second language is discussed with emphasis on our experience with the transition from functional programming to object-oriented programming.

  The curriculum described above was for computer science students only. In the last section, we summarize our experiences and discuss them in connection with the more recent (and far less) experiences we have with an objects-first approach. In this new curriculum, the context is different. The first introductory programming course can be taken by all students at the Technical University of Denmark, and not just the computer science students. With this change of parameters, the first programming course is now a 10 ECTS point Java course, and the following course is a 5 ECTS point course on algorithms and data structures. On top of this, a course introducing functional programming can be taken.

2   A First Semester Course on Functional Programming

When designing a first semester course on functional programming, there are several possible approaches. In [Hughes, 1989], it is argued that two features of "pure" functional languages are particularly important for the construction of well-structured, modular and re-usable programs. One is the concept of *higher-order functions*, (i.e., functions as first class citizens), and the other is that of *lazy evaluation*. Higher-order functions provide a means to parameterize modules, so that they can be specialized to fit a variety of applications. Lazy evaluation supports advanced problem-solving techniques. For example, a program may be modularized into a *generator component* that lazily enumerates a possibly infinite sequence of solutions, and a *selection component*, which chooses an appropriate solution. The two concepts are both independent and together very powerful programming concepts, which are supported by lazy, functional languages like Haskell.

We consider lazy evaluation as an important topic. But, it is an advanced topic that should not have a prominent role in a first semester programming course. On the other hand, higher-order functions should have some attention. It helps to focus on building parameterized modules, on making succinct programs, and, finally, it is certainly possible to relate it to concepts in object-oriented languages (e.g., iterators on collections). Furthermore, more features from functional languages will be introduced in the new version 3.0 of C#.

On the basis of the Scheme [Abelson et al., 1985] tradition in [Felleisen et al. 2001], the rationale behind the course and the book *How to Design Programs* [Abelson et al., 1985], is described. Here, it is argued that the first semester should start with a heavy emphasis on principles and some industrial relevant components should be added during the second semester. The following learning goals, identified in [Felleisen et al., 2001], support our goals that the important concepts of a problem statement should be directly reflected in the programs and program designs, as well as our goal of producing succinct documentation:

---

1. *Students must learn to read a problem statement carefully, to extract information, and to rewrite it into useful pieces:*
   (a) *a concise purpose statement for the program and each of its major pieces;*
   (b) *a description of classes of data that play a role;*
   (c) *a collection of examples that illustrate both the classes as well as the purpose statements.*
   Ideally, the latter should (eventually) make up a rigorous test suite for the program and the functions.
2. *The students must learn to organize programs so that they match the class descriptions in 1b. ...*
3. *....*

Quote from Page 368 of [Felleisen et al., 2001].

Since Scheme is a typeless language where almost every correctly parenthesized expression is a legal program, only little lecture time is needed to cover the syntax of that language. This simplicity has some disadvantages. In particular, there are no language constructs supporting a presentation of the program design, and in the approach of [Felleisen et al., 2001], an *informal* type system is introduced for that purpose.

An alternative to this approach is to use a functional language with a strong type system, such as SML and Haskell, which besides the standard primitive types for numbers, characters and strings, also have powerful features for defining and manipulating structured values like lists and algebraic data types (i.e., trees). Furthermore, the notations of both languages are close to common mathematical notation, and not as Puritan as that of Scheme. This means that it is not too hard for students to learn the syntax of programs. Furthermore, it supports the aim of teaching students to appreciate and to strive for elegant programs, which are understandable and can be communicated to and discussed with other people. Hence, the emphasis should be on understanding and thinking about how to solve a programming problem by using basic, well-understood concepts.

Our approach [Hansen and Rischel, 1999; Hansen et al., 1999; Kristensen et al., 2001] is based on SML rather than on Haskell as, in general, we want an approach capturing both the applicative and the imperative paradigms. Although, we in the first semester course mainly focused on the applicative paradigm.

To solve a programming problem we advise [Hansen and Rischel, 1999] a procedure containing the following three activities:

Problem analysis. Reading of the problem statement leads to a specification of a computational model expressed by types. In the analysis, one must first identify the main concepts of the problem, which are data and functions involved. And then, one must define the model by stating the types of the data and functions.

Programming. Before making a program, one has to analyze the model and turn it into a design. This typically leads to an introduction of further data types and a functional decomposition.

Testing. The functions of the programs are tested according to selected cases. (We mainly focussed on white-box testing in the first semester.)

Notice that these activities match well with the learning goals of Felleisen et al.(2001), which are also stated in the quote on page 34.

Our experience is that the result of these three activities constitutes a good basis for succinct technical documentation. The modelling approach to programming that we follow is inspired from approaches based on formal specification languages like VDM [Bjørner and Jones, 1978; Jones, 1990; Fitzgerald and Larsen, 1998] and Raise Specification Language [the RAISE language group, 1992], where concepts of a broad class of applications are modelled using mathematical concepts like tuples, lists, sets, maps, trees, functions, etc. Using the strength of SML's type system, module system, libraries, and not least the power of the expression language, an important portion of specifications are actually executable. In the next section, we sketch the modelling approach using a simple example.

In *Model-Driven Programming* by Bennedsen and Caspersen, another model-based approach to programming is presented in the context of an objects-first approach. In their approach, the programming activity is also driven by a conceptual model. Their conceptual model is expressed by a class diagram of classes and relationships between classes. In our approach, the conceptual model is expressed in terms of type declarations and signatures for functions, as we shall see in the next section. A major difference of the approaches is in the underlying computational models, where the functional approach is based on an applicative, value-based model of computation, and the object-oriented is based on an imperative, state-based model. Another difference is that in the functional approach, the conceptual model is expressed (to a major extent) in the functional language itself; whereas in the object-oriented approach it is expressed in terms of class diagrams.

3   Programming as a Modelling Activity

The first programming course comprises an introduction to basic data types, like numbers, strings, Booleans, lists, trees, sets and tables (maps), and the recursive functions on these data types. Furthermore, higher-order functions are introduced and used, for example, in connection with program libraries. Notions like binding, environment and step by step evaluation of expressions are introduced, so that students get a clear operational understanding of the meaning of a program.

In examples, applications and exercises, we did not only consider functional beauties like symbolic differentiation, but also a variety of daily life-inspired problems involving non-trivial conceptual modelling, comprising models of data as well as models of operations. Thus, the first course introduced programming as a *modelling discipline* where concepts from applications were expressed by using types for structured values.

We have also exercised abstraction and problem solving using functional decomposition. A non-trivial problem, which the students are able to solve early in the first semester, is a map colouring problem. In Appendix A, we have included a formulation of the problem together with a solution illustrating both abstraction and functional decomposition. We will not go further than that into the language learning parts of the course and the programming techniques taught.

Rather, we will focus on our approach to teaching programming as a modelling activity. We will illustrate the way this is done on the basis of an example - a highly simplified flight reservation system, with the following problem formulation:

> A flight reservation system must contain a register where flights are associated with the persons who have reservations and the persons who are on the waiting list for the flight. The system must provide an operation for the creation of

a new flight with a given number of seats, and operations for making and cancelling a reservation for a given flight. A person who makes a reservation for a fully-booked flight is placed on a waiting list for that flight.

The first point 1) in the quote on page 34 expresses that "students must learn to read a problem statement carefully, to extract information and to rewrite it into useful pieces". The type system of SML supports the specification of the useful pieces, in the sense that type names are introduced for the main concepts in the problem formulation. Also, type expressions for possibly structured values define the concepts and describe the associated data model. Furthermore, the main operations of the problem formulation are specified using function types.

There are of course many ways to model the data in the flight reservation system. One proposal for a data model is given in Listing 1.1 The important thing at this point is that the seven type declarations collected in the figure express our design in a succinct way. The design forms a good basis of precise documentation and for discussions. A point of discussion is whether to represent reservations and waiting lists for a given flight by a single list of persons. The first persons in the list (up to the number of seats) have reservations, and the remaining persons of the list constitute the waiting list.

```
type  person  =  string
type  flight  =  string
type  reservations  =  person  Set.set
type  waitingList  =  person  list  (* without  replicas  *)
type  numberOfSeats  =  int
type  flightData  =  numberOfSeats  *  reservations  *  waitingList
type  register  =  (flight ,  flightData)  Table.table
```

Listing 1.1. Design of a data model for a flight reservation system

A few comments: Reservations are modelled as a set of persons, because the order of the reservations is not considered important. For the waiting list we informally state in a comment that no person can occur twice in the list. The type for **register** is a table type, where flights are keys and flight data are values.

The system must provide commands for creation of flights, making and cancelling reservations, and so on. The evaluation of commands can be specified as a single *evaluation* function:

```
eval:  register  *  command  ->  register  *  result
```

Using **eval** we can compute an updated register *reg'* and result *res* from a given register *reg* and command *cmd*, i.e.

$$(reg', res) = \mathtt{eval}(reg , cmd).$$

The commands are defined by a **datatype** declaration with a constructor for each command:

CmdCreate(*f*, *seats*)
>   Represents the *create* command for flight *f* with *seats* seats.

CmdReserve(*f*, *p*)
>   Represents the *reserve* command for flight *f* and person *p*.

CmdCancel(*f*,*p*)
>   Represents the *cancel* command for flight *f* and person *p*.

Using the types of the data model, a type for commands can in SML be declared by:

```
datatype command = CmdCreate of flight * numberOfSeats
                 | CmdReserve of flight * person
                 | CmdCancel of flight * person
```

The type **result** represents the possible responses from the system, and may be declared as follows:

```
datatype result = ResOK
                | ResUnknownFlight
                | ResAlreadyReserved
                | ResOnWaitList
                | ResAlreadyOnWaitList
                | ...
```

Having a program design, represented by the above declarations, the programming part is a fairly simple task, which we illustrate in Listing 1.2 by the part of the declaration of **eval** which concerns making reservations.

Even for a reader not familiar with SML, the different possibilities which can occur when person *p* makes a reservation for flight *f* are easily traceable in the code. The five different cases are named (a) to (e) in the following list. These names will occur as comments for the related pieces of code in Listing 1.2 (SML code) and Listing 1.3 (Java code).

(a) covers the case where the flight *f* does not exist in the register.
(b) covers the case where person *p* already has a reservation.
(c) covers the case where a free seat is reserved for person *p*.
(d) covers the case where person *p* is already on the waiting list.
(e) covers the case where person *p* is placed at the end of the waiting list.

```
fun eval(reg,cmd) = case cmd of
...
| CmdReserve(f,p) =>
   (case Table.lookup(f,reg) of
       NONE => (reg, ResUnknownFlight)              (* a *)
     | SOME (seats,res,wl) =>
         if Set.member(p,res)
         then (reg, ResAlreadyReserved)             (* b *)
         else if Set.card(res) < seats then
           let val res' = Set.insert(p,res) in
```

```
            (Table.update(f,(seats,res',wl),reg), ResOK)
    end                                                (* c *)
    else if List.exists (fn x => x = p) wl
         then (reg, ResAlreadyOnWaitList)              (* d *)
         else (Table.update(f,(seats,res,wl @ [p]),reg),
               ResOnWaitList) )                        (* e *)
/ ...
```

Listing 1.2. Evaluation function in SML for commands

The other parts of the program declaration are equally straightforward. The full program can be found in [Hansen and Rischel, 1999, chapter16] and on the homepage for that book. With this example we hope that we have illustrated the following:

- the major concepts of the problem formulation are easily traceable in the program,
- SML provides a succinct notation for expressing program designs and programs,
- the use of structured values (tuples, lists, sets, tables) in an application, and
- our approach to programming as a modelling activity.

The example of this section was chosen to give the flavour of our approach and, therefore, a variety of concepts are included. Throughout the course, topics were introduced according to their complexity, starting with simple data types and applications and ending with more complex data types and higher-order functions and their applications. Furthermore, for each topic there was a progression in the difficulty of the exercises solved. The most difficult exercises ranged from modelling exercises as exemplified in this section and the map colouring problem in Appendix A, and to more abstract problems like a tautology checker for propositional logic. In this way, there are exercises for every kind of student, and also enough challenges for the very good ones.

In each class, a group of students appreciated developing succinct functional programs. A group of students was too challenged by the more abstract exercises, like that for the tautology checker. But, that kind of exercises were included for the top students. A group of students told us that during the course they did not understand the relevance of the topics taught. But, at later semesters they appreciated what they have learned. We have not found a way to overcome the last problem. A part of the problem is that students have no frame of reference for judging the relevance of the chosen topics in the first semester.

4   Teaching Java on Top of SML

The Java course following the functional programming course was given as a three week intensive course. The first half was a "pure", language-learning phase also covering graphical user interfaces. Though SML was not used in this part, the students' background knowledge of basic types and structured values, as well as of problem-solving techniques, made this brief language-learning phase possible.

In the final 1.5 weeks, the students should carry out a programming project including design, implementation, test and documentation. The challenges were to make a well-designed class structure and a graphical user interface. In the design phase, the modelling background using SML's type system proved useful. It was natural for students to introduce classes in Java designs, where they would declare types in SML. Taking the flight reservation system as example (see Listing 1.1), the students typically would declare classes for persons, flights, flight data and register, while reservations, waiting lists and number of seats were fields in the class for flight data. In this way, the students automatically achieved high cohesion in their class designs.

Another advantage in their functional background is the habit of making applicative functions. Thus, they tend to declare methods with restricted use of side-effects, resulting in low coupling among the classes. The students' background knowledge of lists, sets and tables leads to their use of the corresponding collection classes in Java, and, for example, skeleton classes for flight data and the register in our example could be:

```
class FlightData
{ private int seats;
  private Set<Person> reservations;
  private List<Person> waitings;
  FlightData(int s) {
    seats = s;
    reservations = new HashSet<Person>();
    waitings = new ArrayList<Person>();
    }
  ... }
```

```
  class Register
{ private Map<Flight,FlightData> reg;
  Register(){ reg = new HashMap<Flight,FlightData>(); }
  ...
}
```

A new design aspect in the object-oriented design concerns placement of operations in classes and decisions on their side-effects. Looking at the evaluation of commands in our example, it could be tempting to place it in the register class, as the various operations may update the register. But, it turns out that branching on the type of commands gets clumsy. Another choice could be to introduce eval in a Command interface, and to have a class implementing the interface for each type of command.

Assuming a suitable enum type Result, we give, in Listing 1.3 below, the eval method implementation, which corresponds to Listing 1.2. In this declaration, the presence of some public methods in class FlightData has been supposed.

These methods change the state of flight data in the relevant register entry. But, we will not give further details here.

```
class CmdReserve implements Command {
  private Flight f;
  private Person p;
  . . .
  public CmdReserve (String fname, String pname) {
    this.f = new Flight(fname); this.p = new Person(pname);
    . . .
  }
  public Result eval(Register reg) {
    //Reserve a seat for person 'p' on flight 'f':
    if (reg.containsKey(f)) {
      FlightData fd = reg.get(f);
      if(fd.hasReserved(p))
          return Result.ResAlreadyReserved //b
      else if (fd.reservePossible()) {
          fd.addReservation(p);
          return Result.ResOK; }                //c
      else if (fd.isOnWaiting(p))
          return Result.ResAlreadyOnWaitList;    //d
      else { fd.addWaiting(p);
          return Result.ResOnWaitList;}          //e
    }
    else return Result.ResUnknownFlight;         //a
  }
  . . .
}
```

Listing 1.3. Evaluation method in Java for commands

4.1 Experiences with the Transition from SML to Java

Experience has shown that the transition from functional programming to object-oriented programming could be performed in an efficient way. First of all we consider the duration of the language-learning phase that is needed for introducing Java (1.5 week) as being very short. Secondly, even though we did not introduce classical object-oriented design methods (e.g., based on UML) the students actually ended up with well-structured Java programs. A reason is that the students' background knowledge about basic types and data structures and of problem-solving techniques from the functional programming course was a good help in the language-learning phase of Java.

Another reason for this smooth transition from functional programming to object-oriented programming is, we believe, that design methods used for functional programs carry over well to object-oriented programs. The conceptual modelling in the functional approach leads to type declarations and specifications of functions. However, the object-oriented approach leads to the definition of classes and operations. The new design aspect in the object-oriented approach deals with the placement of operations in classes and deals with their side-effects.

The students in the Java course were evaluated based on reports documenting the solution to a software engineering problem. Our general experience is that students learn to make useful abstractions in the functional programming course. This helps in writing the program documentation, where major design aspects are presented first, and decisions about implementation details are postponed. It also provides a useful frame of reference when comparing different object-oriented implementations.

5   Discussion

In this section we will summarize and discuss our main experiences on the functional-first approach. In the current curriculum we have experience with an objects-first approach from the last two years. We will relate these two curricula, considering the functional programming and the Java programming parts only.

Considering the first two courses in our *functional-first* approach in the Informatics curriculum, our experience was that students actually learned two very different programming paradigms, and in later courses they were in a position to pick up new programming languages. We observed that it was quite easy for students to learn Java on the basis of the course on functional programming, and we consider the language-learning phase needed for the Java course (1.5 week) a short period for a language of that size and complexity. There are, we believe, several reasons for this. One is that the type systems of Java and SML are "sufficiently alike", so that the students do not start from scratch when learning Java. Another reason is that they are already acquainted with problem-solving techniques from the first course, so they should "only" learn how to formulate their solutions in Java. Though we have little to compare with (see below), we believe that this setting constitutes a coherent framework for learning two programming languages.

A specific goal was to educate students to produce succinct program documentation. Compared to our experience in previous curricula based on the imperative-first approach, the Informatics students' skill to produce good program documentation was improved. The reasons for this are hard to find and to justify. One may very well be that there was more focus on documentation in the Informatics programme than in earlier curricula. But, we do believe that certain aspects in the curriculum supported good documentation. Because, in the functional programming part, abstract views of programs and program design are in focus while more concrete aspects like graphical user interfaces, side-effects, efficiency and persistence of data are taken into account in the second programming course. Hence, students become aware of different levels of abstractions and have means to handle them. This is helpful when making program documentation, which typically starts at an abstract level and then progresses in many stages to a description of an implementation. At last, with the modelling approach to programming, documentation has a natural role from the very start of the development.

The current *objects-first* curriculum is designed so that, in principle, all students at our university can start with the same programming language. Afterwards the computer science students must follow courses on algorithms, program construction and theory. Students from other areas can start on the same curriculum, but stop when their individual needs are satisfied. In this current curriculum, Java was chosen to be the first programming language taught since functional programming occurs in a third semester course on languages and parsing and is intended for the computer science students only. We have just two years of experience with this design. Therefore, and due to the different focus on the two curricula, it is difficult to make strong conclusions from a comparison. Rather, we will make a few observations.

The first course on Java (10 ECTS) also comprises a programming project and graphical user interfaces. In addition to the Java course, the students typically also have a 5 ECTS point course on algorithms before following the language and parsing course in the third semester. Two surprising observations were as follows:

- We could not introduce SML significantly faster in the third semester than we did in the first semester of the functional-first approach.
- Problems that were challenging in the first semester were challenging in the third semester as well.

Explanations of this are again difficult to find and to justify. Was it simply just our own fault?

It is clear that the more challenging problems considered in the functional programming course often were more abstract, in the formulation as well as in solution, than problems considered in the course based on Java. Therefore, many of the challenges were new to the students in the third semester. A second observation was that although students were aware of problem-solving techniques like functional decomposition and divide and conquer, they typically did not master these techniques. They were probably more used to dividing the state space into classes than, for example, solving a problem by combining solutions to simpler sub-problems.

One can, of course, introduce and solve abstract problems and exercise various problem-solving techniques in a first semester course based on Java. But, then there is less time left for other aspects, like the language-learning phase, object-oriented design or graphical user interfaces. The duration of the language-learning phase seems to be a dominant factor in this respect since only few degrees of freedoms are left for choosing among the other aspects. Therefore, the size of an objects-first course based on Java must leave enough space for other topics like modelling and problem solving, as these represent the lasting knowledge of the course. Our experiences were that Java could be taught in a natural manner on top of SML, whereas the reverse order of topics could not be taught as smoothly.

Acknowledgements

We are grateful for comments and suggestions from David Barnes, Lars Bendix, Jens Bennedsen, Aske Brekling, Görel Hedin, Lauri Malmi, Bent Thomsen and Seppo Törmä on earlier drafts of this chapter.

Appendix

A A Map Colouring Problem and a Solution

When a map is coloured, the colours should be chosen so that neighbouring countries get different colours. The problem is to construct a program computing such a colouring. A trivial solution where each country always gets its own colour is not acceptable. On the other hand, the solution does not have to be an "optimal" one.

A *country* is represented by its name, which is a string, whereas the *neighbour relation* is represented by a list of pairs of names containing those pairs of countries, which have a common border. For instance, the list:

```
[("a", "b"), ("c", "d"), ("d", "a")]
```

defines a colouring problem comprising four countries a, b, c, and d, where the country a has the neighbouring countries b and d, the country b has the neighbouring country a, etc.

A *colour* on a map is represented by the set of countries having this colour, and a *colouring* is described by a list of sets of countries. These representations of colour and colouring are indeed abstractions. The above countries may hence be coloured by the colouring:

```
[["a", "c"], ["b", "d"]]
```

where the countries a and c get one colour, e.g. red, while the countries b and d get another colour, e.g. blue.

The problems to be solved are:

1. Declare the SML types country, neighbourRelation, colour and colouring according to the above description.
2. Declare an SML predicate to determine whether two countries are neighbours in a neighbour relation (it is a good idea first to write down the type of the predicate).
3. Declare an SML predicate to determine whether a colour can be extended by a country under a given neighbour relation. (E.g. the colour ["c"] can be extended by "a" while the colour ["a","c"] cannot be extended by "b" given the above neighbour relation.)
4. Declare an SML function which extends a partial colouring by another country under a given neighbour relation. The new country is given the first colour in the colouring, which has not been used for any neighbouring country — or a new colour, if none of the colours can be used.
5. Declare an SML function to colour a map given a neighbour relation.

A complete solution is given here, together with a test example.

1. The type declarations are:

```
type country                = string;
type neighbourRelation      = (country * country) list;
type colour                 = country list;
type colouring              = colour list;
```

2. An auxiliary function

```
member: ''a * ''a list -> bool
```

to test for membership in a list is declared by

```
infix member
fun x member []      = false
  | x member (y::ys) = x=y orelse x member ys;
```

The predicate

```
areNb: country * country * neighbourRelation -> bool
```

to test whether two countries are neighbours is declared by:

```
fun areNb(c1,c2,nbr) = (c1,c2) member nbr
                       orelse (c2,c1) member nbr;
```

3. The predicate

```
canBeExtBy: colour * country * neighbourRelation -> bool
```

to test whether a colour can be extended by a country is declared by:

```
fun canBeExtBy([],_,_)        = true
  | canBeExtBy(c::cs,c',nbr) =
      not (areNb(c,c',nbr)) andalso canBeExtBy(cs,c',nbr);
```

4. The function

```
extndCol: colouring*country*neighbourRelation -> colouring
```

to extend a colouring is declared by:

```
fun extndCol([],cnt,_) = [[cnt]]
  | extndCol(col::cols,cnt,nbr) =
          if canBeExtBy(col,cnt,nbr) then (cnt::col)::cols
          else col::extndCol(cols,cnt,nbr);
```

5. Two auxiliary functions to get a list of countries without repetitions from a neighbour relation

```
addElem: ''a * ''a list -> ''a list
countries: neighbourRelation -> country list
```

are declared by:

```
fun addElem(x,ys) = if x member ys then ys else x::ys;
fun countries [] = []
  | countries((c1,c2)::nbr) =
          addElem(c1, addElem(c2,countries(nbr)));
```

Two functions to generate colourings are specified by:

```
colCntrs: country list * neighbourRelation -> colouring
colMap: neighbourRelation -> colouring
```

and they are declared by:

```
fun colCntrs([],_) = []
|  colCntrs(cnt::cs,nbr) =
                    extndCol(colCntrs(cs,nbr),cnt,nbr);
fun colMap nbr = colCntrs(countries nbr, nbr);
```

The function colMap can be applied directly from an interactive SML interface:

```
- colMap [("a","b"), ("c","d"), ("d","a")] ;
> val it = [["c", "a"], ["b", "d"]] : string list list
-
```

Learning Programming with the PBL Method — Experiences on PBL Cases and Tutoring

Esko Nuutila, Seppo Törmä, Päivi Kinnunen, and Lauri Malmi

Helsinki University of Technology (TKK),
Laboratory of Software Technology,
P.O.Box 5400, FI-02015 HUT, Finland
{esko.nuutila,seppo.torma,paivi.kinnunen,lauri.malmi}@hut.fi

Abstract. In the *seven steps method* of problem-based learning (PBL), students work in small groups and learn about the problem domain by trying to make sense of complex real-world cases. We have been using the seven steps method for several years to organize the learning in an introductory programming course. In this chapter, we outline the evolution and the arrangements of the course, and give examples of possible cases. The requirements for PBL cases are analyzed, as it is not straightforward to identify good cases in the area of programming. The analysis focuses on the concept of "open-ended, real-world problems" and its interpretation in the domain of programming. We relate the cases to different aspects of programming skills and present student feedback on the cases. We also report about experiments with tutorless PBL that were carried out to see if the method could scale up to courses with large numbers of students. The results were not encouraging. Student questionnaires reveal possible reasons. Firstly, when a tutor is not present, the students become insecure if they are progressing in a fruitful direction and thus, they become frustrated and lose motivation. Secondly, the behaviour of a group may deteriorate (i.e., become unbalanced or turn into irrelevant chatting).

1 Introduction

Problem-based learning (PBL) is a term that has been used in different, but closely-related meanings in the literature:

1. Learning that is *stimulated by descriptions of real-world problems* [Schmidt, 1983]. The problems are presented in the form of *cases*, which are narratives of complex real-world challenges common to the discipline being studied [De Gallow, 2007]. Each case raises issues that *require explanation* and that need to be *understood* in order to solve the problem described. The focus is on acquiring *knowledge* to gain an understanding of the problem, without directly solving it (which may be impossible without further details and tests).

J. Bennedsen et al. (Eds.): Teaching of Programming, LNCS 4821, pp. 47–67, 2008.

2. Learning by *creating solutions to real-world problems.* The solutions are domain artefacts such as computer programs or program designs. Students work in groups to solve open-ended, multi-answer problems. The aim is to develop *skills to solve problems and to create designs* in the domain.

3. Learning by working on complex, real-world tasks [Fekete et al., 1998; Greening et al., 1997; Kay et al., 2000a; Lambrix and Kamkar, 1998]. This approach resembles *project-based learning.* The work involves different phases (e.g., analysis, synthesis, implementation, presentation) and usually takes weeks to finish, whereas in the previous interpretation (2), the time span is much shorter. Typically, the aim is that students will activate and integrate the material they have previously learned and, in addition, learn *work practices and tools* that are effective in the domain.

When PBL is mentioned in connection with computer science education, the meaning is usually related to the two latter ones. However, in medical faculties, where PBL is most extensively used, the term is interpreted in the sense of the first meaning. We have used PBL since autumn 1999 in one of our introductory programming courses [Lambrix and Kamkar, 1998; Nuutila et al., 2005], and as we adopted the method from the medical school of the University of Helsinki, it was also based on the first of the above meanings. However, our implementation has gained aspects of the other meanings, since in computer science it is also natural to use cases that require the students to create a solution (or design) to some problem. In addition, since programming is a skill and needs to be rehearsed, the students are assigned programming exercises and an individual programming project towards the end of the course.

Our implementation of PBL is based on the *seven steps method* [Schmidt, 1983], which is widely used in medical faculties. Groups of 7 to 10 students gather weekly to discuss real-world cases related to programming. Each group defines learning goals for itself to understand and to explain what is essential in the case or to create a solution for the problem presented in the case. A new case is opened every week and closed next week after each member of the group has studied independently to achieve all the specified learning goals. See Section 3.2 for a detailed description of the method.

During one semester, students process ten cases with each focusing on some important aspects of programming. When compared with traditionally organized courses, the PBL sessions replace the lectures and provide the rhythm and social organization for the course. *PBL is thus the central learning method in our course, even though it is supplemented with other methods, such as programming assignments, essays, concept maps, a personal programming project and a portfolio.* In this chapter we focus on the PBL part of the course. See [Nuutila et al., 2005] for a detailed description of the other learning methods, such as personal programming exercises and a personal programming project, that we have found necessary for the development of programming skills.

Regarding the applicability of PBL to education in general, Bereiter and Scardamalia (2003) note: *Whereas in medical education it is possible to select cases that engage students with problems very similar to those they will encounter in later work, this is not a realistic possibility in general education.* This is indeed true to computer programming as well. Typical professional programmers do not encounter and solve "cases" in the day-to-day work, but instead, they work on large and extended software projects. As a consequence, while there are collections of medical case reports, the most curious ones of which can be used as PBL cases, there are no such resources available in the field of programming.

Some applications of PBL in computer science courses have been reported in the literature. At the University of Sydney, foundation CS courses have been implemented with an approach that consists of two project like cases per semester [Fekete et al., 1998; Greening et al., 1997; Kay et al., 2000a]. The authors define PBL as "learning by solving a large, real-world problem". At Linköping University PBL has been used in a course that integrates computer science studies with other engineering disciplines [Lambrix and Kamkar, 1998]. This course is based on a single large scenario that is processed through four major themes. Neither of these approaches is based on the seven steps method. Instead, they are primarily characterized by problem solving focus and resemble project-based learning. However, similar, overall benefits are reported as follows: learning generic skills, familiarity with group work, and ability to deal with vaguely specified problems.

The main contributions of this chapter are the following:

1. We *describe a successful implementation of an introductory computer programming course that uses the PBL as the main learning method.* We give an overview of the course organization, and present some example cases. We also describe the experiences gained during 1999-2005. The supplementary learning methods and results of the course are described in more detail in [Nuutila et al., 2005].
2. Due to scarce tutoring and classroom resources, we have experimented with a *tutorless version of PBL* during 2001-2002 to find an approach that would scale up better than the tutored version of PBL. *The results of the tutorless version turned out to be worse than those of the tutored version.* Based on student questionnaires, we present possible reasons for the failure.
3. Since computer programming is a domain where no natural PBL cases exist, it is not clear *how to come up with good cases.* We analyze what the requirement of "open-ended, real-world problem" means in connection to programming and present *some conceptual distinctions*: whether the content or the implied task comes from the real-world, whether the content talks about issues inside or outside a software system, and whether the implied task is explanation or design.

Our approach deals with similar questions that are considered in several other chapters in this book. One of the key issues in PBL is discussion and collaboration in small groups. This is also an important part of *Apprentice-Based Learning* presented by Kölling and Barnes, as well as Thomsen's method of having students discuss the material together in on-line tutorials (*Using On-line Tutorials in Introductory IT Courses*). In all these chapters, students reflect their learning jointly, which is a very important aspect of learning. Apprentice-Based Learning also emphasizes the importance of setting up practical non-trivial and open problems for students of which they also have some control of where they proceed. The same elements can be found in our PBL method. Finally, Hansen and Kristensen discuss programming as a modelling activity, which they emphasize already in their introductory course. We have also identified conceptual modelling as an activity that fits well with PBL, and our observations have demonstrated to us that student groups are well capable of conceptual modelling very early in their programming course, when PBL is used.

The structure of the chapter is as follows. First, to provide a background for the subsequent discussion, we discuss the essential aspects of programming skills. The implementation of our course then is presented, followed by some observations we have made on the method —including the role of the tutor— during the past five years. We provide a sample collection of different kinds of cases, followed by a discussion on the characteristics of the cases. We then relate the PBL cases to the aspects of programming skills and describe what other learning methods may be needed. Finally, we present student feedback on our cases.

2   Aspects of Programming Skills

Why is it so difficult for many novice students to learn computer programming? We should first note that it has —both as a cognitive activity and as a practical activity— many elements that are foreign to novices.

According to [Blackwell, 2002], the difficulties stem from the indirect nature of programming and the resulting need for abstractions. In other problem-solving tasks that students face —for instance, in mathematics or physics— the solution is created by directly manipulating the model describing an instance of the problem. In programming, the benefits of this kind of direct manipulation are lost. Quoting [Blackwell, 2002]:

> The situation in which the program is to be executed may not be available for inspection, because it may be in the future, or because the program may be applied to a greater range of data situations than are currently visible to the programmer. While acting on a single situation is concrete (actions have visible effects in the current situation), programming is abstract (effects may occur in many different situations, not currently visible).

This indirect nature of programming requires a specific type of thinking that novice students are not familiar with. Instead of focusing just on the intended execution path of the program, the student must also consider all the unintended or exceptional situations that may be encountered in the execution and the possibility of exceptional data objects that the program has to deal with.

The testing and branching operations present in modern programming languages reflect this fact: many aspects of the situation that the program is dealing with are only revealed during the execution and many decisions of required operations must, therefore, be postponed to the execution time. The problems with complex patterns of control flow have led to various structured control mechanisms (conditionals, iteration, exception handling). To tackle the indirectness, abstraction mechanisms (e.g., procedures, classes) have evolved into programming languages. They can be used to instantiate common data or to control patterns based on the execution time information. To have even rudimentary programming skills, these kinds of mechanisms need to be understood well enough that they can be used when writing new programs.

However, these mechanisms are not something that students know in advance. There are a large number of *new, abstract concepts and mechanisms* that a novice programmer needs to learn and to understand. Few of these concepts are self-evident, as it took decades before they were invented. It is, however, important to master these concepts to the extent that they can be correctly used in programming work. The concepts are interdependent and often describe different aspects of the same dynamic or structural mechanisms related to the programming language (for example to method invocation or parameter passing) and to the data structures and algorithms (for example, to the structure of and operations on a stack or a binary tree).

[du Boulay, 1989] separates the difficulties of learning to program into the following five areas: (1) *orientation*: the purpose of programs, types of problems that can be solved, and the benefits of programming skills; (2) *the notional machine*: the nature of the abstract machine that needs to be controlled; (3) *notation*: the syntax and semantics of the programming language; (4) *structures*: idioms, patterns, and plans to achieve small scale goals; (5) *pragmatics*: skills for specifying, implementing, testing and debugging programs by using appropriate tools. A major challenge in orientation is to have the students adopt the mindset of an engineer: to build mechanisms to solve practical problems. The previous education of novice students usually contains few activities of that kind.

The notational difficulties are caused by the *strict syntax and semantics of programming languages*. The notation of programming languages differs from that of natural languages, and often seems complex for beginning programmers. Moreover, they are usually unfamiliar with any tasks that require similar meticulous and careful attention to details as the use of programming language does. No errors in syntax and semantics of programs are tolerated.

Many difficulties relate to the pragmatics of programming. Novice programmers seldom have any experience of any activity that requires *continual use of problem solving and design skills* in a manner that programming does. In other disciplines (e.g., mathematics and physics) students primarily solve *closed problems* (i.e., small problems defined by the teacher) that typically have only one correct solution. Moreover, the teacher evaluates the solution, which means that getting an almost correct answer is usually sufficient. The student does not need to use the solution anywhere. Furthermore, there is no need to rephrase or to improve an existing solution.

In programming, the problems are usually *open-ended*: they have a large number of possible solutions, some better and some worse. To design a program, the student must define sub-problems by him or herself, solve these sub-problems, and use the solutions as part of a larger program. Even minor flaws in the solutions will almost certainly lead to an erroneous program. When combining partial solutions, there is often a need to rephrase or to improve them. Moreover, program design typically requires definition of new abstractions, which can be regarded a particularly demanding cognitive task [Blackwell, 2001]. The unfamiliarity with the methods in this area often leads the student to stare at the blank computer screen with no idea of what to do next.

Programming requires familiarity with a set of *specific tools* —editor, interpreter or compiler, debugger, and a manual browsing tool— and appropriate *work practices*. For example, students should learn to use an iterative development style —composing the program of pieces with frequent editing, compilation, and testing cycles— instead of attempting to write a complete program before the first attempt to compile it. However, the iterative style should be used in a proper, goal directed manner, instead of resorting to ineffective, trial-and-error style (so-called *bricolage* [Ben-Ari, 1998]).

Programming cannot be learned without some level of parallel progress in *all the above-mentioned areas*, even if the mastery in the skill only comes after years of practice. Given the strange nature of computer programming as an activity, it is not surprising that results of introductory programming courses leave usually a lot to be desired.

3   Implementation of a Programming Course Using PBL

In 1999 Helsinki University of Technology (TKK) established an interdisciplinary degree program of information networks. The program combines information technology with business management, sociology and communication. At the time when the studies for the new program were planned, we became familiar with the PBL method used at the medical school of the University of Helsinki. Centred on real-world problems, the method appeared to match with the interdisciplinary character of the new degree program. Moreover, the small number of students in the program (the enrolment is about 30 students per year) made it possible to experiment with a learning method that is radically different from traditional teaching based on lectures.

There are different specific ways for implementing PBL. We adopted the approach from the medical school of University of Helsinki, where PBL was based on the seven steps method developed at Maastricht University [Schmidt, 1983]. The method is designed to foster learning by

1. connecting the learning to *specific problem situations* that may be encountered in practice
2. *activating prior knowledge* of students about the topic to learn
3. making the students *elaborate on the material* that they have learned.

The seven steps method is a process designed to satisfy these requirements as described below in more detail.

3.1   Course Organization

The course has evolved over several years. In the following, we describe the current state of the course organization.

The students are divided into groups of 7 to 10 members. Each group is supervised by a *tutor* who is either a faculty member or a student who has taken the same PBL course before.

The primary role of a tutor is to act as a *domain expert* who can answer questions in the domain or correct the direction of the discussion that has taken a wrong path. Often an appropriate question — "how do you know that X", "can you think of other factors besides X", "what are the causes/parts/properties of X" — is enough to set the group into a more fruitful direction.

The secondary role of a tutor is a *facilitator* of the group process. If the discussion is unbalanced or unproductive, the tutor can try various approaches to improve the behaviour of the group. For example, the tutor may require that the students sit in different places in each meeting, do not bring books to the meetings, or that each student writes at least five notes during the brainstorming. We have also occasionally used some cooperative exercises to improve the atmosphere of the group.

Since programming is a skill, it needs to be rehearsed. Thus, already in the first course version (autumn 1999) we supplemented the PBL cases with programming assignments and a personal programming project. Solving the programming assignments is supported by weekly meetings with the course assistants. In addition, students write essays and draw concept maps about key mechanisms of the programming language.

Based on the material they have produced in these tasks, they finally prepare a portfolio, in which they summarize and reflect their learning. The students are evaluated based on the programming assignments, the programming project, a small exam and the portfolio.

We do not believe PBL to be a magic solution for learning programming, but it has a more central role than other learning methods mentioned above. It is the main organizing method in the course, and the weekly PBL sessions establish a social organization among the students and the teachers, which seems to be very important.

3.2   The Seven Steps Method

Each group meets once a week in a PBL session lasting for three hours. There are few requirements for the setting. A group needs a meeting room equipped with a white board or a flip chart. Self-stick notes and white board markers should also be provided for every student. The meeting starts with the closing session of the previous case, if any. Then a new case is opened. The processing of the case goes through the sequence of steps shown in Table 1.

One person in a group may act as a secretary that stands up and places the self-stick notes on a white board. Another student may act as a chairman, whose main role is to see that the group proceeds through all phases within the allocated time frame. However, once the students are familiar with the method, there is no real need for a chairman anymore. Even a secretary is not necessary if all members have room to stand up during the steps when the self-stick notes are placed or reorganized on the white board.

Table 1. The sequence of steps used to process each of the cases

Opening session — half an hour, in the group
Step 1. **Examination of the case**. The group familiarizes with the case material.
Step 2. **Identification of the problem**. An initial title related with the key issues of the case is specified.
Step 3. **Brainstorming**. The students present their associations and ideas about the problem to activate their previous knowledge about the topic. The ideas are said aloud and written on self-stick notes, which are posted on a white board.
Step 4. **Sketching of an explanatory model**. The gathered knowledge is systematized into a model that explains what happens in the case.
Step 5. **Establishing the learning goals**. Based on the explanatory model, the structures, gaps, weaknesses and inconsistencies are identified and the central ones (within the context of the course) are chosen as learning goals for the group.
The intended outcome: a set of learning goals, initial understanding of the domain based on prior knowledge.
Study period — one week, each student working independently
Step 6. **Independent studying**. Each student independently studies to accomplish *all* learning goals. This phase includes information gathering and usually a substantial amount of reading (*e.g.*, 50-150 pages).
The intended outcome: individual understanding of the domain to the extent that each student is able to answer the learning goals.
Closing session — one to two hours, in the group
Step 7. **Elaboration**. Equipped with the newly acquired knowledge, the group reconvenes to discuss the case. The discussion includes *explanation* of central concepts and mechanisms, *analysis* of the material, and *evaluation* of its validity and importance.
The intended outcome: the confidence that the understanding is basically correct, more thorough understanding of the domain, awareness of the provisional status of existing knowledge (different approaches and theories, problems, open questions, and so on).

3.3 Results

In a questionnaire (autumn 2002), the students reported that group work in PBL improved the motivation, provided emotional support and gave a social context for the course. A measurable benefit of this learning method has been a much lower drop-out rate than in our traditional programming courses, 17%

versus 45%. Both the students of the PBL course and the students of the traditional programming courses subsequently take the same advanced course in Java programming. The average scores for the students coming from the PBL course have been slightly better, but the difference is not significant.

3.4   Experiences and Problems

Below we describe our experiences with the different steps of the seven steps method. Steps 1 and 2, examination of the case and identification of the problem, are straightforward and should not take longer than a couple of minutes. Only in the first few cases should the students have any difficulties in finding a title for the case. The tutor may indicate that the exactness of the title is not important. It is crucial to get the process in full motion and not get stuck with these steps.

In Step 3, brainstorming, the goal is to connect the case with the previous knowledge and experience of the students. Brainstorming is a divergent and exploratory activity: the aim is to cover different areas and aspects of the domain. It is essential that the students do not criticize each other's —or their own— ideas. In fruitful brainstorming there are parallel and freely combining streams of ideas. The process is unconstrained and requires no centralized coordination, apart perhaps from a secretary that places self-stick notes on a white board. In our experience, brainstorming is usually the least problematic step of the method. However, a prerequisite is that the case has connections to something that the students already know. As a result of brainstorming, the group usually has 20 to 40 self-stick notes on a white board, each of which names some concept or presents a statement or a question.

Brainstorming is an example of the power of *distributed cognition* [Hutchins, 1995]. Since multiple people are working on the same cognitive task, it contains an element of *social distribution*, and also *physical distribution* because an external representation is constructed. The representation, a collection of unrelated self-stick notes, is appropriate when considering the divergent and exploratory nature of this task.

Step 4, sketching of an explanatory model, is a convergent activity where students try to systematize the material generated in brainstorming into a connected whole. The group must focus into one common issue after another. The secretary works on the white board and constructs the model by moving the self-stick notes and making drawings and annotations on the board. Contrary to the previous step, evaluation and criticism of the ideas can be expected. Typically, during this process some new concepts or questions arise and a few new notes are added.

The typical performance of the student groups in this task has not been satisfying. Given that the result of brainstorming is a bunch of loosely connected ideas and concepts, one would expect students to reflect about the material and end up reorganizing it into a more coherent and meaningful whole. However, that rarely happens. The students usually confine themselves to simply regrouping the self-stick notes. A typical result is two to four different categories, with a general title for each of the categories.

Recently, we experimented with concept maps [Novak and Cañas, 2006] in sketching the model. The results have been encouraging as follows: new abstractions and relationships emerge among the ideas and less fruitful ideas are left out. It would also be worth a closer study as to whether the tutor could take a more active role in guiding the sketching process. It is important, however, that the group, and not the tutor, provides the content of the explanatory model since the purpose of the model at that point is to reveal what weaknesses or gaps there are in the current understanding of the group.

Step 5, establishing the learning goals, is based on the explanatory model the group has created. The model works here in different ways as follows: it gives an idea of how the domain can be divided into sub-topics, it can show that certain areas of the domain are not understood as well as others (gaps and weaknesses), and show that there are inconsistencies in the understanding. Generally, with the aid of the tutor the students have been able to identify relatively good learning goals. However, if the explanatory model is weak, there may be important issues not seen by the students that the tutor must explicitly include as learning goals. The tutor may also point out if some learning goals seem too general. Such a problem often arises within the first cases because students have not gained enough experience on defining learning goals explicitly enough.

In this method it is important that all members of a group will study to independently fulfill all the learning goals. The goals are thus not split between the members, but everyone has the same goals. The idea is that the students will be able to discuss and to elaborate on what they have learned and not that they will teach different parts of a complex topic to each other. Sometimes it is possible, however, that the learning goals are categorized to central goals and optional goals (to be studied if time permits), but often this is not necessary. After the learning goals have been defined, the group should identify material - books, articles, and web sites - for independent studying. This is a task in which the tutor can and should help the group.

Step 6, independent studying period, is the most crucial of the steps. It is by far the longest step and most of the learning takes place during it. The importance of self study and that all group members study to achieve the same learning goals should be emphasized to the students from the beginning and the morale should be kept high throughout the course. In addition, this should be taken into account when designing the overall syllabus for the students. There should be enough time reserved for independent studying.

The quality of Step 7, discussion about learned material, is directly connected to the amount of self-study. Optimally, each student is so familiar with the facts, concepts and mechanisms of the domain that the discussion is mostly focused on reflection on the meaning, importance and the use of learned material. In the other extreme, if Step 6 has failed, then the group may even seem to know less about the subject than in the opening session. A typical observation, however, is that the discussion tends to stay on a level of recalling facts and observations instead of delving into deeper levels of knowledge. This is obviously related to lack of experience in programming. Moreover, many programming textbooks do not emphasize reflecting the importance of various concepts. Rather, they concentrate on presenting the language features. However, here the tutor may assist the group by presenting occasionally suitably targeted questions.

The material should not be fixed too rigidly in Step 5. It is actually beneficial if students use various sources of knowledge during independent studying. When multiple viewpoints exist, the quality of the discussion in Step 7 will improve. It will be better motivated and more thorough. The students' metacognitive skills —evaluation of difference sources, resolution of conflicting viewpoints, and so on— will be rehearsed. The whole method will be more robust since errors or weaknesses in source material are more likely to be revealed and corrected.

It is worth noticing that the group work in this method is completely different from what our students are accustomed to in high school where the splitting of the work seems to be the norm. In the PBL method each student is responsible for his or her own learning. Therefore, the problem of group-work called "free riders" (i.e., members that avoid responsibility or contribution) does not arise in the same way as in the groups that need to produce common results. Naturally, the activity of different students in the participation to discussion varies, but that has not been a major problem in our course.

3.5 The Role of the Tutor

Our experience suggests that the tutor should not be too active. Otherwise the PBL session starts to resemble a lecture, and the students begin to see the tutor as responsible for their learning. Indeed, in the best PBL sessions the students take charge of the process from start to finish and the tutor is mostly a passive observer. Even in these cases, however, *the presence of the tutor* is important because it helps the group to overcome difficulties and prevents the group from breaking up.

In the questionnaires filled by the participants of our PBL courses [Kinnunen, 2004], students report that the tutor

1. is a safety net against incorrect knowledge and reasoning,
2. may provide wider or new perspectives to the subject and helps to focus on essential content,
3. helps the group to proceed to a more fruitful direction, if it gets stuck,
4. helps in group dynamics and social issues by maintaining a balance in participation between different members of the group, and
5. just by being present, creates additional pressure for the students to work harder in the self-study phase.

However, a problem is that the PBL implementation we have described above does not easily scale up to large courses due to lack of tutoring and classroom resources. A course of 200 students would already require 60 hours of tutoring and allocated meeting rooms per week, both requirements that in our university prevent the use of PBL in most computer science courses.

To solve this problem, we carried out experiments with the *tutorless version of PBL* [Kinnunen and Malmi, 2002] in which students held the PBL sessions without tutors and at places they chose themselves, for example, in a meeting room of a university library or possibly even in the apartment of one of the students. The goal was to find out if the important properties of the PBL method could be preserved without prohibitive resource requirements.

During the years 2001 to 2002, three prototype versions of a tutorless PBL course were given. Each group was assigned a teaching assistant taking charge of the group. The assistant was present as a tutor only in the first two PBL sessions to ensure that the group would learn the seven steps method. Thereafter, the group gathered to PBL sessions weekly in a place of its own choice. If the group had any difficulties, it had the possibility to meet the assistant once a week to discuss the problematic issues.

Students in the tutorless groups were subsequently interviewed to find out how they felt about the method. It turned out that following the seven steps method did not cause any difficulties for them. However, they often reported being uncertain about the correctness of the presented knowledge, which led to frustration. Some groups seemed to digress into discussing irrelevant matters, which ultimately led to the breaking down of some groups. As a whole, the differences between groups' working styles were considerably larger than between groups where tutors were always present.

These observations were in line with the dominant problems in tutorless PBL groups listed in [Woods et al., 1996]. First, the group can end up in a conflict due to a perception that all members are not putting in their fair share of the work. This affects attendance in the group as well as the trust and reliability among students. Second, it is also more difficult to establish common work goals and standards among students in a tutorless group. Due to the poor results of the tutorless PBL, no further courses using that approach have been arranged. Tutoring seems to be an essential part of the method.

One possibility to somewhat relieve the lack of tutoring resources is to recruit the tutors from the best students (those with highest grades) of the previous year. This has turned out to be a successful approach. It is not, however, a similar solution to resource problems as tutorless PBL since the tutors are paid a normal salary. Furthermore, with organized tutoring it also seems natural to provide the groups with meeting rooms.

In the first two years of the course, all the tutors were members of the teaching personnel. Their strength was in the amount of technical knowledge about the area. The drawbacks were that they had not studied in a PBL course themselves and they did not have a good memory of the difficulties they have had in the beginning of their programming career. In addition, they were often pretty busy with other responsibilities.

In autumn 2001 we hired the best students from the previous years to work as tutors. Before the semester begins, a couple of meetings with the prospective tutors are held to explain the changes to the course arrangements, PBL cases and programming exercises. However, no additional training for the tutors is arranged.

The experiences have been good. Students are often eager to become tutors and they are thoroughly familiar with the method. The recruited students have possessed quite sufficient technical knowledge about the area. Moreover, they typically have a good feeling about the difficulties that novices face in the course. They are also familiar with different kinds of practical problems, for example, related with the use of the student computer systems. In addition, they seem to be able to cope with problems in the group process as well as the teaching personnel.

4   PBL Cases in the Domain of Programming

In this section, we give examples of PBL cases that we have used. We analyze different characteristics of the cases and discuss their relation to different aspects of programming skills. Finally, we present student feedback concerning the cases.

4.1   Example Cases

The course currently consists of ten cases (see [Nuutila et al., 2005] for a complete listing). Below we give examples of different types of cases.

Hamburger restaurant: This case is related to modelling software systems by using objects and classes. The main goal is to make the students understand the concepts of object and class and the difference between them.

The students are asked to provide "some kind of conceptual and functional model" of a hamburger restaurant. In choosing the learning goals, the students should pay attention to presenting the model by a diagram and in Java code.

If the students find this task difficult, the tutor may ask them to think what kinds of concepts are related to hamburger restaurants. If the students describe very abstract concepts, the tutor may ask them to list things that they have seen in hamburger restaurants. Sometimes the students mistake subclasses for objects - for instance they may think that hamburger is a class and cheese burger is the instance of this class.

The reason for choosing the hamburger restaurant domain was that it is familiar to most students and it consists mostly of discrete objects such as hamburgers, which can be categorized in a class hierarchy. There are also some interesting composite objects such as hamburger meals.

Java code: In this case, we give the students the listing of some simple Java classes (about 60 lines of code in total), a partial UML class diagram and the corresponding program execution. In the previous case, the students learned the concepts of an object and a class. The aim here is to make them more familiar with the structure of Java programs and the exact Java syntax, to introduce constructors, methods, and variables, and to present the idea of program compilation and execution. The students typically detect some connections between the program code and the program execution, but find the program syntax incomprehensible. The learning goals are mostly related to Java syntax.

A robot in a maze: The students are asked to design the control logic for a robot walking in a maze. They are presented pictures (grids) of different kinds of mazes. To make the task easier, they are told that the robot can turn itself left or right and step forward if it is possible. The students should first identify objects and classes needed for presenting the maze and then describe the control logic.

Although the design tasks are not easy, the students get fairly good algorithms. They usually choose for their learning goals to be able to define the objects and classes needed and the control logic in Java.

WWW bookstore: The students are asked to design a way to present data in a WWW bookstore. They need to present the available products, the customers and their shopping carts. Obviously, collections of objects are needed here. The students sometimes seem to have difficulties in distinguishing between classes and collections since objects somehow "belong" to both classes and collections. The tutor may have to point out their differences. The learning goals are related to presenting collections in Java.

Computer file system: The goal is to introduce hierarchical object structures and recursion and to make a distinction to the class hierarchy. The students are explained that a computer file system consists of files that are of two different types: 1) documents and 2) folders. A folder can contain a set of files (either documents or folders) and each file belongs to some folder. Typical operations on files are move, rename, copy and delete. The size of storage required by a file can be presented to the user. The students should model the file system by Java classes and methods.

The problem here is to find a minimal set of classes —only three are needed— and to design the file operations. The concept of recursion, which is not familiar to the students, is needed when copying folders and counting the size required by a folder. In the opening session, the students realize the need for recursion, but cannot yet formulate it. Further, they seem to have difficulties in understanding the idea of objects that refer to other objects and form a tree-like structure.

4.2   Characteristics of PBL Cases

Below, we discuss some interesting characteristics that can be used in designing and analyzing PBL cases. PBL cases are characterized as "open-ended, real-world problems". What does this mean in connection to programming? Is it sensitive to whether the focus of the case is on explanation or design?

Reality: An essential aspect of PBL cases is that they are from the real world. Even when the goal is to teach an abstract concept or mechanism, the case should introduce it in a concrete and specific situation.

Reality has many important benefits. A good case often has an element of *surprise* [Hafler, 1998] in that it describes something that is against students' expectations. If the case is invented, the surprise does not arouse the students' *curiosity* (since anything can be invented) in the same way as when the students know that the case has actually happened. Moreover, the reality helps to ensure the *relevance* of the case and consequently helps the students to *transfer* the learned material to situations they will encounter in their work. Reality also fosters the *activation* of previous knowledge in cases where an abstract concept needs to be learned. Furthermore, the requirement of reality leads to *pedagogically more effective cases* [Hafler, 1998]; they are more likely to contain contradictions and incompleteness that force the students to think in a more *reflective and open-ended* manner.

What does the requirement of reality mean for the selection of programming cases? If we consider the cases as real-world challenges faced by a professional programmer, we can identify two aspects that make a case closer to reality:

1. *Real-world content*: The case requires students to *think* about the kinds of *issues* that programmers need to *think* in their work.
2. *Real-world task*: The case requires students to *do* the kinds of *tasks* that programmers need to *do* in their work.

The first one of these, content realism, has to take into account the artificial character of computer programming. Herbert Simon calls engineering oriented disciplines such as computer programming "sciences of the artificial" [Simon, 1969]. Their focus is not on how things are (like in descriptive sciences), but on artificial constructs, artefacts that can be created. A major part of programmers' work centers around artefacts such as requirement specifications, program designs, program code, and program documentation. Examples of issues that a programmer needs to think in his or her work are program structure, abstractions, algorithms, data structures, correctness, the representation of domain objects in a program, input, storage and output of data, mechanisms of user interaction, testing and debugging methods, system performance and ways to determine and to improve it and so on.

However, an interesting and important property of computer programs are that they can be *about* some objects or phenomena outside of computer (e.g., people, organizations, physical products, activities of a project, accounts, risks, probabilities and so on). A part of programming work (e.g., problem analysis) deals with understanding the structure of a particular domain outside a computer to the extent that the relevant aspects of the domain can be represented inside a computer.

There is consequently another interpretation of the term "real-world problem" as an *outside-world* problem such as a case that talks about things outside software systems (i.e., something not related to computers, computation, or programming languages). There is nothing particular that the programmer needs to know about outside-world, but he or she needs to be able to make a connection between the relevant properties of outside-world and the structure of the program.

How does this distinction between issues inside and outside a software system relate to PBL? Since the novice students do not know much of anything about the internals of software systems and do not even grasp the concepts involved, the use of outside-world problems may be necessary if we want to activate any prior knowledge about anything. Once the students have learned something about the internals of software, cases that rely on knowledge of those internals are possible.

Another aspect of real-world cases, task realism, relates to the kinds of tasks that programmers do in their work. Examples are analyzing a domain, creating specifications, creating a design, specifying data structures and/or algorithms, implementing a program, testing and debugging a program and so on.

The allocated time frame, the group work nature, and the typical tools (i.e., whiteboard and self-stick notes) available in PBL sessions constrain the kinds of tasks that can be carried out. Programming, for instance, is difficult to do in such a setting, but a design of a small program can actually be produced quite well. We have used many cases that concentrate on the task of design.

A real-world case should have either content realism or task realism or both. If a case has content realism, but not task realism, it can be used to develop understanding about the domain. If a case has task realism, but not content realism, it can be used to develop design skills. Such cases can use artificial or invented figures (such as an imaginary robot in an imaginary maze) while preserving the essential structure of a real task.

Open-endedness: An open-ended case does not have a single correct solution to the presented problem. There are several different possible solutions, some worse and some better. Moreover, an existing solution can often be improved in many different ways, by making it more detailed, efficient, robust, elegant/understandable and so on.

Every problem determines *constraints* that the possible solutions must satisfy. Constraints are only accidentally just tight enough that there is only one possible solution. If the constraints are less tight, there are multiple possible solutions (problem is under-constrained), and if they are tighter, there are none (problem is over-constrained). When multiple solutions exist, there is often a need to rate these solutions according to some *evaluation criteria* in order to distinguish a better solution from a worse one. In case the solution is searched for iteratively, there is also a need for *stopping criteria* to tell when a solution is good enough to quit for the further search. The tutor may be in an important role to give the students feedback about the solution, such as when some parts are good enough, when something is lacking, when something could be improved, when some ideas are not fruitful or improvable, and so on.

Open-endedness is a property of a PBL case that makes the group work more meaningful. In a group it is likely that more than one solution is identified. The discussion about the merits and drawbacks of different solutions, or whether some proposed solution is satisfactory are of great pedagogic value.

The open-endedness can be controlled by the case description. Each case has a short textual description, which includes the title of the case, and possibly guidelines to learning goals. The description has an effect of the activity of the group. It is a mechanism to control the direction of the group effort.

The more specific the description is, the less freedom the group has in the processing of the case. The danger is that the case turns into an ordinary assignment and the opening session becomes somewhat irrelevant. On the other hand, a loose description can make it difficult for a group to proceed in any direction and students may become frustrated. An example of a too specific description was a case titled "Objects and classes in Java". Perhaps not surprisingly, the groups typically specified learning goals such as "objects and classes" and "how objects and classes can be used in Java".

If we analyze the cases described above in this aspects, we note that the computer file system is the most specific and least open-ended. Although this is an interesting example of the power of recursive definitions, the case description does not leave many options for the students. They should find out three classes and a set of methods. The robot case is a bit more open-ended since there are different algorithms for the task. The case description is rather specific. The description of the hamburger case is less specific, and the problem is rather open-ended. This seems to confuse the students, especially since the case is presented at the beginning of the course. In the Java code case, the description is the least specific as the students are only given a set of Java files without any further guidance. However, the problem does not seem to be too open-ended. The students seem to understand that the aim is to learn program syntax and its relation to program execution.

Focus of work: In traditional PBL cases, the main focus of work is to produce an *explanation* for the problem described in a case. In order to do so, the students need to *acquire knowledge* to *gain understanding* of the problem. An explanation is what [Bereiter, 2002] calls a *conceptual artefact* or a *knowledge object*. From the point-of-view of education, these kinds of artefacts have value as such, since they improve the understanding of the students and facilitate the further learning of that topic.

A case can also require the students to produce a *solution* to a problem, for instance, a program design in the form of a diagram of classes. Such a solution is a *domain artefact* and it does not have any particular educational value as such. However, to create the artefact the students need to (1) *know* the target representation (i.e., notation for building blocks of the design and the ways to put the elements of design together) and (2) have *skills* required by the creation of the artefact (i.e., design skills). The skills required by the design work are rehearsed already in the opening session of the case, and may further be enhanced in the self-study phase. Thus, the whole case focuses on developing skills instead of improving knowledge, even though most such problem or design-oriented cases include the latter aspect too.

If the representation of data/information in the case is foreign to the students, the group may need to acquire knowledge about it. Learning is not focused on explaining a problem, but *knowing "all about"* the representation [Bereiter, 2002]. In our experience, all design-oriented cases do not lead to natural learning goals.

4.3   Effects on Programming Skills

Above we identified the following aspects of the programming skills that students find difficult:

- new and abstract concepts and mechanisms
- continuous use of problem solving and design skills
- strict syntax and semantics of programming languages
- programming tools and work practices

The cases whose work focus is explanation, lead to learning factual and conceptual knowledge of the subject area. In an introductory programming course, conceptual learning is more critical of these. These kinds of cases rely on background knowledge of programming, and in the beginning of the course many cases of this character must use outside-world problems.

The cases whose work focus is in producing a design, lead to improvement in the design skills of the students as well as in improved conceptual understanding about the elements that are used to express the design. The design work carried out in a group is often surprisingly effective, namely, the group does not get stuck with minor problems as easily as individual students do. It also resembles the actual design processes that occur in real software teams. Students soon learn the right "design mindset" and learn to ask the right questions that drive the design forward. This seems to be most helpful to the students that initially are less oriented to computer programming.

If the case contains problem-solving aspects, the problem solving skills of the students are rehearsed. Again the group interaction is beneficial, even though problem solving may also require solitary activity when students think the problem through themselves.

Some aspects of the programming skills require the use of supplementary learning methods. Supervised programming exercises are essential to teach the use of programming tools and effective work practices. The application of the material learned in the cases also requires exercises and —in our experience— a larger programming project.

Some difficult conceptual topics may benefit from using essays and concept maps as learning methods. We have good experience of the use of concept maps as specified by [Novak and Cañas, 2006]. However, we have later on developed a notation called *text graphs* [Nuutila and Törmä, 2004] that better supports the representation of conceptual relationships that exists in domains, such as computer science, where complex technical mechanisms are in central role.

There has been some controversy whether lectures can be fruitfully combined with ordinary PBL. The students may perceive that lectures tell what the really important issues are to be learned and PBL sessions are not essential in specifying the learning goals. In our experience, carefully designed supplementary lectures help to give the students a wider perspective to the topic of a case, especially in tutorless PBL where a tutor is not available during the sessions to provide a wider perspective. Lectures can also be used to teach certain technical concepts, such as exceptions, interfaces and I/O libraries, since such concepts do not fit well to PBL cases. The problem with them is that such concepts are technical solutions to problems in designing and implementing large programs, an experience far beyond the level of our students. Therefore, the students cannot see a need for such concepts in the opening sessions.

4.4   Student Feedback

Students were asked to give feedback concerning the cases and grade the cases on a scale from 1 (completely uninteresting) to 5 (very interesting). Below is a summary of the comments of the students as well as the average grade received by the cases.

Hamburger restaurant: average grade 2.1. This was regarded as the most uninteresting case. Students felt that the case was unclear, disorganized, disconnected and vague. The case led the discussion to non-essential issues. Moreover the case was regarded laborious. Note that this was the first case presented for the students.

Java code: average grade 3.7. This case was given in an early phase of the course. The case awoke positive feedback. It was regarded as more interesting than the average case. Students liked the topic and the case was considered helpful.

A robot in a maze: average grade 4.1. This was regarded as the most interesting case. The case was well prepared. It had a concrete and well-defined problem. It generated lots of different kinds of thoughts that were discussed together. Nobody was able to solve the problem alone. Instead, all members of the group discussed together. The case also generated concrete experiments with different kinds of search algorithms.

It was especially good that all students were able to participate in the discussion because the case did not require previous knowledge about computers or programming. Instead, the case was more about logical reasoning than about programming. Moreover, students were required to apply discussed/learned issues into a programming exercise given slightly later in the course. Thus, they were able to apply recently learned knowledge into practice.

WWW bookstore: average grade 2.9. This case was regarded slightly less interesting than the average case. Students felt that the case was boring. The topic was regarded as simple, but abstract.

Computer file system: average grade 2.7. This case, again, was regarded slightly less interesting than the average case. Although the case generated a good group meeting, students felt that the aim of the case was unclear. The case was considered abstract and, therefore, hard to put together, which caused frustration.

5   Summary and Conclusions

We have described experiences of using problem-based learning, especially the seven steps method, in introductory programming courses. Since 1999 we have tested various types of PBL cases and combinations of PBL and other learning methods. We have also experimented with PBL without using a tutor. The aim has been to identify the best practice methods to implement a PBL course in programming.

Our main findings are the following. First, the PBL method can be successfully applied in an introductory programming course. Compared to traditional education, the main role of PBL is replacing lectures either partially or wholly, whereas programming exercises are still necessarily needed to learn programming skills. A PBL course may well include a few lectures, especially on technical details, but the role of the lectures should remain as a source of information for students when they are searching for information to their learning goals. The key difference here is that in PBL the students their own learning goals, whereas in traditional lecture courses the goals are set up by the teacher. PBL thus emphasizes students' responsibility of their own learning.

Second, the PBL method applies well to learning some aspects of programming skill. These include problem-solving and program design skills. The group interaction within the PBL group supports this.

Third, appropriately designed PBL cases can be used successfully to initiate learning many important programming concepts. In the beginning of the course, however, such purposed cases must use problems outside an immediate programming context due to students' lack of experience on programming.

Fourth, programming concepts that have been designed to aid managing large software products, such as exceptions or interfaces, are not applicable to PBL cases. Students do not have enough experience to anticipate the need for such constructions.

Fifth, the PBL method has to be supplemented with practical programming exercises to rehearse coding skills enough. Also, learning syntactical issues and the use of programming tools are better practiced in programming exercises than in PBL sessions. Finally, a tutor is highly important resource for the students in PBL sessions, even though the tutor need not necessarily be actively participating in the discussion during the sessions.

The PBL approach has several similar aspects as the *Apprentice-Based Learning* by Kölling and Barnes. Group interaction is highly important in both methods and both emphasize real, open problems. But, there are differences as well. In the latter one, the central idea is to start from studying expert code, learning from it and extending it, whereas in our PBL approach the joint sessions are not used in coding. Even though some cases may include inspecting code, the main emphasis in the PBL cases is elsewhere such as identifying learning goals, discussion on important concepts and practicing design. Coding is carried out in parallel, but separate programming assignments.

In the heart of designing a PBL based course is finding and defining good cases. We have presented examples of cases that we have used. To be able to come up with good cases, we have analyzed the properties of the cases. Since computer science is an example of the "sciences of the artificial" [Simon, 1969], the reality aspect has a different role in learning programming than in natural sciences and medicine. A "real world" case in a programming course is something that might occur as a design task for a professional software engineer.

Open-endedness of the case is crucial to meaningful group interaction. It can be controlled by the specificity of the case description. Open-endedness is possible regardless of whether the focus of work in the case is on producing an explanation or a design. Finally, in learning computer programming, cases that mainly lead to acquiring knowledge are not so central as in medicine. Instead, the cases often have problem-solving or design focus.

Using On-Line Tutorials in
Introductory IT Courses

Bent Thomsen

Department of Computer Science, Aalborg University,
Selma Lagerlöfs Vej 300, DK-9220 Aalborg Ø, Denmark
bt@cs.aau.dk

Abstract. Many universities offer introductory IT courses covering an
introduction to programming and the use of applications such as spreadsheets, presentation tools, word processing and databases. Teaching such
introductory IT courses is, for many Computer Science lecturers, an extremely difficult task. The pedagogical challenges include institutional
setup, reduced teaching resources, the perceived ease of IT, a growing
number of students, a reduced student effort and a growing motivational
gap. Although applications have become easier to use, they have also become more advanced with a growing list of advanced features. Similarly,
programming technology has improved with new programming languages
such as Java, but the fundamental concept of programming is still difficult to grasp for many students. This chapter reports on two pedagogical experiments using on-line tutorials in combination with lectures and
hands-on exercises. Although it is still the early days, the results seem
to suggest that the approach could contribute to establishing a best -
practice for courses of this nature. The approach seems especially suited
for motivating and activating the growing number of students whose will
to learn is low, the so-called "minimalist students".

1   Introduction

Most universities offer an introductory IT course covering an overview of what
a computer is and can do, with introductions to useful applications such as
word processing, spreadsheets and databases, the web and an introduction to
programming. This is evident by the growing list of textbooks intended for such
courses (e.g., [Beekman, 2005; Capron and Johnson, 2002; Snyder, 2004]). Such
courses can be characterized as CS0 courses as these are often given to non-CS
students or given to CS students as a precursor to traditional first programming
courses, and are often referred to as CS1 courses.

I suppose many CS lecturers will agree that teaching a CS0 course is a daunt-
ing and unthankful task. This is especially the case if the physical and institutional setup dictates a traditional lectured course style of teaching, where large
numbers of students are expected to attend lectures, to solve exercises and to
study at home by reading books. However, such a setup leaves little scope for
variations in the pedagogical approach.

J. Bennedsen et al. (Eds.): Teaching of Programming, LNCS 4821, pp. 68–74, 2008.

In 2002 and 2003, I gave an introductory IT course to around 400 first year science and engineering students at Aalborg University. The course was given to students studying civil, mechanical and electrical engineering, but not to students in Computer Science and Software Engineering. The course was accredited 2 ECTS (European Credit Transfer System) in a 30 ECTS semester. The course consisted of 10 modules, where each module comprised two 45 minute lectures, a two hour exercise/lab session and about one hour of reading. The course was given to around 400 students, but due to space limitations each module was repeated three times for up to 140 students each time. In each module, I gave the lecture and during the exercise session, two to three teaching assistants and I circulated among the students. Exercises were not handed in for formal assessment. In fact the course did not have a formal assessment as it was considered a course in support of the students' project work in their main field of study (e.g. civil, mechanical or electrical engineering). The course covered topics such as advanced word processing for project report writing by using Word and LaTeX, Excel for engineers, and introduction to databases and an introduction to programming (using JavaScript and PHP). This is quite a common curriculum according to textbooks intended for such courses [Beekman, 2005; Capron and Johnson, 2002; Snyder, 2004.]

I observed a general trend that the first couple of modules would have full attendance. But rapidly, the number of students attending the latter modules would drop considerably in most cases to less than half. In one run of the course, in fact, attendance dropped to only 15 students attending the last lecture. Clearly, the course received poor comments from the students and I was very unhappy.

In the rest of this chapter, I will describe my analysis of the problems surrounding introductory IT courses, or the so-called CS0 courses for non-CS students. I will describe what I did to overcome these problems, give my own evaluation of the outcome and report on the students' evaluations. I will conclude the chapter with a list of suggestions that other lecturers facing the challenge of "the introductory IT course" may use as a guide towards a best-practice.

2   The Problems

As noted by [Millwood, 1996], classrooms and lecture theatres have not changed much over the past 100 years. The layout still consists of rows of chairs and desks facing the front with the lecturer speaking to an (expected) attentive audience. This physical layout often dictates the format of courses where large numbers of students are expected to attend lectures, to solve exercises and to study at home by reading books.

At Aalborg University, most lectured courses, including previous versions of the introductory IT course, follow a rather rigid format. They are given in modules of four hour sessions, usually divided into two 45 minute lectures followed immediately by a two hour exercise session. Students are also expected to spend between one and two hours preparing for each session (e.g., readings in a text book) ideally before attending the lecture.

The above is the expected course of events during a session. However, the reality in introductory IT courses is that most students do not read before attending the lecture, in fact only a few students do so even after the lecture. Most students do, however, attend the lecture, but they are ill-prepared for the exercises and often do not get the expected learning outcome. In many cases, they even give up trying to solve the exercises. The students can do the exercises in PC labs or in group rooms if they bring their own computer. Most students do the exercises in group rooms as there are a limited number of PC labs, most with an unattractive, physical location. However, for students doing exercises in group rooms, the problems are further exacerbated since it is often the case that one or a few students "lead" the exercise session with the rest as spectators. Or even worse, some may sabotage the session by distracting and even discouraging their fellow students from doing the exercises.

Furthermore, Introductory IT courses today have the problem that students often come with different IT skills levels. Some students have already made advanced use of IT tools at primary school and high school level, and a few have done a bit of programming. Thus, introductory IT courses run the risk of missing the target as some students may have little or no IT knowledge to build on, and thus, may feel the course is too difficult. However, others may have lots of IT experience, and thus, become bored and uninterested. Although in a different setting, this problem has been observed by [Ruefli and Leibrock, 1999] from their experiences of teaching introductory IT courses to MBA students. They see the students' diverse IT background both as a potential to be drawn upon, but also as a potential problem. They even suggest that some amount of "un-learning" may be needed for students who feel technically fluent.

For the majority of students, there is another factor as well. They may have used IT since primary school, but the use of such IT has become easier and easier over the years. Thus, this may have left many students with an impression that learning how to make advanced use of IT tools, especially programming, is not necessary or should be straight forward This is leading to an increasing, motivational gap between the institutional expectations and the requirements for the students to master advanced use of computers along with the students' expectations of the need, or rather perception of no need, to learn and to benefit from such use. On the one hand, all science and engineering disciplines nowadays rely heavily on advanced computing. On the other hand, freshmen students, although used to computers from an early age, seem to have an expectation that programming and an advanced use of IT is only for Computer Science and Software Engineering students.

Finally, learning to program is difficult. Many papers have been written on this subject so I list only a few of these difficulties and refer the reader to good references such as [Jenkins, 2002] and [Dijkstra, 1989]. Programming is not a simple skill, but a complicated set of interrelated skills such as requirement analysis, specification, algorithm design and program code construction. Introductory IT courses naturally focus on code construction; however, even this skill is complicated and easily degenerates to low level issues about syntax and language peculiarities. It is well-known that students have a high investment and a low return feeling about learning to program.

Combine this with the growing number of "minimalist students", or those students whose will to learn is low [Lauvås, P., 2003,Biggs, 2003], and I think most lecturers can understand the problems with which we are faced.

3   Incorporating On-Line Tutorials

Faced with the analysis of the problems and the experiences from two previous runs of the course, the following changes to various aspects of the course were agreed upon:

First of all, it was decided to split the course into two separate courses. These were ITV (an introduction to IT tools for project work) and Java (an introduction to programming using Java). Each course would be given as five modules equivalent to 1 ECTS. The argument for changing this was to signal clearly to the students the difference between the two topics: the advanced use of IT applications and programming respectively (there was also a request to teach programming by using Java). By splitting the course into two courses, the students who felt they were sufficiently fluent in advanced IT applications could elect to skip this course. Similarly, students who felt they could program or that they had no need for programming could elect to skip this course.

I also decided to re-organize the way each session was run. I realized that there was hardly any point in assuming that the students would read before attending the lecture. At the same time, I felt that the most important aspect of the course was for the students to gain some experience of using the tools presented in the course, so they would be able to apply them in their project work and be able to do programming exercises. Therefore, I found the exercise session to be the most important, which is a view shared by other researchers (see *Apprentice-Based Learning* by Kölling and Barnes).

To bridge the gap between what the students can learn during the lecture without reading beforehand and doing the exercises, I introduced the use of on-line tutorials. But, I did not have time to develop my own tutorials and there was no budget to buy "professionally" developed on-line tutorials. Thus, the on-line tutorials that I used were available at no cost on the web.

For the ITV course, I used the online tutorials from the Danish website Kend-DinPC (English translation: GetToKnowYourPC) on `http://www.kenddinpc.dk/`. For the Java course, I used the online version of the Java Tutorial from Sun Microsystems on `http://java.sun.com/docs/books/tutorial`. Neither of these tutorials are highly interactive, but are rather straightforward, hyperlinked documents. But, each contains a fair amount of simple "try this" type exercises. The latter tutorial even comes in book form [Campione et al., 2000]. In the ITV course, I used a format based on two 30 minute lectures, followed by the students reading the online tutorial and solving small training exercises posed in the on-line tutorial that are interleaved with the reading content. The students usually spent 1 to 1.5 hours following the tutorials, followed by more complex exercises relating to their semester projects.

I observed that attendance in the latter part of the course was no longer dropping significantly. The students read the online tutorial while in the group rooms and discussed issues as they appeared, thus often helping each other clarifying points, and also ensuring that questions for the lecturer and teaching assistants were much more pointed. They also managed to complete the exercises, in most cases both the training exercises, and applying the techniques to their project work.

As the Java course was given after the ITV course was completed, I had time to refine the format further. I reduced the lecture part further to one 45 minute lecture, followed by the on-line tutorial. I also divided the exercises into two categories: group discussion exercises and individual technique/programming exercises. Again, I observed that students read the on-line tutorial while in the group room and discussed questions as they arose. The group discussion exercises further supported this. Most students also managed to do the individual exercises and some even started programming in Java for their semester projects in their main line of study (e.g. civil, mechanical or electrical engineering). An additional advantage with the Java Tutorial is that it is full of program examples. Thus, it seems to be intentionally supportive of a "literacy" approach as opposed to the more common "syntax free" approach towards teaching programming [Fincher, 1999]. Having the many program examples on-line meant that students could easily cut, paste and compile them to try them out or even to make simple modifications to explore their own ideas without having to write a lot of code. I noted that most students appreciated this approach.

This is not to say that programming is taught only as "cut-paste-compile" programming. The above remark is only a reflection on the reading process that can be interweaved with quick "let's see how it works" experiments, which often trigger an "aha" experience. This is something that students seldom, if ever, would do had they read the material in a book because this would require them to type in the example, which is a slow an error prone experience. Clearly, the students will also have to program from the ground up, as well as extend others' programs, much in the spirit of the approach described in *Apprentice-Based Learning* by Kölling and Barnes.

As development environment I used JDK 1.4.2, command line prompt and NotePad, the first trail in the Java Tutorial explains how to install the JDK and how to use NotePad and a command line prompt. Many students downloaded and installed an IDE, such as JBuilder, Eclipse or NetBeans. On reflection, I think I will use an IDE in future versions of the course as many students are unfamiliar with the command line prompt and frustrated with the simplicity of NotePad. The plethora of different IDEs led to some confusion and choosing one and sticking with that throughout the course may resolve these issue, especially as most IDEs come with good "getting started" online tutorials of their own.

4   Evaluation

Following the ideas in [Lauvås, 1996], I asked the students at the end of each course to fill a questionnaire and there was, in general, a high level of satisfaction with the new versions of the courses. From the answers regarding the ITV course, I could see that about two thirds of the students followed each session, whereas one third had been selective regarding which lectures they had attended. In the Java course, the majority of the students followed all sessions (which I also expected as there is a necessary progression from lecture to lecture). Several students reported that they used the on-line tutorials to catch up with their fellow students if they had missed a session.

I was particularly interested in knowing if it would be possible to do away with the lectures, but only a few students felt that they would have preferred an "on-line only" course. It seems that most students used the lectures to gain an overview of the contents for the sessions. Although they might not have understood what they heard during the lecture, they felt that when they then read about the subject in the tutorial, they gained a better understanding than they would have done without the lectures.

During the first two lectures of the Java course, I showed only "precooked" programs during the lecture. Several students suggested that I program "live" so they could get a feel for the programming process. However, in a short lecture, programming live easily takes up too much time. But, I could imagine using recordings of "real" programming based on the techniques described in *The Programming Process* by Bennedsen and Caspersen would be useful. As the Java course was very short (5 sessions), I was only able to cover a very small part of the Java language. But, several students reported that they had continued learning aspects of Java by following the more advanced on-line tutorials available from Sun Microsystems on their own or within their project group.

I was also interested in knowing if they would have preferred more professionally developed tutorials and if they would be willing to pay to use such tutorials. However, as I somewhat expected, the majority of the students rejected the idea of paying for on-line material and felt that the available tutorials had been very professional. A few students reported that they would be willing to pay to use online material if the costs were reasonable. One student expressed reasonable costs as "not more expensive than a traditional book".

5   Conclusion

It is obviously far too early to draw general conclusions from one (or rather two) teaching experiments. They clearly need to be repeated. But, as preliminary conclusions and possible guidelines for establishing a "best practice" in introductory IT courses for non-CS, science and engineering students, these experiments suggest the following:

1. That the introduction of on-line tutorials was a success, in the sense that they lead the students to read and to try out examples, thus increasing the

activity level. However, the answers from the students indicate that they do not eliminate the need for the lectures. They are rather a replacement for a text book.

2. Having the tutorials on-line means that the students can easily switch between reading about a subject and trying out small examples, often by easy cut and paste from the tutorial. This also seems to have overcome some of the students' aversions against getting started with complex tasks. These were tasks that students in the previous years had given up completing because they perceived them to be far beyond their capabilities.

3. Reading the tutorials while in groups (which I have never seen students do with book-based material) means that they can discuss questions with each other as they arise, introducing a level of peer-learning. This behaviour can be stimulated by introducing a number of group discussion exercises as well as the more traditional hands-on exercises. This way of working seems to appeal to the minimalists as most students read the on-line tutorials. It also means that the questions they put forward to the lecturer and the teaching assistants are much more pointed.

4. Splitting the introductory IT course in two, one focusing on advanced use of applications and one focusing on programming is preferable because:

   (a) Students get a clearer idea of what the course is about.
   (b) Students who feel they already master the topic can skip this course.
   (c) Students who feel they do not need to learn programming can skip this course.

5. Unfortunately, students do not expect to or are not willing to pay for on-line material, and thus reducing the incentives for lecturers or others to develop such material. This is rather surprising as students are used to paying for books and even printed lecture notes. However, for introductory IT courses there are plenty of on-line tutorials available free of charge on the Internet.

6. Questionnaires, following the suggestions in [Lauvås, 1996], are worthwhile and can help a lecturer understand in detail what students like and dislike.

Overall, I will recommend others facing the challenges of giving an introductory IT course for non-CS students to structure the course as outlined above and to make use of the growing number of on-line tutorials.

Part II

Introducing Object-Oriented Programming

Introduction to Part II
Introducing Object-Oriented Programming

The practice of teaching programming at universities, colleges and high schools went through a major change roughly in the mid 1990s: The teaching of object-orientation in introductory courses slowly became mainstream. Fairly soon, the *Object First or Objects Early* school of thought was formulated, stating that teaching object orientation by discussing objects from the very start is a good thing.

However, many experienced teachers find that transitioning to teaching objects and teaching objects first is a difficult task. We have to ask, "Why is this the case?" To answer this question we must distinguish between inherent and accidental complexity.

Object-orientation, or the teaching thereof, is made complex by the following two factors: intrinsic complexity caused by the nature of the problem and accidental complexity caused by external factors such as the use of inadequate languages, tools, teaching strategies, lack of experience by teachers, and so on.

Whether actual problems with teaching OO stem from intrinsic or accidental complexity is an important question. If it were intrinsic complexity, then it cannot be fixed, and an objects first approach would indeed be too hard for beginning students. If it is accidental complexity, then we can fix it.

We believe that most of the problems many teachers currently observe originate almost exclusively in accidental complexity. We use non-optimal programming languages, inadequate software tools, many textbooks are appallingly bad, many teachers have no experience or training in object-orientation themselves, pedagogical strategies used were developed for entirely different paradigms, and so the list goes on. Good books, tools, and pedagogical approaches do exist, and they get used in some courses, but they do not get used routinely or widely enough.

However, there is also inherent complexity in teaching introductory object-oriented programming. This is because the basic concepts are tightly interrelated and cannot easily be taught and learned in isolation. Furthermore, the basic object-oriented concepts represent a higher level of abstraction. Together, this results in a higher threshold for the learner in order to grasp the basic concepts.

This part consists of four chapters in which we tackle different aspects of the accidental and incidental complexity of teaching introductory, object-oriented programming. The first two chapters address many of the same issues, but from two different perspectives: the perspective of the teacher and the perspective of the programming tool designer. Both chapters present principles and guidelines which help to overcome most of the accidental complexity of object-oriented programming. The third chapter presents a model-driven approach to teaching introductory object-oriented programming. By making modelling the basis for programming, the inherent complexity stemming from the tight interrelatedness

J. Bennedsen et al. (Eds.): Teaching of Programming, LNCS 4821, pp. 77–79, 2008.
© Springer-Verlag Berlin Heidelberg 2008

of the basic concepts of object-orientation is attacked conceptually up-front and made a primary concern of the course. The fourth chapter presents a specific solution to the so-called "big-bang problem" of getting started, which is particularly challenging because of the interrelatedness of the basic concepts.

The first chapter, *Transitioning to OOP/Java — A Never Ending Story*, is an honest description of challenges, difficulties and obstacles encountered when transitioning from teaching procedural or object-oriented programming. The chapter presents 11 principles for the design of an introductory, object-oriented programming course classified in three categories: high-level goals for course design, tools, and pragmatics. The motives behind the principles are explained and the experience from their concrete implementation is discussed. The chapter concludes with a summary of the lessons learned thus far in the never ending process of transitioning to and refining an introductory object-oriented programming course.

The second chapter, *Using BlueJ to Introduce Programming*, is a description of the BlueJ system, which is developed specifically for teaching introductory object-oriented programming. There are several such systems, but BlueJ is by far the most widespread. Furthermore, the system is accompanied by a textbook and several other resources including a set of examples and projects. Behind it all is a framework of pedagogical principles, which guides the development of the tool and the accompanying materials. The chapter contains a description of the BlueJ IDE and a presentation of eight pedagogical guidelines. Furthermore, the chapter presents a sequence of increasingly complex projects, which can be used in an introductory object-oriented programming course spanning a period of up to one year. The chapter ends with a discussion of traps, pitfalls, and lessons learned from the BlueJ project.

The third, *Model-Driven Programming*, chapter is a description of an introductory, object-oriented programming course designed in the spirit of the Scandinavian school of object-orientation. According to the Scandinavian school, conceptual modeling is the defining characteristic of object-orientation and provides a unifying perspective and a pedagogical approach focusing upon the modeling aspects of object-orientation. The chapter presents an introductory, object-oriented programming course based upon modelling. The progression in the course is defined by increasing complexity of class models rather than being dictated by a bottom-up ordering of language constructs, which is the prevailing approach. The alternative organization helps overcoming one of the most challenging inherent complexities of object-orientation – the tight interrelatedness of the basic concepts – by making them the primary concern and focus of the course.

In the fourth chapter, *CS1: Getting Started*, we specifically address the problem of how to get started in an introductory object-oriented programming course. The interrelatedness of the basic concepts introduces a challenge, which is most prominent in the very first weeks. To help overcome this challenge, the authors have designed an object-oriented version of the well-known turtle graphics. The chapter describes how the turtle abstraction can be used in the first couple of weeks to practice programming and at the same time provide an intuitive understanding of fundamental programming concepts such as class, object, state, behaviour, specification, implementation, message passing, control flow, and polymorphism. The chapter concludes by demonstrating how the turtle abstraction can be used as a primitive graphics library later in the course when discussing more thoroughly advanced topics such as recursion, delegation, inheritance, and application frameworks.

Michael E. Caspersen

Transitioning to OOP/Java — A Never Ending Story

Jürgen Börstler, Marie Nordström, Lena Kallin Westin, Jan-Erik Moström,
and Johan Eliasson

Department of Computing Science, Umeå University, Sweden
{jubo,marie,kallin,jem,johane}@cs.umu.se

Abstract. Changing the introductory programming course from a traditional imperative model to an object-oriented model is not simply a
matter of changing compilers and syntax. It requires a profound change
in course materials and teaching approach to be successful. We have
been working with this transition for almost ten years and have realized
that teaching object-oriented programming is not as simple or "natural"
as some proponents claim. In fact, it has proven difficult to convey to
the students the advantages and methodologies associated with object-
oriented programming. To help ourselves and others in a transition like
this we have developed a number of "course design principles" as well
as teaching methods and examples that have proven to have positive
influence on student learning outcome.

1 Introduction

The object-oriented paradigm has become the most common programming paradigm for introductory programming courses[1][de Raadt et al., 2004; Stephenson
and West, 1998; Chen et al., 2005]. The transition to this paradigm has proven to
be more difficult than expected. Traditionally, programming concepts have been
systematically introduced one after one, each building nicely on the concepts
already learned. Abstract and advanced concepts (e.g., modules and abstract
data types) were deferred to later courses. In the object-oriented paradigm, on
the other hand, the basic concepts are tightly interrelated and cannot easily be
taught and learned in isolation [Roberts et al., 2006], as illustrated in Figure 1.
Furthermore, the basic object-oriented concepts are on a higher level of abstraction[2]. Together, this results in a higher threshold and steeper learning curve for
the learner.

It is generally accepted that transitioning to the object-oriented paradigm is
not just a programming language issue. Object-oriented development requires a
new way of thinking [Bacvanski and Börstler, 1997]. This is particularly important in education. A syntax-driven approach can take the students' attention

---

[1] Even in upper secondary school (high school).
[2] Whether this is an advantage or disadvantage for teaching or learning is unclear.

J. Bennedsen et al. (Eds.): Teaching of Programming, LNCS 4821, pp. 80–97, 2008.
© Springer-Verlag Berlin Heidelberg 2008

(a)   (b)

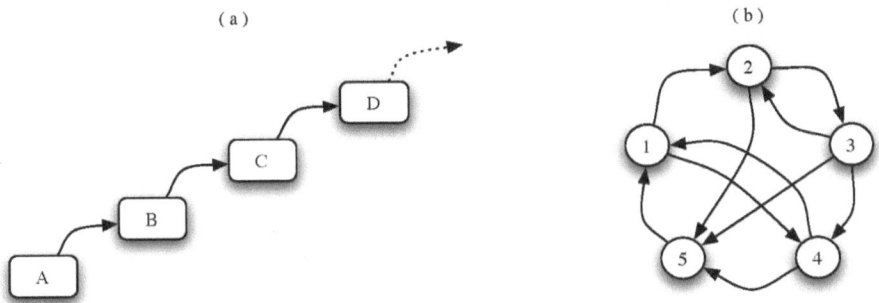

Fig. 1. Dependencies between basic concepts to be introduced in imperative - (a) and object-first approaches (b), respectively

away from the underlying concepts and principles (see also *Model-Driven Programming* by Bennedsen and Caspersen and *CS1: Getting Started* by Caspersen and Christensen). Studies show that there is a mismatch between the programming language used and the paradigm that is actually taught. In Australia for example, about 82% of the introductory programming instructors used an object-oriented language, but only about 37% taught their courses by using an object-oriented approach [de Raadt et al., 2004]. Approaches for teaching introductory programming courses are still heavily discussed [Bruce, 2005].

In this chapter, we describe our experience transitioning from a traditional approach using (Turbo) Pascal to a true objects-first approach in Java. The advantages of using object-orientation for teaching are many. It provides powerful mechanisms for the structuring and organisation of models (in particular designs and code) and decreases the conceptual distance between problem and solution models. This makes it much easier to communicate models and keep them consistent [West, 2004].

However, these advantages come at a price. The basic object-oriented concepts are highly interrelated and cannot easily be taught or learned in isolation (as illustrated in figure 1(b)). There also is no commonly accepted pedagogical approach to overcome this problem [Bruce, 2005]. It is furthermore very difficult, if not impossible, to develop "simple" examples. A proper and meaningful object-oriented example requires quite some overhead [Westfall, 2001]. Many textbook examples are, therefore, unnecessarily complex, not meaningful, or not even "truly" object-oriented [ACM-Forum, 2002; Hu, 2005]. During our "journey from Pascal to Java" we stumbled across these and other problems and made a few detours before realising that the object-oriented approach not only requires a new way of thinking, but also, a new way of teaching.

There are more factors contributing to a student's success or failure than the course material and how a course is taught. We have observed that our students as a group are less motivated and not as well prepared[3] compared to a few

---

[3] This problem has been observed by most math, science and engineering programs.

years ago. Attendance rates at exams, lectures and other scheduled events have decreased. Reading assignments are neglected to a high degree and mandatory assignments are submitted late. We introduced Supplemental Instruction (SI) [Arendale, 1997] to increase student activity and thereby improve course outcome. SI is a non-mandatory part of the course. In some course offerings, only half of the students participated in the SI programme while in other the majority of students participated. In all course offerings, students participating in SI have a higher attendance rate at exams and also get higher grades on average than the group of students not attending SI [Nordström and Kallin Westin, 2006].

The remainder of this chapter is organised as follows. First, we briefly explain the motives behind the principles we used for designing our new course, and how these were actually implemented. In section 4, we evaluate how well this new course worked with respect to our original principles. Section 5 summarises the lessons we have learned since we made the transition to the object-oriented paradigm in 1998. In sections 6 and 7, we discuss external factors affecting student performance and related work, respectively. The chapter concludes with a summary of our experience.

2   Principles for Course Design

Prior to our transition, we introduced object-oriented concepts in our data types and algorithms[4] course, following the introductory programming course. However, this was not sufficient to enable students to effectively use the object-oriented paradigm. Most students perceived object-orientation as a simple extension to imperative programming. They did not realise that object-oriented programs are conceptually different from strictly imperative ones and that using object-oriented syntax does not automatically lead to object-oriented programs.

When switching to the object-oriented paradigm in our introductory programming course in 1998, we only made minor changes to our traditional course design. Initially, our students did very well on this course, but we soon realised that their ability to develop code true to the object-oriented paradigm was not satisfactory. After several course offerings with unsatisfactory learning outcomes, we decided to develop a "truly" objects-early approach. When proficiency in a certain paradigm is the major learning goal of a course, it seemed sensible to start with that paradigm as early as possible [Bruce, 2005; Bergin, 2000b].

To support the design of such a course we developed a list of principles, to guide course development. These principles were either based on our teaching experience [Bacvanski and Börstler, 1997; Börstler et al., 2002; Börstler and Sharp, 2003; Kallin Westin and Nordström, 2003, 2004] or the collected advice and experience from the literature in computer science education (see e.g., [Bruce, 2005; Westfall, 2001; ACM-Forum, 2002; Guzdial, 1995; Holland et al., 1997; Kölling and Rosenberg, 2001; Kölling, 2003; Turk, 1997; and *Using BlueJ to Introduce Programming* by Kölling]).

---

[4] More or less similar to a CS2 course.

2.1   High-Level Goals

No magic (P1). We must provide a correct and consistent frame of reference, so that the students always can make sense of new material. The students must be able to associate the new material with something familiar or wellknown. The succession of learning units and topics must be carefully worked out. The frame of reference must be refined or extended accordingly. The current frame of reference should always be sufficient to understand new material and validly explain what is going on [Zull, 2002]. Everything requiring a comment like "don't worry now, you'll understand later," must be revised or delayed. Language specific complexities should be hidden until students are sufficiently mature to understand the underlying language design issues.

Students will always try to make sense of new material. If we cannot provide them with a correct and consistent frame of reference, they might construct invalid explanations by themselves. This can easily lead to persistent misconceptions about object technology and programming [Holland et al., 1997; Börstler, 2005; Clancey, 2004; Ragonis and Ben-Ari, 2005].

Objects from the very beginning (P2). Everything should build on the notion of objects, since they are at the very heart of object-orientation. Therefore, objects should be introduced in the very first lecture. The earlier we start with the most important concept, the more often we can reinforce it and the more time we give students to fully understand it.

General concepts favoured over language specific realisations (P3). Learning units should be based on the teaching and learning of general object-oriented concepts. Although the mastery of a particular programming language is an important learning goal, it is secondary to the understanding of the underlying concepts. Focusing on concepts does not necessarily mean to move strictly from concept to syntax for each new topic. It is, however, important to stress fundamental principles and techniques and not the elements of a particular language. This can, for example, be achieved by means of moving from concrete to abstract as proposed in *CS1: Getting Started* by Caspersen and Christensen.

No exceptions to general rules (P4). By general rules, we not only mean the definitions that constitute the object-oriented paradigm[5], but also design and programming guidelines and all the other pieces of advice we provide to our students. We must always "do as we say," only use sound and meaningful objects, only show well-designed classes, and certainly not do unnecessary `main`-programming. Concepts must never be introduced or be reinforced by using flawed examples (see also P6).

2.2   Tools

OOA&D early (P5). It is necessary to provide students with simple tools to approach a problem systematically and to evaluate alternative solutions before

---

[5] Like for example "objects are instances of classes with state, behaviour and identity," or "in object-oriented programs, problems are solved by objects sending messages to each other."

starting to code. Early OOA&D conveys to the students that responsibilities are distributed amongst the objects that solve a problem [Börstler, 2005; Andrianoff and Levine, 2002.]

Exemplary examples (P6). All examples used in classes and exercises should comprise well-designed classes that fill a purpose (besides exemplifying a certain concept or language specific detail) [Holland et al., 1997; Nordström, 2007]. Consequently, examples should be non-trivial and involve multiple classes. All examples should be made available for experimentation, e.g., by making the source code available for download from the course web page.

Easy-to-use tools (P7). Students should be provided with tools that support object-oriented thinking. The tools must be easy to learn and easy to use. Tool usage must add as little cognitive load as possible to the students' tasks. Usability should be favoured over any "bells and whistles."

2.3   Pragmatics

Hands-on (P8). Programming is a skill that must be "trained." Topics should be reinforced by means of practical exercises. Lectures should be followed by supervised in-lab sessions. For each session, step-by-step instructions and exemplary examples should be provided.

Less "from scratch" development (P9). "Reading before modifying before coding." All software development takes place in context (see also *Using BlueJ to Introduce Programming* by Kölling). Reuse is an important aspect of the object-oriented paradigm and should be emphasised early. To be able to read, to understand, and to modify existing code is, therefore, as important as developing understandable code.

Alternative forms of examination (P10). Assessment should support learning. It is very important to evaluate actual programming skills as well as conceptual understanding. Furthermore, assessment should not be separated from teaching. For example, peer evaluation or peer marking can call the students' attention to alternative ways of solving certain problems. It is important to realise that there rarely is a single, correct solution to a problem.

Emphasise the limitations of computers (P11). Students should learn that computations can produce erroneous or unexpected results due to limitations in data representation, even in logically correct programs.

To summarise, our main goal was to follow an object-oriented approach in a true and consequent way. In addition, we wanted to provide our students with easy-to-use tools supporting "object thinking" and the systematic development of proper object-oriented code (see also *Model-Driven Progamming* by Bennedsen and Caspersen).

3   Implementation

The first course, based on these principles, was offered in spring 2001. After a case study in summer 2001 [Börstler et al., 2002], we have refined our teaching approach and successively implemented it in all our introductory programming courses[6]. Some of the principles are very difficult to implement, or even in conflict with each other. In particular the principles *No magic (P1)* and *Exemplary examples (P6)* still cause a lot of work.

From an organisational point of view, we made four major changes to our original course as follows:

1. We introduced BlueJ [BlueJ, 2007], a programming environment particularly designed for the teaching and learning of object-oriented programming to novices (P7) [Kölling and Rosenberg, 2001; Kölling et al., 2003]

2. We introduced CRC-cards, a simple informal tool for collaborative object-oriented modelling (P5, P7) [Beck and Cunningham, 1989]. The strength of the CRC-card approach lies in its associated scenario role-play activities [Börstler, 2005; Andrianoff and Levine, 2002]. During the role-plays the students explore hypothetical, but concrete situations of system usage (scenarios). They enact the objects in the model, much like actors following a script when playing the characters in play. This supports "object thinking" and helps the students to develop a mental model of the workings of an object-oriented program (P1-P4) [Börstler and Schulte, 2005].

3. To accommodate for more practical training (P8), we substituted our traditional lecture room exercises by guided, hands-on exercises in computer-labs.

4. The traditional pen and paper exam was split into a shorter one, half way through the course, and a computer-based exam was used at the end to test actual programming skills (P10).

In addition to these changes, we started to offer Supplemental Instruction (SI) [Kallin Westin and Nordström, 2003] to improve students' study skills and to make them more active participants in the course. SI is targeted towards historically difficult classes to help students master content while developing and integrating strategies for learning and studying [Arendale, 1997]. This is done through sessions guided by a model-student, the SI leader.

A major difference between SI and other forms of collaborative learning is the role of the SI leader. Rather than forming study cluster groups and then releasing them in an unsupervised environment, the SI leader is present to keep the group on task with the content material and to model appropriate learning strategies that the other students can adopt and use in the present course, as well as other ones in future academic work.

Since the "roll out" of our teaching approach, we have made several changes to our introductory programming courses (see Figure 2 for an overview). For example, we have postponed graphics and event handling to a newly developed advanced programming course. We have also slightly adapted our course for non-CS majors. However, we are still faithful to all our principles.

---

[6] We offer introductory courses in object-oriented programming for three different technical degree programs.

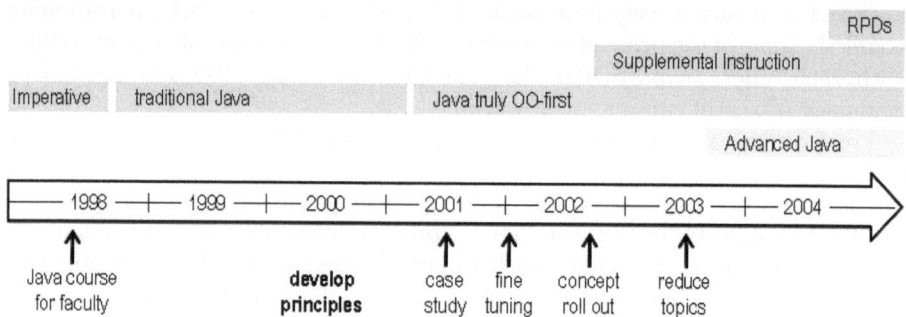

Fig. 2. Major steps in the evolution of the introductory programming course

4   Evaluation

In this section, we restrict our discussion to an evaluation of our principles as defined in section 2. Overall, we conclude that changing to a "truly" object-oriented approach according to our principles worked well. However, there are many factors not directly related to the teaching and learning of object-oriented programming itself that affect course design and outcome. Many important factors are difficult to control like prerequisites and attitudes of the students entering our programs, for example. This will be discussed in section 6.

4.1   High-Level Goals

In common for all high-level goals (P1-P4) is the urge to be "truly faithful" to the object-oriented approach. This means to avoid concepts or examples that seem to question or even contradict the idea of object-orientation, such as objects without meaningful state or behaviour, excessive use of static methods and public attributes, Singletons[7], etc. [Westfall, 2001; Hu, 2005]. To be "truly faithful" also means to strive for meaningful objects in realistic contexts.

No magic (P1). Our ambition has always been to use examples and contexts not only simple enough for the students to understand, but that also emphasises the object-oriented paradigm. BlueJ is an excellent tool for this since it allows teachers and students to concentrate on the object-oriented aspects instead of dealing with editors, configuration files, compilers, etc. BlueJ achieves this by visually representing classes and objects and manipulating them directly using its graphical user interface (see figure 3). Unfortunately, this approach has some limitations that can generate misconceptions that can be harmful and great care has to be taken to avoid them. A short example will illustrate the problem.

Since the very beginning we have used an example with geometrical shapes supplied with the BlueJ environment [Barnes and Kölling, 2003; and *Using BlueJ to Introduce Programming* by Kölling]. In BlueJ, objects are represented by red

---

[7] A Singleton is a class with one single instance only.

blocks in the object bench (see for example c: Circle in figure 3). Actually, to be more precise, these red blocks represent object references and not the objects themselves. This is a small, but important difference as explained below.

One can send messages to objects in the object bench by right clicking them. This will display a menu with the methods defined for this object. When selecting makeVisible(), a graphical surface is created ("automagically") and a representation of c is drawn on it (see Window BlueJ Shapes Demo in Figure 3). Whenever the state of an object is changed, its representation is changed or animated accordingly. This gives immediate feedback and helps students to understand the difference between classes and objects. On the other hand, it blurs the difference between the objects themselves and their references. Furthermore, the details of the graphics are quite involved and too complicated to understand ("magic") for a novice.

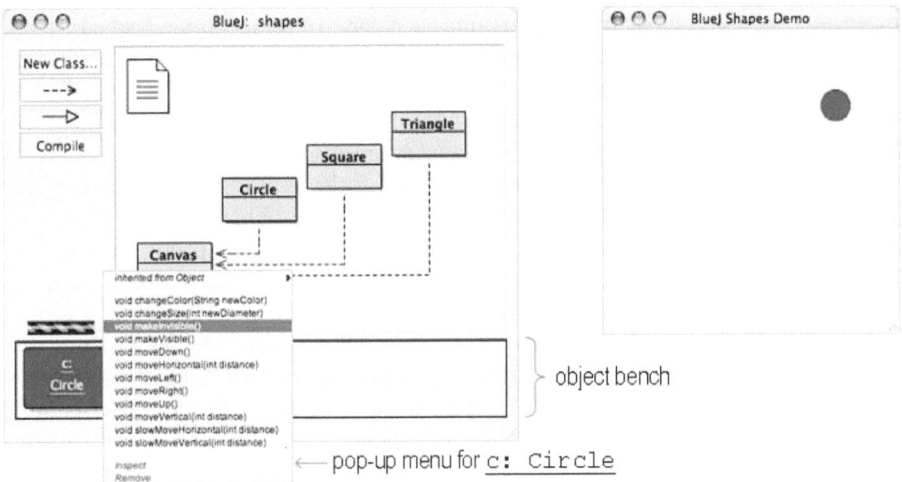

Fig. 3. Screenshot of the Shapes example

Another problem with the Shapes example is the cognitive difficulty to differ between the visual representation of an object (the circle in window BlueJ Shapes Demo) and the object itself, which actually cannot be seen. If, for instance, the reference to the object (the red block in the object bench) is removed, nothing happens in the drawing. This is puzzling for the inexperienced because the coloured dots on the canvas are mistaken for the object itself! Misconceptions like this are very hard to deal with. Other examples of difficulties are discussed in [Ragonis and Ben-Ari, 2005].

This example shows how difficult it is to create assignments early in the course, without (unintentionally) introducing magic or material not taught yet.

Objects from the very beginning (P2). To make the students immediately acquainted with the idea of objects, we use a kind of interactive exercise the first lecture [Andrianoff and Levine, 2002; Bergin, 2000a]. Without previous explanation, the students are asked to discuss in general terms, something that needs to be modelled like, for example, a ticket machine or an employee. During the discussion the lecturer collects specific and general characteristics and behaviours on the whiteboard. At the end of the lecture, these things are pointed out as "properties" belonging to a single object or a class, respectively.

Nevertheless, it is difficult to convey to the students that they are working with an isolated "component" in a larger program, instead of a whole program. Many students, particularly those with previous programming experience, find it quite frustrating that there is no "program" to execute like they are used to. They seem to have difficulties focusing on the properties and responsibilities of objects without controlling its context at the same time [Guzdial, 1995].

General concepts favoured over language specific realisations (P3).
The learned programming and problem solving should be transferable to other programming languages. It is important, therefore, to focus on general concepts. We try to highlight general concepts, knowledge and skills and to avoid language specific details and idiosyncrasies.

This has resulted in using elementary UML-notation throughout the course, instead of some kind of simplified temporary notation. However, we do not explicitly introduce UML. We just use its most intuitive parts consistently.

Furthermore, semi-formal syntax-diagrams are used. This makes it much easier to talk about the syntax, semantics and pragmatics of programming languages. Information hiding is also stressed as a general (design) concept and the usefulness of Boolean variables to formulate easy to read expressions.

On the other hand, topics like anonymous objects and classes are not discussed. These concepts require a thorough understanding of object-orientation and are saved for later courses. We try to avoid language idiosyncrasies as long as possible in particular shortcuts like ++, +=, ?:, etc. and forced returns out of for-loops and methods. They just make code harder to read and, therefore, their use is actually discouraged.

No exceptions to general rules (P4). It is important to be consistent with the frame of reference we provide to our students (see P1 in section 2.1). Students will hopefully adopt what the teachers present to them eventually. It is important, therefore, not to misguide them (see also P6). We must never present any material, explanation or example that we might reject as an answer or solution from a student.

Unfortunately, Java courseware in particular is littered with examples that contradict the "rules" or "styles" we want our students to adopt. The concept of objects, for example, should not be exemplified by using Java strings. In Java, `String` objects cannot be modified and do not posses all the characteristics we require from proper objects [Thimbleby, 1999]. Since `Math` has only `static` methods and there are no objects of this class type, its use should be postponed until the students have a firm understanding of the concepts class and object. The `main` method is an atypical method since there is no object it belongs to.

Thus, the method is never invoked explicitly and its parameters seem to be supplied by magic forces (see also P1).

4.2   Tools

OOA&D early (P5). The purpose of this principle is twofold: showing the students a systematic way to develop a solution for a given problem, and providing them with a tool to reason about object-oriented solutions without the need of actual code.

By using CRC-cards [Beck and Cunningham, 1989], we can do both. The object-as-person metaphor helps students with "object thinking" and to develop a conceptual model of the inner workings of an object-oriented program [West, 2004; Börstler and Schulte, 2005]. Another advantage of this approach is that it does not require any prerequisite knowledge.

A problem noted in [Bellin and Simone, 1997] and described in detail in [Börstler, 2005] is that CRC-cards are used as surrogates for classes (in the modelling activities) as well as for objects (in the role-play activities). This conflicts with the *No exception* principle (P4) and can easily confuse novices.

To address these problems, we enact a live CRC session in front of the class to give the students a feeling for the dynamics of such a session. In addition to that, we have developed so-called Role-Play Diagrams (RPDs) to support and document the role-play activities [Börstler, 2004]. RPDs combine elements from UML object and collaboration diagrams [OMG, 2003]. However, the notation is informaland much less extensive. In RPDs, we use specific object cards to denote objects and thereby, avoid the double role of the CRC-cards. Although the enhanced "method" is more complicated than the original one, the students have fewer problems using it. The RPDs also provide an excellent documentation of the role-play. To give the students some practical experience in CRC-card role-playing, we schedule two CRC exercises where the students develop designs for small problems. One of these designs is later implemented as an assignment.

Exemplary examples (P6). As discussed in *No magic* (P1), it has turned out to be difficult to find or to develop suitable problems and examples for the initial introduction of objects. The range of concepts and syntactical elements known to the students is still very limited. Examples should also be small and to the point, so that students do not lose sight of the concept exemplified. This limits the degree of freedom for defining "realistic" objects. For example, what would constitute a reasonable context illustrating the concepts of loops? What kind of object would have such behaviour? Immediately the example grows to justify the use of a simple construct and tends to conceal the small component it was intended to show.

Another problematic example is the usage of Singleton classes, like the popular Pig-Latin translator [Nordström, 2007]. One might ask whether it is reasonable to have a class `PigLatinTranslator`? How many objects of this class would anyone need? Singleton classes do probably not qualify as good examples. The main idea behind classes is instantiating as many objects as necessary. Singletons are special cases, i.e. an exception to the general rules (c.f. P4). Their treatment should, therefore, be delayed to more advanced courses.

Many examples use print statements to present some result. This is not a representative way to illustrate objects and classes. Usually, results are returned and used by other objects. In an object-oriented program, objects communicate to fulfil a task. Objects that use printing to present results are rarely useful in other contexts. Students are not able to reuse such examples as prototypes or templates to solve more general problems.

Exploiting the "naturalness" of the object-oriented approach can also be difficult. Object-oriented models of real-life objects might have behaviours and responsibilities their real life counterparts never would or could have. Therefore, it is very important to make a distinction between the model and the entity being modelled. A typical example of this could be the model of an employee in an economy system for a company. The model of the employee could have the responsibility to know its salary, the number of remaining days of vacation and so on. This is conflicting to how things are in real life. No company would rely on their employees to be the only source of information for the payment of salaries. So, how could it be possible for the inexperienced designer to foresee this responsibility in the model?

Easy-to-use tools (P7). Some of the advantages of BlueJ turned out to be disadvantages for the students (initially). The interaction with entities is done by right-clicking a class or an object. The problem for the student is to understand the equivalence of right-clicking and generating the same action in code. Another problem is to realise the difference between classes and objects [Ragonis and Ben-Ari, 2005]. However, as the students continue to practise their skills using BlueJ they realise the strengths of this simple, but powerful, interaction with objects.

The ability to write code must not depend on the tools we provide to our students. Students must not be "locked" into BlueJ for example. This is also highlighted by the BlueJ developers (see also *Using BlueJ to Introduce Programming* by Kölling). They should develop and run at least one complete application outside BlueJ. Although experienced students tend to dislike BlueJ, we think they should be encouraged to at least try it. They might very well get some new insights into the object-oriented paradigm.

4.3   Pragmatics

Hands-on (P8). The initial idea of guided in-lab sessions directly following the lectures did not work as expected. The students complained about lack of time to think about the new material before using it. Most students actually had difficulties applying the ideas presented. They merely consumed the presentation at the lecture.

In later years, we have thus rescheduled the lab sessions. We still have the same number of hands-on sessions, but they are no longer scheduled on the same day as the corresponding lectures. We also developed very detailed guides to make sure students succeed with initial tasks and so they can gain some confidence in working with the environment. Too detailed guidelines or fill-in-the blanks exercises, however, can be counter-effective. Students might be enabled to perform successfully without actually understanding their answers and activities. Students and teachers as well might get a faulty feeling of mastery of the subject.

Less "from scratch" development (P9). The practise of reading and manipulating existing code before actually writing own code turned out to be a major problem for our students. Inexperienced students acquired a passive practice and had difficulties writing complete programs on their own. It is important then to train some programming from scratch. Experienced students, on the other hand, often want to have full control over their programs and might reject "foreign" code [Guzdial, 1995]. However, code reuse is a crucial practice that requires code reading and understanding and needs to be trained as well.

Alternative forms of examination (P10). The content of the course is initially focused on object-oriented concepts, while the second half is heavier on actual problem solving and programming. To reinforce the need to work with and to understand basic concepts early on, we divided the examination into two parts. Halfway through the course a written (theoretical), closed-book test is given and at the very end, a practical problem solving and programming test is given. The results of the two tests are added and graded as one. In addition to this, the students have mandatory assignments and some of them orally assessed. The idea of splitting the examination into two tests with rather different focus was appreciated by the students. Furthermore, the exam results better reflect student skills than a single pen-and-paper test.

Emphasise the limitations of computers (P11). This principle had its origin in the numerical tradition of our department. We make students aware of problems and limitations in data representation and how these can lead to erroneous computations. We emphasise this by discussing examples leading to unexpected results in logically correct programs.

5   Lessons Learned

In this section, we briefly summarise the practices that worked particularly well for us. We have grouped them together into recommendations to make them easily accessible to the reader.

Teach "object thinking" and modelling explicitly.

- Start the first lecture with a modelling or role-play activity (no syntax involved). Students can be asked then to describe (model) an employee or a ticket-machine to illustrate the basic object properties (state, behaviour and identity).
- Introduce CRC-cards and scenario role-plays. This provides students with a framework to think in terms of (active) objects and their responsibilities. Furthermore, it teaches them basic modelling/ problem solving skills.

- Introduce role-play diagrams so that students easily can track and document scenario role-plays. This also helps to prevent some problems inherent in the original CRC approach [Börstler, 2005; Börstler and Schulte, 2005].

Schedule guided and supervised lab activities. Programming is a skill that needs to be trained extensively. Students should visit the labs as frequently as possible and receive immediate help when getting "stuck."

- Reduce the number of traditional lectures and introduce supervised lab sessions instead. Guide students through practical exercises in the labs. We provide for example step-by-step guides, including reflective questions, which the students have to work through. Lecturers and teaching assistants should always be present to discuss and resolve problems.
- As much as possible, move supervising time from office rooms to the computer labs to force students to visit the labs to ask questions.

Use and utilise a suitable programming environment. The environment must be easy to use and to support the object-oriented paradigm. However, it is also important to show how programs are developed and executed outside such an environment. We have used BlueJ [BlueJ, 2007] successfully since 2001.

Examine the "right" things. It is important to assess actual and individual programming skills in addition to conceptual and syntactical knowledge. This can be done, for example, by practical computer based tests (problem-solving and programming) and individual oral demonstrations of mandatory assignments.

There is no course design that fits all target groups. Different groups of students need different types or flavours of courses. It is important to be sensitive to changes in the field as well as the context and the environment of a course [Forte and Guzdial, 2005; Jenkins and Davy, 2000; and *Using On-line Tutorials in Introductory IT Courses* by Thomsen]. Our principles have been a useful guideline to us when adopting the course to different student groups. The principles make sure that the core of the course is the same and taught in roughly the same way, regardless of lecturer and student group.

Do not lull students and teachers into false security. Fill-in-the-blanks guides and exercises can give a faulty feeling of students' subject mastery. Too much help or undemanding tasks can lead to mechanical answering. If no reflection or second thought is necessary, then students can successfully complete such exercises without learning anything. Also, teacher expectations about what the students really have learnt might be too high.

Good examples are crucial, but very hard to develop. Truly object-oriented examples are very difficult to find or to develop. Educators should resist constructing examples "on-the-fly" (for example to exemplify a specific feature), since they rarely will follow principles P1, P4 and P6.

- Programming in a true object-oriented style often leads to overly (unnecessary) complex examples, due to the additional layers of abstraction imposed by the paradigm. This can be frustrating to students since they cannot understand why the different abstraction layers are necessary (e.g., "Why should I do it like that, it's easier and faster to read the information directly from the database"). It is a challenge for the teacher to explain that optimization is secondary to a good object-oriented design. Our main goal is to devise a good solution that fulfils certain quality criteria and not to simply make it work somehow. Students are not mature enough to differ between optimizations and proper design.
- Although often claimed, there is no 1:1 relationship between real-world objects and their corresponding software abstractions. A physical book for example is removed from the library, when it is checked out. A book object in a (software) model, however, stays in the library and is only marked as "on loan." Furthermore, in a "real world" library, we would never make the borrowers responsible for keeping track of their unpaid overdue fines. In a (software) model however, this might be a good design choice since trust is no issue there.

Keep students active. Data collected during the SI-projects shows without a doubt that student attendance and activity correlate with course results [Arendale, 1997; Kallin Westin and Nordström, 2003, 2004.] Mandatory in-lab exercises and a two-stage examination keep the students alert and active from the start. SI gives the students opportunities to work with the course material in a structured way and helps them to recognise the strength of collaboration. After introducing SI, the attendance rate on the examination rose from 80 percent to above 95 percent (see Section 6, in particular Figure 4).

6 Discussion

When analysing student performance over the years (see Figures 4 - 6) our case for a "truly-objects-first" approach does not look convincing. However, there are also external factors affecting student performance. These factors have lead to considerable changes in the student population in recent years.

Assessment consists of mandatory assignments, a pen-and-paper test and a computer-based test (see P10 in Section 4.3). In Figure 4, the passing rate after the first opportunity to finish the course is shown as a solid line. Java was introduced in 1998 and our "truly" object-first approach was introduced in 2002 (see Figure 2). The dashed line in Figure 4 shows the attendance rate on the exam (i.e. the proportion of students submitting at least one mandatory assignment or attempting at least one test). SI was introduced in 2002 to raise attendance rates and it seems to have an effect[8]. Participation in SI correlates with overall student

---

[8] In 2001, the seemingly high attendance rate was due to an examination system where handing in assignments (not necessary correct ones) gave credit points on the final exam. The numbers for 2001 in figures 4 - 6 must be seen, therefore, as statistical outliers.

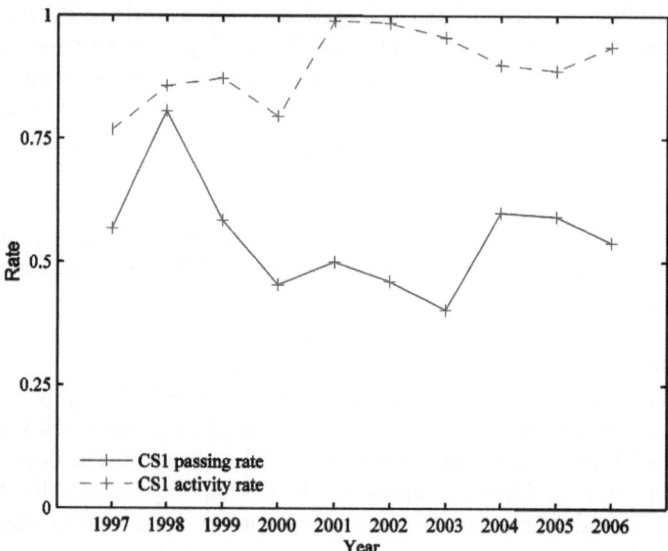

Fig. 4. Performance data for CS majors on our introductory programming course. The solid line represents the passing rate after the first opportunity to finish the course. The dashed line represents the proportion of students submitting at least one mandatory assignment or attempting at least one test.

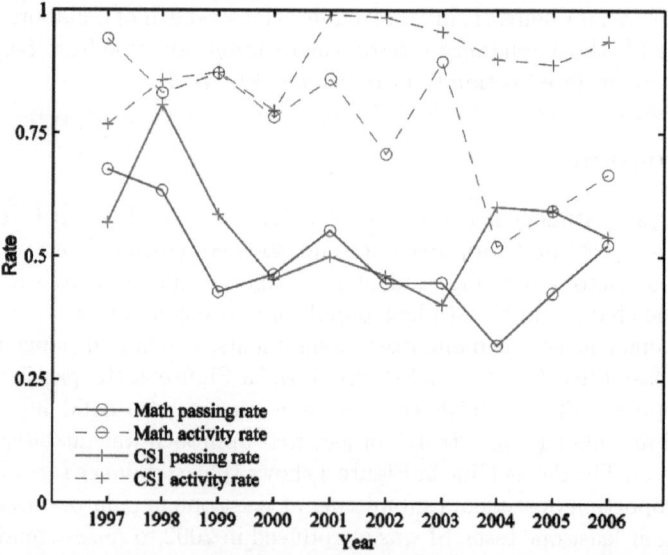

Fig. 5. Performance data for CS majors on the discrete mathematics course, compared to our introductory programming course (cf. figure 4)

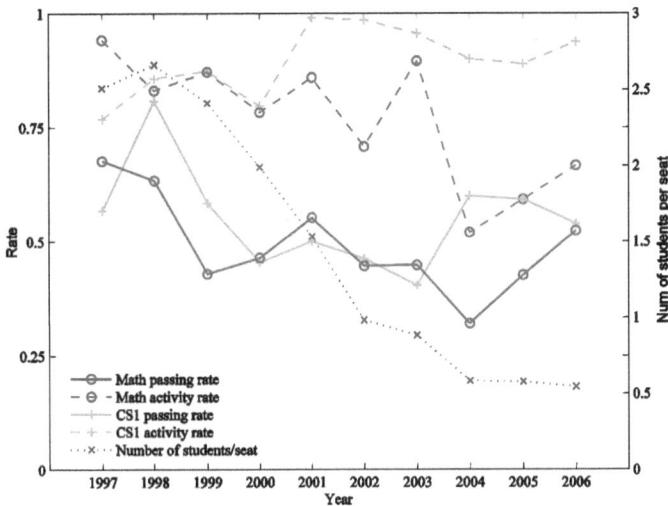

Fig. 6. The number of students per seat on our programme is shown as a dotted line added to Figure 5

performance. Unfortunately, the weakest students seem not to be motivated to participate in SI. An investigation of the students with severe problems in keeping up with the pace of the curricula of the programme showed that a vast majority had not attended SI at all, or only tried it a few times.

Another factor is that knowledge and skills in mathematics have been decreasing in general [Högskoleverket, 1999; Helenius and Tengstrand, 2005]. It is believed that mathematical ability is strongly connected to performance in introductory programming [Denning, 2004]. Skills, like (array) indexing and creating series of numbers seem to be more of a problem nowadays. Students also have a weak understanding of functions, in particular, their parameters and return (computed) values. This lack of understanding might result in the assumption that the only possible way to get something out of a method is by printing a string to the screen. We strongly believe this contributes to the lower passing rates, especially for mandatory assignments.

Our CS majors take a course in discrete mathematics in the same term as their introductory programming course. In Figure 5, we can see that the students also have problems in the discrete mathematics course. Attendance rates are even lower in discrete mathematics where students only have a single traditional exam at the end of the course. However, in the introductory programming course, a student needs to attend only one of the three exam parts to be counted as "active". This might falsely indicate high attendance rates.

The dotted line in Figure 6 represents the number of students per seat. In Sweden, each programme has a fixed number of student seats available. The applications to IT-related programmes have severely suffered from the turbulent situation within the IT business. Practically, this means that all students applying are admitted as long as they fulfil the basic prerequisites. Historically, we have had 2 to 3 applications for each seat available, resulting in a higher grade average for the students admitted.

A further factor is a shift in motivation among novices. In a study we performed in 1994, the main reason for students applying for our programme was an interest in the subject itself (or in mathematics). In a later study, the motivation had shifted to "want high salary," "want to be a civil engineer," and other reasons not connected to the subject or the programme itself. Thus, students' interest in computing science is far from obvious [Kallin Westin and Nordström, 2001, 2003; Eliasson et al., 2006a,b]. Similar trends are reported internationally [Forte and Guzdial, 2005; Jenkins and Davy, 2000].

7   Related Work

There have been several attempts to explain why students are having difficulties in their first Java course. Three common explanations are the following:

- The students can program, they are just having problems with the design part [McCracken et al., 2001].
- We are not teaching object-orientation the correct way, we need to teach the subject in a pure, object-oriented way [Bergin, 2000a; Kölling and Rosenberg, 2001.]
- Java has so many special cases, like `public static void main` and string handling so that it becomes difficult for the students to remember and to understand all the special cases [Bruce et al., 2005].

In a multi-national cross-university study, [McCracken et al., 2001] investigated how well students actually could program. They proposed a list of five steps that students should be able to follow successfully after passing CS1.

- Abstract the problem from its description.
- Generate sub-problems.
- Transform sub-problems into sub-solutions.
- Recompose the sub-solutions into a working program.
- Evaluate and iterate.

The results from this study were disappointing. The students' programming skills were at a much lower level than expected. Somewhat surprising, the most difficult part seemed to be the first step (e.g., to abstract the problem).

[Lister, 2004] followed up on these results and investigated students' ability to read, to understand and to modify existing code. Here, the results were disappointing also. A surprisingly large proportion of the students had difficulties completing even the most basic tasks. It seems that students not only have problems with the abstraction step, they also have problems with the more basic task of reading and understanding code.

[Lister, 2004] also investigated the annotations students made while solving the problems. In general, it turns out that students who carefully trace executions are more likely to provide correct answers than those who do not. However, there are considerable differences between universities [McCartney et al., 2005]. Students from some universities used annotations (traces) to a very high degree while others did not.

Considering the scope of this book it is interesting to note that the two universities with the least annotations are in Sweden and Denmark. Despite the low annotation level, these students performed on average compared to the students from other universities. Whether this is a coincidence or due to differences in object-oriented programming education needs to be further investigated.

8 Summary and Conclusions

The transition to object-orientation is not easy. It is not sufficient to simply change the language of instruction in an otherwise traditional introductory programming course. The strong relationships between basic, objected-oriented concepts constitute a high threshold to the learning and teaching of programming. Considerable changes to the course design are necessary to convey to the students the real power of the object-oriented approach.

We have presented and evaluated a set of eleven principles for course design that have helped us to stay on track in our efforts continuously to improve our introductory programming course. We have seen several factors that influence the results of an introductory programming course apart from the course itself. Attendance rates drop on all parts of the course and many students seem to think that knowledge can be acquired passively.

It is our firm believe that it is necessary to be faithful to the object-oriented approach. Tools that help students to "think in objects" are very important for successfully teaching basic object-oriented concepts. We must provide our students with a consistent frame of reference. This frame of reference will change with the knowledge and skills the students acquire. However, its core (i.e., the basic rules) should not be constantly contradicted by our own exercises and examples.

Using BlueJ to Introduce Programming

Michael Kölling

University of Kent, Canterbury, Kent CT2 7NF,
United Kingdom
mik@kent.ac.uk

Abstract. This chapter describes the BlueJ system. The discussion includes both the software tool aspects of BlueJ, as well as pedagogical approaches that should be considered when teaching with BlueJ. Pedagogical changes that have been suggested go deeper than merely introducing a new software tool: they include changes to a more software-engineering-oriented course, removal of considerable chunks of traditional material, and the introduction of new skills and approaches. We discuss experiences of using the system over eight years at various institutions, and discuss successes and failures as seen retrospectively today.

1   Introduction

In this chapter, we describe our experiences with the BlueJ system. BlueJ is, at its core, an integrated development environment (IDE). In practice, it has grown to become much more. When we started our work on BlueJ, we did not realise what it would grow into. For us, BlueJ as it stands now, is a software tool, a set of examples and resources, a framework of pedagogical principles and a distinct pedagogical approach to introductory programming.

At the start of the project, we had the intention of creating a software tool that was designed along some clear, explicitly formulated guidelines, which in turn were based on pedagogical principles. BlueJ, which started in 1998, was a direct copy of its predecessor system, Blue [Kölling, 1999b]. Only this time, it has Java as the supported language.

One goal was to design a system that allowed a different approach to teaching. Instead of wading through a sea of syntactic detail at the start to be able to make it to the solid ground of programming concepts, we wanted to create a visible exposition of those concepts upfront and to be able to deal with those first. BlueJ (and Blue before it) succeeded in doing that.

Our —retrospectively naïve— expectation was that we would publish this tool, and people would take it and start teaching their courses differently. This did not happen, however. We published BlueJ and after some time, it received a reasonable amount of visibility and attention. Some institutions started using it. At first, we were delighted to see our system being used, and then, we were horrified.

The revelation that things were not going as expected came when we looked more closely at what people were actually doing with BlueJ. What we found was

J. Bennedsen et al. (Eds.): Teaching of Programming, LNCS 4821, pp. 98–115, 2008.

that teachers would use BlueJ, but would still introduce material in exactly the same order and in the same manner as they had always done.

BlueJ's main goals, in our mind, were the following three things:

- To make the environment truly object-oriented by representing objects and classes as first-class entities in the user interface. This visualisation was intended to create a mental emphasis on class and object relationships, instead of concentrating on the positioning of semicolons and parenthesis.
- To allow interaction with individual objects to encourage small-scale experimentation. We believed that frequent interaction with single objects and methods would almost automatically lead to a better understanding of the inner workings of any program in particular and Java in general.
- To simplify the user interface of the environment to a degree that presents minimal distraction from the principles of programming. While learning to deal with IDEs is a worthwhile goal for a whole curriculum, it should not be forced on students simultaneously with learning their first programming concepts. It is a question of ordering. We wanted to free the teaching from the environment overhead.

In observing teachers using the BlueJ IDE in the first years following its release, we found that many of them were using BlueJ exclusively for the third reason. They appreciated the simpler interface to the editor and compiler, but did little to exploit the potential of the visualisation or interaction mechanisms. To our mind, this was missing the majority of the benefit of the tool.

At that stage, we realised that it was not enough to give people a new tool and to expect them to discover new teaching methodologies automatically, or to change their habits on their own. After some time, we became convinced that this was in fact the much harder part. Designing the tool was not the challenge, but figuring out how to use it to the best effect. How to change the pedagogical approach to teaching pro-gramming was where the real difficulty lay.

At that time, we got into a pattern of travelling around universities and conferences and giving workshops. We tried to tell people how we thought BlueJ should be used, and what our underlying ideas about teaching were when we designed it. The workshops were generally well received, but it was a slow process. The number of people we could reach in this way was limited. It became clear that we really needed a detailed, written description of our approach to teaching - a textbook. In late 2002, this textbook was published after being written with David Barnes [Barnes and Kölling, 2005].

In this chapter, we try to summarise what we have learnt from the whole BlueJ experience until today. We describe the BlueJ IDE as well as some of the pedagogical ideas of the project. We then discuss some experiences, later developments and end with some observations and thoughts about the future. This chapter expands on several previous papers with a different focus and a differing amount of detail. Some prior papers describe the BlueJ IDE [Köllingetal., 2003,] and some discuss approaches to teaching with BlueJ [Kölling and Rosenberg, 2001.]

2   Background

When we started designing BlueJ, many teachers expressed that they found teaching object-orientation more difficult than teaching procedural programming. This is, in fact, still the case today eight years later. Many teachers still find it more difficult. Our hypothesis has always been that teaching object-orientation is not intrinsically more complex, but that it is made more complicated by a number of external factors. Two of these are a profound lack of appropriate tools and pedagogical experience with this paradigm.

To start our discussion, we summarise the problems we have found in other environments for object-oriented languages as they were when we started working on this project. For a more detailed discussion, see [Kölling, 1999a]. The observations presented here are not much different today. Some small progress has been made, and we will discuss the more recent developments towards the end of this chapter.

The fundamental problems with most existing environments can be summarised in the following three key points:

1. The environment is not object-oriented.
2. The environment is too complex.
3. The environment focuses on building user interfaces.

We discuss each of these in some more detail.

2.1   Object-Orientation

An environment for an object-oriented language does not make an object-oriented environment. The environment itself should reflect the paradigm of the language. In particular, the abstractions students work with should be classes and objects. In most existing environments, students deal with files and an application instead. They are forced to think about the operating system's file system and directory structure. Setting up projects can be difficult. All this creates overhead that hinders teaching and distracts from the important issues. When students work in such environments, their interaction is exclusively with lines of source code, not with objects. Consequently, they come to view programming as dealing with lines of code rather than dealing with object structures. Objects as interaction entities are not commonly supported. Yet, they are one of the most fundamental abstraction concepts.

2.2   Complexity

Many teachers do not use an integrated environment because of problems with finding a suitable one. Students must work from a command line (using Sun's Java SDK) and spend considerable time becoming familiar with Unix or DOS instead of learning about programming. The result is a loss of valuable opportunities for improved teaching and learning through the use of better tools. The

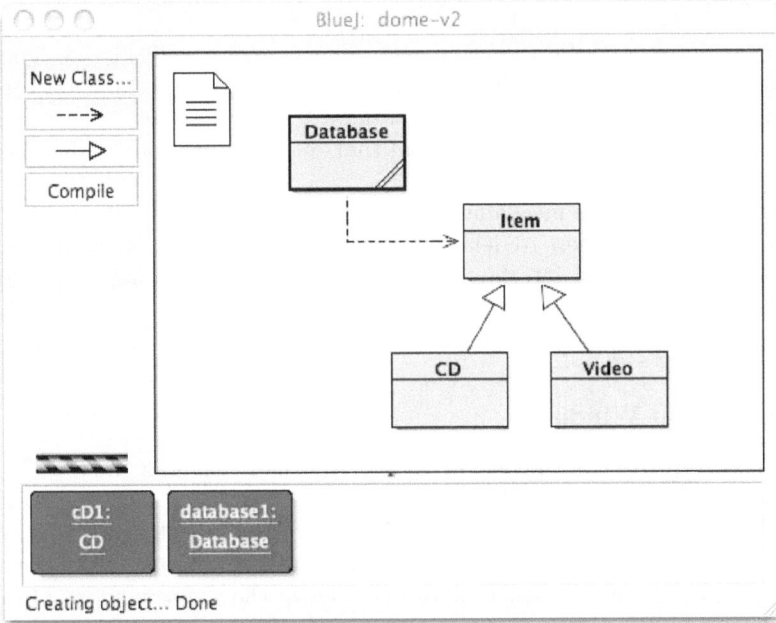

Fig. 1. The BlueJ main window

converse problem is that many other environments are developed for more professional users and present an overwhelming set of interface components and functionality. Students are lost in these environments, and the effect can be as bad as having no integrated environment at all. Other environments are really modifications of non-object-oriented (procedural) environments that offer the wrong set of tools and abstractions. Thus, the tools are too minimalist, too complicated or inappropriate and cause considerable problems.

2.3   User Interface Building

Many environments that are using graphics use them for the wrong tasks. In particular, many environments concentrate on building graphical user interfaces (GUIs). Building GUIs from the start conveys a very distorted picture of programming and object-orientation. Students spend their time dragging buttons rather than thinking about building an application. In discussions about the value of IDEs for teaching, people often equate environments with GUI builders. This is a dangerous trap that should be avoided carefully when discussing IDEs. There are more useful tools for learning object orientation than GUI builders.

One of the most beneficial uses of graphics is often neglected: a display of class structure. Object-oriented program structure can be represented graphically in a way that makes it easier to understand and to discuss design issues. Few existing environments make good use of this.

3   BlueJ

BlueJ is an integrated Java development environment specifically designed for introductory teaching. BlueJ is a full Java environment. It is built on top of a standard Java SDK, and thus uses a standard compiler and virtual machine. It presents, however, a unique front-end that offers a different interaction style than other environments.

BlueJ offers a unique mechanism of direct parameterised method calls. This mechanism allows teachers to delay the introduction of other interface technologies such as text based interfaces, GUIs or applets until a more appropriate point in the course. The environment's interface facilitates the discussion of object-oriented design and aids in using a true "objects first" approach.

3.1   The Main Window

When a Java project is opened in BlueJ, the main window shows a Unified Modelling Language (UML) class diagram visualising the application structure (Fig. 1). Users can then interact directly with classes and objects. A class icon can be used to execute a constructor, which results in an object being created and placed on the object bench at the bottom of the main window. Once the object has been created, any public method can be executed (this is discussed in more detail below).

A double-click on a class icon opens a text editor that lets users read or edit the class's source code. A simple click on a "Compile" button will recompile all changed classes and execution can start again. Compile-time errors are displayed directly in the editor by highlighting the corresponding line and showing the text of the error message.

The following sections discuss some of the most important aspects of the system in more detail.

3.2   Creating Objects

Clicking on a class icon with the right mouse button displays a class menu (Fig. 2). This contains some environment operations (such as compiling, editing and removing the class) as well as entries to invoke the constructors of the class.

When a constructor is invoked, a dialogue is displayed prompting the user for a name for the object (a default name is supplied) and, if appropriate, the parameters. Fig. 3 shows the dialogue for a constructor with two parameters.

Once the dialogue is confirmed, the constructor is executed and the resulting object is placed on the object bench.

3.3   Calling Methods

A right-click on an object displays an object menu (Fig. 4). The object menu contains two environment operations ("Inspect" and "Remove") and an entry for each public method is defined in the object's class. Inherited methods are placed

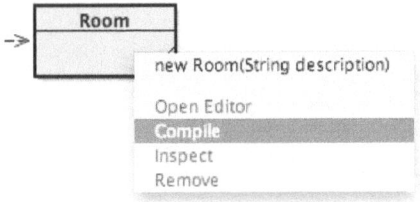

Fig. 2. The class menu

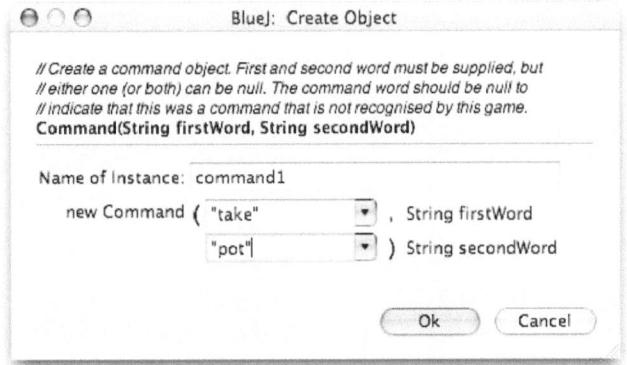

Fig. 3. A creation dialogue

in submenus. Selecting one of the methods results in that method being executed. If the method expects parameters, a dialogue similar to that shown for object creation is displayed to let the user specify the parameter values. Parameters can either be typed in (any valid Java expression is allowed) or other objects from the object bench can be chosen. Objects are specified as parameters by supplying their name (a simple click on the object is a shortcut to inserting the object's name into the parameter dialogue).

If a method has a non-void return type, the result is displayed in a method result dialogue. If the result value itself is an object type, the object can be placed on the object bench for further interaction.

BlueJ also provides a mechanism to instantiate classes from the standard Java class library. Users can then interact with these objects in the same way they do with objects from their project. This allows students to explore and experiment with library classes and objects. They can, for instance, directly interact with string objects or hash tables to observe their behaviour.

3.4   Inspection

The interaction mechanisms allow sophisticated and detailed testing of classes. Once a method has been written, it can immediately be tested without the

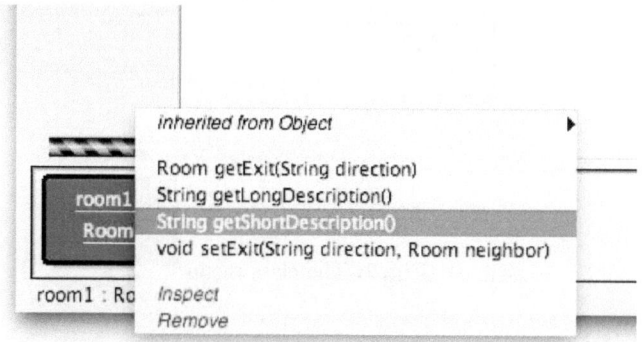

Fig. 4. The object menu

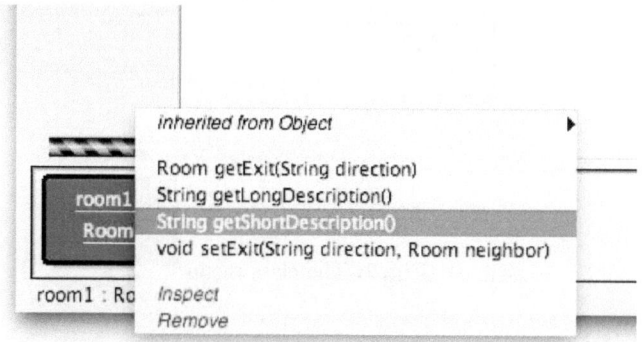

Fig. 5. Object inspection

overhead of writing test drivers. Sometimes, however, a user wants to test a method that alters the state of the object while no accessor methods are available to directly observe the state. For example, a constructor has just been written and no other methods are implemented yet. But, we would like to test the constructor before proceeding.

In this case, object inspection can be used to check the effect of the method. The "Inspect" operation from the object menu opens the object inspector, which displays the values of all instance fields of the object (Fig. 5). Any fields that are themselves objects can be recursively inspected.

3.5 Visualisation

One of the central aspects of the BlueJ environment is the class structure display in its main window. This forces students to recognise and to think about structure from the very first time they see a Java program. When showing students the very first example, it becomes immediately clear that an application is a set of cooperating classes.

Traditionally, one of the hard-to-explain (but very important) issues is the difference between classes, objects and their relationships. Using BlueJ, a teacher can interactively create multiple objects of a class and inspect and interact with every one of them. The relationship between classes and objects usually becomes clear very quickly. Without the need to talk much about it, students see that the class is used to create objects (as many objects as desired), and that the objects contain data. They also notice that the type of data in each object of the same class is the same while the actual values are different.

It also becomes apparent that objects are manipulated by invoking operations on them (which they provide) that alter their state. Some operations return information about the state. Thus, visualising the important abstraction entities of object-orientation (classes and objects) and allowing direct interaction with each serves to illustrate the OO concepts in a powerful and easy-to-understand manner without the need for long, dry explanations.

3.6 Simplicity

The third cornerstone of the BlueJ architecture (besides interaction and visualisation) is simplicity. The major problem with many existing environments is their complexity. Most environments were designed primarily for professional programmers, and the complexity of their tools overwhelms beginners. Beginning students need different tools than professional software engineers. This issue has been discussed in detail in the context of the original Blue system [Kölling, 1999b] on which BlueJ is based.

BlueJ is designed specifically for beginners. The central aim is that we want to teach about OO programming, not about using a particular environment. With BlueJ, students can start using the environment on their own almost immediately. After the first half hour of the first tutorial, we never talk about the environment again, and students are able to competently use it. We have traded some advanced functionality not needed in first year courses for ease-of-use, resulting in an environment not necessarily suitable for professional development, but much better suited to first year teaching.

3.7 Regression Testing with JUnit

BlueJ's object interaction facilities provide a very low cost entry to testing on an informal level, but lack support for more organised testing. There is a growing recognition of the value of the use of unit testing frameworks such as JUnit [JUnit, 2002].

JUnit is a small framework that allows organised regression testing through writing of test methods. It provides functionality to easily execute test banks, to express assertions on the results and to be notified of failing test cases. The JUnit test framework has recently become very popular in the Java community as a tool for organising testing, partly because of its extensive use in the extreme programming (XP) process [Beck, 1999].

BlueJ includes an integrated implementation of JUnit to support the teaching of organised testing to students [Kölling and Patterson, 2004]. The interaction mechanism described above supports ad-hoc testing in a convenient way, but is not suitable for more organised repetition of test cases. The integration of JUnit overcomes this problem. The result is not only the sum of these two test mechanisms, but the creation of a new quality of test tool through the combination of both. Thus, interactive test sessions can now be recorded and automatically saved as JUnit test methods to be replayed later for regression testing.

3.8   The Extension Mechanism

A continuous tension exists between requests for additional features being added to the BlueJ environment and our desire to keep BlueJ simple and small.

This tension has led to the development of an extension (sometimes called "plug-in") interface. Using this interface, third party developers can now write extensions to the BlueJ environment. Extensions have access to most of the BlueJ constructs and can be notified of user or environment actions via an event mechanism. Examples of available extensions are a project submission system and a code style checker.

3.9   Other BlueJ Features

BlueJ includes a variety of other features, which we will not discuss in detail here. Some of the most important are an integrated, easy-to-use debugger, integrated support for Javadoc generation, sophisticated support for generating and executing applets and an export function that can create executable jar files. The applet support includes automatic generation of an applet skeleton, and automatic generation and loading of an HTML page. It also includes the ability to run the applet in web browsers and applet viewers. Details can be found on the BlueJ web page [BlueJ, 2007] and in the BlueJ documentation (available from that web page).

4   Pedagogical Considerations

So far in this chapter, we have concentrated on presenting the technical details of the BlueJ environment. There is, of course, no single "right" or "wrong" way in which to use these tools. There are, however, known problems with introducing object-oriented programming to beginners. Many of these problems are related to mastering the inherent complexity of object-orientation, Java and the software tools.

Maybe the greatest single problem with teaching Java is the large number of circular dependencies of language concepts and constructs (as discussed in *Transitioning to OOP/Java - A Never Ending Story*). It sometimes seems that to understand anything, you have to know everything. This characteristic makes especially the first few weeks of a course hard to deal with.

Over time, we have identified a set of five guidelines that help in designing a course in a way that avoids some of the most common problems. These were presented in an earlier paper [Kölling and Rosenberg, 2001]. Some of the guidelines are independent of BlueJ, but some assume a BlueJ-like environment. Here, we briefly summarise those guidelines.

Guideline 1: objects first. Start talking about objects from the first day. Objects and classes are the fundamental concepts that students need to understand. Do not obscure this by talking about syntax first. Everything else can then be introduced in the context of classes and objects.

Guideline 2: don't start with a blank screen. If students start writing projects from scratch, they have to structure the problem first. In effect, they have to do design. Design is hard and requires experience. This is not a task that students can master at the beginning.

Guideline 3: read code. Reading code is an essential skill for any software developer. This skill can (and should!) be trained as any other programming-related skill. It is the first thing students will be required to do when they enter a software development job in industry. Teach it explicitly. Students can learn a great deal from reading code.

Guideline 4: use "large" projects. One of the major benefits of object-orientation lies in the ability to structure problems into independent modules (classes). Beginners cannot understand the purpose and the character of object-orientation from looking at single-class examples. Show multi-class examples from the start to convey the right ideas. Linn and Clancy describe a similar approach [Linn and Clancy, 1992].

Guideline 5: show program structure. The internal structure of applications lies at the heart of understanding object-oriented programming. Spend a large share of time discussing this.

Some specific applications of these guidelines to particular areas are important enough that we formulate them as explicitly expressed corollaries to the general guidelines:

Corollary 1: don't start with "main". The main method is the worst code example to study when trying to understand object-orientation. It has nothing to do with objects —it is a quirk of history.

Corollary 2: don't use "hello world". Hello World teaches nothing about objects. If the problem really was to produce the words "Hello World" on the screen, an object-oriented language is the wrong tool. If the purpose is to simply illustrate the edit-compile-execute cycle, then choose more reasonable examples to demonstrate this.

Corollary 3: be careful with the user interface. Dealing with user input and output is a difficult issue. Text I/O can be complicated, GUIs are complex to program, and applets are mysterious. BlueJ provides a mechanism that allows data input and output without explicitly programmed I/O code. Use this first and then carefully introduce programmed I/O. Delay GUIs until students can fully understand them.

5   The Project-Driven Curriculum

In this section, we present an example of a sequence of projects, which build on each other and drive the contents of the course. Other course activities, such as lectures or lab classes, are structured largely to support and to enable the projects. In that sense, the introduction of class material is problem-driven and closely related to problem-based learning approaches [Kay et al., 2000]. The sequence of projects presented here is designed to span two courses over two semesters.

The sequence presented here is a true "objects first" approach: students start seeing and interacting with objects as the very first thing, even before being confronted with Java syntax or source code. True "objects early" approaches, even though popular in theory, are difficult to implement in practice. With most environments, the syntax that is required to arrive at the first objects represents a real problem. In addition to syntax, the required Java code exposes concepts such as the main method, array parameters, object creation, variable declaration and dot notation for method calls.

The BlueJ environment, through its interaction facilities, allows the opportunity to avoid this problem. Interaction with objects can be presented first, leading to detailed discussions of the main concepts of object-orientation, before the need to deal with source code. (The same idea has been discussed in *CS1: Getting Started.*) Students can interact with object as their first task. From there on, students go through a sequence of progressively more complex activities. They are as follows:

- make small modifications to existing methods;
- implement complete method bodies where method signatures are supplied;
- add new methods to existing classes;
- add new classes to existing projects; and
- finally, create a complete project.

All of this work is done in the context of relatively "large" projects. Students get used to reading and modifying existing code from the very beginning. Many of these activities conform to an educational pattern called "Fill in the Blanks" [Bergin, 2000].

Another characteristic in which students are introduced to more advanced (and more realistic) concepts is the introduction of group work. Whereas the first few steps are done as individual work, the last step or two are carried out as group work projects. This adds the usual challenges of group coordination.

1 Getting your feet wet: executing code. The first project should be designed to achieve two things: to familiarise students with the environment, and to convey the basic concepts underlying object-orientation. The abstractions students are expected to encounter are objects, classes and methods.

Our example for this stage is a project called "shapes". This project contains classes for creating circles, squares and triangles, which are represented on screen. These can be moved, resized and changed in colour by interactively invoking methods on the separate shape objects. Students interactively manipulate these objects to create a picture on screen. In doing this, students practice creating objects, calling methods and passing parameters. They also get a first hint at types: integer and string types are used as parameters. In addition, we let students inspect objects (that is: view the values of the internal variables).

Some of the most fundamental Java concepts are illustrated through this activity: that Java applications consist of a collection of classes; that classes can be used to create objects; that many objects can be created from one class; that objects have operations (methods); that methods may have parameters and return values; and that objects have a state (fields with values that may change through method calls).

Note that there is no need at any stage of this project to deal with Java syntax. We show the classes' source code at the end of this project, but only to illustrate the existence of source code as an underlying construction mechanism. We do not expect students to understand any of it at this stage.

2 Manipulating source code. The purpose of the second project is to familiarise students with source code, Java syntax, and to introduce the first few programming constructs and the edit-compile-run cycle. In our example sequence, we use a class that implements a simple ticket machine to achieve this. Students can investigate the behaviour of the class, and they quickly notice that the program has several bugs: in our example, the ticket machine sometimes collects too much money, and sometimes it prints tickets without proper payment.

When investigating the source code, students are able to map the methods they discovered through experimentation and observation with object instances to the relevant source code sections. We then analyse the existing code. Students start to understand structure and syntax, and we begin to introduce new constructs needed to improve the behaviour of the faulty class (conditional statements, in this case).

During this stage, students learn about basic Java syntax, variables, constructors and methods, assignment, the 'return' statement, simple arithmetic operations and 'if' statements.

3 Creating new behaviour —the next step. After fixing or adding code within an existing method, students are now ready for the next step: adding new methods. For this stage, we typically provide students with partly implemented projects, which students have to extend or complete in obvious ways. These extensions involve the addition of new methods, as well as modification of existing ones.

Over time, we have used a number of different projects for this stage. They include a calculator program similar to that described by [Reges, 2000], which is an image manipulation example (e.g., a simplified Tetris game, an Eliza-like dialogue system, an encryption/decryption system and an electronic auction system).

In a typical course, we do three of these projects in sequence in increasing order of complexity. At this stage, the projects typically do not require students to write GUIs (they are either provided or the example is text-based). The number of language constructs required for the solution increases steadily.

4 Building blocks: adding more classes. The next step is a project where students create complete classes (again as part of an existing project). Here, we have often used a simple, text-based adventure game called "The World of Zuul" similar to that described in [Adams, 2002]. A basic framework is given to students that implements different rooms, input of commands and movement through rooms.

Students are asked to invent a game scenario, add items to rooms, the ability for players to carry items (up to a certain weight), etc. A number of more interesting challenge tasks is set such as implementing non-player characters, adding dialogue with game characters, adding random transporter rooms, various scoring systems, and many others. The scope for challenge tasks is endless.

One crucial aspect is that some of the tasks clearly require the addition of new classes, the most obvious one being an "Item" class. Students also go through exercises in reading and understanding the existing code. They have to make changes in most (but not all) of the classes, but they have to figure out themselves what they have to change and where. We have done this stage as individual tasks or as group tasks at various times. Both variants can work well and the choice depends largely on the goals of the course.

This has been one of the most successful assignments, with surprisingly elaborate student submissions both in inventiveness of story telling and technical implementation.

5 The master test. The last step is a project where students work in groups and create a whole application from scratch. This time, only a brief problem description is given, and students have to go through the whole development process, including the class design (with a lot of guidance). We have used a variety of continuous event simulations as projects. They included a supermarket checkout simulation, a traffic intersection with traffic lights, a lift simulation, emergency evacuation from buildings, a marine life simulation and others.

At this stage of the course, we don't discuss small scale programming issues very much anymore. The low level code writing is assumed to be mastered by students, and the project serves as a practice ground for applying these skills. The really new and challenging issues at this stage are application design and group work.

Simulations are an ideal example for practicing object-oriented design, because almost all objects needed in the application have corresponding objects in the real world, and are very easy to recognise with fairly simple methods. We use the noun/verb analysis and CRC cards [Beck and Cunningham, 1989] for class discovery (see also *Transitioning to OOP/Java — A Never Ending Story*).

Small scale problems are usually solved by groups internally, while the lecturer and tutor concentrate on discussing analysis, design and group work issues. It is made very clear that the group work aspect is not a coincidental side issue, but one of the important study topics of this course. Well-organised group work processes are expected to be set up and documented.

This is the first time students do design, but not the last. In the following year of study, there is a whole subject about analysis and design. We go through their first design with a lot of advice and attention to make sure that all groups arrive at a solution that is implementable within their given time.

This project is by far the longest of the assignment projects. Students are given eight weeks to complete the project, and the deliverables include a report and a demonstration.

6   Traps and Pitfalls

There is no light without shadow, and all we do has to balance at the end. Thus, when we introduce something new, something old has to give way. It is no different when introducing objects-first teaching with BlueJ. We are introducing new methods and new content, and so, necessarily something else is lost. Our observations show that students in our course have a better grasp of object concepts and general software engineering issues, but are in danger of being weaker in other areas. Some of these weaknesses were expected and accepted, other were accidental and had to be addressed.

The planned trade-off involved treatment of data structure implementation and searching and sorting algorithms. This has traditionally been second semester material in many institutions. With the shift to a software engineering focus in the course by using an object-first methodology, we have removed a significant part of this material from the first year. We now discuss competent use of data structures (as provided in the standard Java library), but not implementation of these. This topic has been moved to later courses in the curriculum.

Other problems that we did not anticipate, but which we observed or were reported to us by other BlueJ teachers, include transition issues out of BlueJ, complete application development and treatment of low level coding issues. These are discussed below.

6.1   BlueJ Dependency

BlueJ is intended as an introductory learning environment. Mastering the use of BlueJ has no value in itself —it is a tool for a purpose. A professional software engineer or computer scientist should be familiar with more professional development tools and be able to cope with minimal installations, such as command line environments and plain text editors for the purpose of developing programs. Thus, it is important that students learn to use professional tools before leaving the university.

We observe a reluctance to change in some students. For example, students cling on to the use of BlueJ and use it at inappropriate levels. (Other students are only too happy to migrate to more powerful tools!)

The design goal for BlueJ was to support programming in the first year. The optimal exit point for BlueJ is not entirely clear and can depend on a variety of factors. We feel, however, that BlueJ should rarely be used beyond the first year. We consider it essential that students mature out of BlueJ and are forced to gain experience with professional development tools afterwards.

We include a segment towards the end of our first year that requires students to develop and to run an application without BlueJ by using just an editor and command line tools. This is their first glimpse at the "other world" out there. This, we feel, is essential, but it is not sufficient for moving students on who have comfortably settled into their environment. Second or third year courses should ensure, by setting appropriate requirements, that students gain confidence with more professional tools.

6.2   Change Is Painful

Requiring a change to another environment does not guarantee a successful transition. Often curricula require use of different tools, but little explicit support is provided to master these. Our experience shows that merely requiring use of a professional environment can leave some students with problems.

We have found it beneficial to explicitly address the transition to the next environment in discussions. Expecting students to transfer the concepts on their own, obvious as they might seem to the teacher, is not always successful. We have repeatedly observed an effect where students who were successful in the use of BlueJ have difficulty applying the same concepts in a more traditional environment.

Discussing the transition and the transfer of concepts does not take much time. In fact, a single one-hour lecture is usually enough. Such a proactive approach, however, seems to make a big difference.

6.3   Self Sufficiency

In our course sequence, a large part of the activities consist of making modifications and extensions to existing code. The main driver classes of projects are often provided. Students experience the challenge of starting from scratch with a blank screen only towards the end. Developing a complete application is easily underrepresented in this curriculum.

The effect of this can be that students have difficulty to structure and to implement a complete application from scratch. This is especially the case if the last activities in the course (where this is practiced) are done as group work. It is possible to overcome this problem if it is consciously addressed. Regular exercises should be included early on, where students are required to develop small, but complete applications.

6.4   Control Structures

Feedback from some teachers indicates that they are worried about a decrease in student ability in handling low level coding structures, such as control structures or parameter semantics. We speculate that the reason for this is not intrinsic in the BlueJ environment, but in the way a BlueJ course may be structured. In our BlueJ-related publications (such as in this one), we often concentrate discussion on object concept issues. It is not our intention to suggest that these issues should replace lower level programming skills, but rather that the environment facilitates a reordering of topics. There seems to be a danger, however, that teachers focus on object-oriented concepts to such an extent so that basic writing of algorithms is somewhat neglected.

It is a general problem that more and more concepts are introduced into modern introductory programming courses (such as group work, testing, GUIs, concurrency, design issues, etc.). This necessarily leads to a reordering that results in some traditional material being moved into another semester or being dropped altogether. This is an issue independent of the environment used. The point to note is that important skills —the competent use of control structures, algorithmic thinking, recursion, etc.— still need the same amount of attention they needed in previous course structures. The use of an objects-first-approach does not lead to students magically mastering these issues.

7   Inspiration and Related Systems

Inspiration for the direct interaction techniques in BlueJ came from early Smalltalk environments and the Monads system [Keedy and Rosenberg, 1989], both of which also allow direct interaction with objects. Neither, however, had a graphical representation of objects. Smalltalk's interaction usually assumed a multi-window GUI, but strangely still represented classes, objects and their relationships purely textually. Monads was a persistent object-oriented system that included its own hardware, operating system and programming language with a purely text-based user interface.

Later Smalltalk versions, such as Squeak [Ingalls et al., 1997], have added extensive graphical visualisations, far beyond the functionality of BlueJ. Self [Ungar and Smith, 1987] is another integrated language and environment that provides much of BlueJ's functionality and much more sophisticated visualisations with emphasis on different aspects.

A number of object-oriented design tools exist that provide class structure visualisation such as Rational Rose [IBM Rational Rose, 2003] and JBuilder [JBuilder, 2003]. These systems, however, are aimed at professional developers and lack the ease-of-use needed to make them appropriate for introductory teaching. They also do not support interaction at an object level.

More recently, several systems were published that allow direct interaction with Java objects. Most notable among these are BeanShell [BeanShell, 2003] and DrJava [DrJava, 2003]. Both of these are Java interpreters that allow interactive evaluation of a series of Java statements similar to BlueJ's code pad functionality. Their interface resembles that of a Unix shell or a traditional Lisp read-evaluate-print loop.

The main difference between Java source interpreters and BlueJ is the level of conceptual abstraction provided by the user interface. The abstraction used for interaction in Java interpreters is lines of source code. The conceptual abstractions used in BlueJ are classes and objects, represented graphically.

We believe that the initial focus on higher level concepts benefits a deeper overall understanding of object-oriented programming. The early fixation on source code can distract from important issues and hide the bigger picture. We are, however, not aware of a formal study to confirm or to reject these assumptions.

8   Reflections

Was the BlueJ experiment successful? Well, that depends on your criteria. We like to think so. But it's not all roses. Or, in other words, "There's good news and there's bad news."

Do I think students have learned better using BlueJ? Yes. Do I think BlueJ has helped me in my teaching? Most certainly. Are our problems with teaching object-orientation solved? Not at all.

Assessing the effect of BlueJ is a very difficult task. I am not aware of any serious study into the effects of BlueJ on learning that included meaningful indicators, such as a control group or properly set up evaluations. Setting this up is an inherently difficult task. If an experiment were run within an actual teaching situation with a control group where both groups were taught with different methodologies (one with BlueJ and one without), then difficult ethics problems arise. Even the suspicion on part of the teacher that one method may be better than the other would make it unacceptable to use the weaker method for a group of students. If, on the other hand, the test was done in voluntary, extra-curricular activities, the situation would probably be significantly different because of self selection of participant groups. The most realistic chance would probably be when teaching methods change in a single course between one year and the next, but setting up a meaningful experiment in this situation is also not easy. Firstly, one would have to run the first part of the experiment a year before the change to get the control group, which requires a level of planning that rarely exists in a typical institution. And secondly, it almost never happens that individual aspects of a course are changed separately. Usually, when a change is done, several aspects (e.g., programming language, paradigm, teaching approach, teacher, textbook, software tools) change simultaneously so that meaningful results are hard to extract.

That said, there are some results that we can report. Firstly, there is adoption. The BlueJ software is now used at more than 800 universities, and the number of downloads is still rising every year. This indicates that user numbers are increasing, which in turn seems to indicate that current users are happy enough with the system to not switch away from it (at least not in larger number than new adoptions).

When BlueJ was first used at Monash University, Australia in 1999, students taking this course were invited to participate in a series of surveys to evaluate the environment. A detailed summary of this evaluation was presented by [Hagan and Markham, 2000]. Student perceptions were that the environment was helpful, particularly the object bench functionality and integration of the compiler error messages and source editor.

A study by [Madden and Chambers, 2002] that was surveying student attitudes to learning Java contained data showing that students found BlueJ significantly easier to use than a second environment that was used, JBuilder. (70% of students responded that BlueJ was easy to use, compared with 39% who found JBuilder easy to use.)

In addition to this, there is a lot of anecdotal feedback we receive from teachers, which is overwhelmingly positive. On the other hand, there seems to be a backlash slowly developing in the computing education community of teachers in general reporting unexpected difficulties in teaching object-orientation. While some are happy with their courses, others have concluded that object-orientation is too complex in principle to be taught at introductory level [Astrachan et al., 2005.]

Our conclusion at the moment is that the art of teaching object-oriented programming has a long way to go. We are firm believers in the benefits of doing this, and we believe that it is possible to succeed. But, it is clear that the required change is much greater than just changing a software tool. New approaches to teaching are needed, and it will take time for those to mature in our profession.

Model-Driven Programming*

Jens Bennedsen[1] and Michael Caspersen[2]

[1] IT University West
Fuglesangs Allé 20
DK-8210 Aarhus V
Denmark
jbb@it-vest.dk
[2] Department of Computer Science
University of Aarhus
Aabogade 34, DK-8200 Aarhus N
Denmark
mec@daimi.au.dk

Abstract. Conceptual modelling is the defining characteristic of object-orientation and provides a unifying perspective and a pedagogical approach focusing upon the modelling aspects of object-orientation. Reinforcing conceptual modelling as a basis for CS1 provides a course structure to integrate the core elements from a conceptual framework for object-orientation and a systematic approach to programming. Both of these are helpful to newcomers. The progression of the course is defined by the growing complexity of the conceptual model, which is to be implemented. The focus is not on conceptual modelling per se, but on the use of conceptual models as a structuring mechanism and a guide for the implementation. In this article we discuss different ways to structure an introductory programming course and give concrete examples on how a course where the complexity of the conceptual model is defining the structure.

1 Introduction

Over the years there have been ongoing discussions on the content and the structure of an introductory programming course, what programming language and tools to use in such a course, as well as the pedagogy to apply. There have been many suggestions [Bell and Scott, 1987; Evans and Patterson, 1985; Koffman and Wolz,1999; Oldham, 2005; Shaffer, 1986; Henze et al., 1999; Fjuk et al., 2004.] Most of the suggestions are structured according to the complexity of the programming language and are focused on the syntax of the programming language. In this chapter we will describe and discuss what we have found to be a useful structuring mechanism for an introductory programming course, namely the complexity of the class model to be implemented.

---

* This chapter is partly based on Bennedsen, J. and Caspersen, M.E. Programming in Context — A Model-First Approach to CS1. In *Proceedings of the Thirty-Fifth SIGCSE Technical Symposium on Computer Science Education*, Norfolk, Virginia, USA, March 3-7, 2004, pp. 477-481.

J. Bennedsen et al. (Eds.): Teaching of Programming, LNCS 4821, pp. 116–129, 2008.

1.1   Three Implementations of a Programming-First Curriculum

In order to define a common computer science curriculum, including an introductory programming course, ACM and IEEE established the Joint Task Force on Computing Curricula 2001. The charter was "to review the Joint ACM and IEEE CS Computing Curricula 1991 and develop a revised and enhanced version for the year that will match the latest developments of computing technologies in the past decade and endure through the next decade". In the final report [Engel and Roberts, 2001], the role and place of programming in the curriculum is discussed. Is programming what needs to be taught first (what they call a programming-first approach) or are there other topics that need attention first? The conclusion is that "the programming-first model is likely to remain dominant for the foreseeable future" (p. 24).

The report describes three implementations of a programming-first curriculum based on three of the following programming paradigms: The imperative, the functional and the object-oriented paradigm. The object-oriented paradigm has gained much interest in the past decade resulting in many textbooks (e.g., [Arnow et al., 2004,Barnes and Kölling, 2006,Horstmann, 2001, Hosch and Niño, 2002]) and much interest among teachers on implementing the object-first strategy (e.g. [Alphonce and Ventura, 2002, Cooper et al., 2003]).

1.2   Objects-First Curriculum

Objects-first is not a well-defined term. It seems that every CS1 teacher has his or her own interpretation of the term (e.g., [Cooper et al., 2003, Jones et al., 2003, Kölling and Rosenberg, 2001, Schmolitzky, 2004]). The Joint Task Force [Engel and Roberts, 2001] described it as "an objects-first approach that emphasizes early use of objects and object-oriented design" (p. 28). However, what does early mean, and what is meant by object-oriented design?

To add to the confusion of the objects-first concept is the problem that students often struggle with, namely the concepts of "class" and "object". They see and work with the program text and, therefore, work mostly with the classes and not objects directly. To have students understand the difference between the class as the concept at compile time and the objects at run-time is a major challenge [Fleury, 2000, Holland et al., 1997]. We have experienced that the explicit use of the conceptual framework for object-orientation and talking about it helps the students to understand it, e.g., by talking about a concepts extension, intension and designation [Madsen et al., 1993, p. 291] and to use a tool that supports intuitive and easy creation of objects from the classes (see *Using BlueJ to Introduce Programming* by Kölling).

[Lewis, 2000] discusses nine myths about object-orientation and its pedagogy; one is that the phrase "objects first" is well-defined. The author writes that "no matter what your definition of objects first is, it is likely to be different from that of the person next to you" (p. 247). Similarly, the author also states the following:

The phrases 'objects first' and 'objects early' are bandied about in a variety of contexts. When discussing a CSI course they are often used to convey the general idea that objects are discussed early in the course and established as a fundamental concept. Beyond that, however, these phrases seem to take on a variety of meanings, with important implications (p. 246).

Our definition of objects-first is:

- Objects from day one - in the beginning the students uses predefined classes to create objects, then they imitate the implementation of a class and finally they create classes.
- A balanced view on the three perspectives on the role of a programming language (see next section)
- Enforcing the use of a systematic way to implement a description of a solution (see section 1.4 Contracts)

1.3   The Role of the Programming Language

In [Knudsen and Madsen, 1988], three perspectives on the role of a programming language are described as follows:

Instructing the computer: The programming language is viewed as a high-level machine language. The focus is on aspects of program execution such as storage layout, control flow and persistence. In the following, we also refer to this perspective as coding.

Managing the program description: The programming language is used for an overview and an understanding of the entire program. The focus is on aspects such as visibility, encapsulation, modularity and separate compilation.

Conceptual modelling: The programming language is used for expressing concepts and structures. The focus is on constructs for describing concepts and phenomena.

These represent a widespread, three-level perspective on object-oriented programming as represented by the three abstraction levels for the interpretation of UML [Rumbaugh et al., 2004], class models [Fowler and Scott, 2000]. These consist of a conceptual level, a specification level and a code/implementation level.

When designing a programming course, one decides how much time, effort and focus are given to each of the three perspectives. It is possible just to focus on the first, instructing the computer, and to ignore the two others. This results in a course where the details of the programming language are in focus, but where the students do not learn the underlying programming paradigm. If, on the other hand, one just focuses on conceptual modelling (using a CASE-tool to generate code), the result is a course where the students cannot produce code by themselves. We find it vital to balance the three views on the role of the programming language. The primary advantages are

- A systematic approach to programming
- A deeper understanding of the programming process
- Focus on general programming concepts instead of language constructs in a particular programming language.

Most of the descriptions and discussions of the object-first strategy tend to focus on instructing the computer and managing the program description [Robins et al., 2003]. To our knowledge, no introductory programming textbook exists that addresses conceptual modelling, and we have been able to find only a few articles discussing the adoption of conceptual modelling in CS1 (e.g., [Alphonce and Ventura, 2002, Knudsen and Madsen, 1996, Sicilia, 2006]). It is our experience from many years of teaching CS1, that the inclusion of a conceptual modelling perspective has a major impact on the students' skills and their understanding of the programming process. Aspects of conceptual modelling are mentioned only briefly in CC2001 and the recommended time to be used on the subject is four core hours! It is our conviction that the general omission of conceptual modelling is one of the major reasons for the problems identified by CC2001 as can be seen by the following quote:

> *Introductory programming courses often oversimplify the programming process to make it accessible to beginning students, giving too little weight to design, analysis, and testing relative to the conceptually simpler process of coding. Thus, the superficial impression students take from their mastery of programming skills masks fundamental shortcomings that will limit their ability to adapt to different kinds of problems and problem-solving contexts in the future. (p.23)*

1.4   Contracts

We identify contracts [Meyer, 1992] and techniques for the systematic creation of object-oriented programs at four (six) different levels of abstraction:

1. *Problem domain* → **conceptual model:** Create a UML class model of the problem domain, focusing on classes and structure between classes
2. *Problem domain* → **Dynamic model:** Create a UML state chart to capture dynamic behaviour
3. *Conceptual model and dynamic model* → **specification model:** Specify properties and distribute responsibility among classes.
4. *Specification model* → **implementation:**
   a. *Specification model* → **implementation of inter-class structure:** Create a skeleton for the program using standard coding patterns for the different relations between classes.
   b. *Specification model* → **implementation of intra-class structure:** Create class invariants describing the internal constraints that have to be fulfilled before and after each method call.
   c. *Specification model* → **implementation of methods:** Use algorithm patterns for the traditional algorithmic problems (e.g., sweeping, searching). Use loop-invariants for the systematic construction of loops.

In the introductory programming course, focus is on the fourth level. Beginning students cannot design [Pattis, 1993], and therefore, we provide a specification model as the basis of almost every programming assignment in the course.

We reinforce the notion of contracts at each level:

- At the conceptual level, the contract is expressed as relations between classes; this contract is between the use and the programmer.
- At the specification level, the contract is expressed as functional specifications of the interfaces (classes) in the model; this contract is between clients and implementations of interfaces.
- At the implementation level, the contract is expressed as assertions in the program text (e.g., general assertions, class invariants, and loop invariants).

In the intro course we focus on contracts at the conceptual level and the implication of these contracts for the implementation in Java. It is our experience that the notion of contract in the context of a model-driven approach is a great help to beginning students.

2   Conceptual Modelling

In [Madsen et al., 1993], object-oriented programming is defined as follows:

> A program execution is regarded as a physical model, simulating the behaviour of either a real or imaginary part of the world.

The key point here is model. An object-oriented program is a model, and this model can be viewed at different levels of detail characterized by different degrees of formality as follows: An informal conceptual model describing key concepts from the problem domain and their relations, a more detailed class model giving a more detailed overview of the solution, and the actual implementation in an object-oriented programming language.

Object-orientation has a strong conceptual framework (notions of concepts and phenomena, identification of objects, identification of classes, classification, generalization and specialization, multiple classification, reference- and part-of composition). One of the advantages of the conceptual framework is that it gives an integrating perspective on analysis, design and programming, thus making it much easier for the students to understand these normally fuzzy concepts. Analysis is the process by which you create a conceptual model of the problem domain, design is the process where you fit the model to the restrictions of the particular programming language and implementation environment, and implementation is coding the design model. Omitting this integrating perspective and focusing only on object-orientation for implementation will leave out one of the most important assets of object-orientation.

We focus on the conceptual modelling perspective by emphasizing that object-orientation is not merely a bag of solutions and technology, but a way to understand, to describe and to communicate about a problem domain and a concrete implementation of that domain. The integration of conceptual modelling and coding provides structure, traceability and a systematic approach to program development, which strongly motivates and supports the students in their understanding and practice of the programming process.

The course is still a programming course and not a course on how to create conceptual models of given phenomena. We do not expect the students to create conceptual models of the referent system [Madsen et al., 1993, p. 286] that is to perform the activity they call analysis (p. 310). Nor do we expect the students in the beginning to be able to create a design for the program. We supply them with the program design described as a class model, and then they implement this design in a systematic way.

3   Structure of a Model-Driven Course

In this section we discuss different aspect of a model-driven programming course. These include progression, goals, and an example of a model-driven course describing the progression in terms of the concepts from the object-oriented conceptual framework.

3.1   Progression

One of the key problems in designing a programming course is to define the progression —what to start with, what next and so on. Traditionally, one starts with the simple things, but that quickly raises the question, "Simple related to what?" Traditionally, the answer is "Simple programming language constructs" (i.e., the progression is defined by the complexity of the programming language). [Robins et al., 2003] conclude that "typical introductory programming textbooks devote most of their content to presenting knowledge about a particular programming language" (pp. 141). That is to say, the majority of them are based on an "instructing the computer" or "managing the computer" perspective.

The approach taken here is to use the three perspectives on the role of the programming language as a guide for the structure of the course. In the first half of the course, roughly speaking, focus is concurrently on understanding and using a conceptual model as a blue print for programming and actual coding. In the second half of the course, the primary focus is on internal software quality, i.e. managing the program description. The answer to the question on "simple related to what" is, therefore, simple related to the complexity of the underlying conceptual model.

In section 3.3 entitled "A concrete implementation of a model-first course," our course design is presented. The interpretation is what we find simple and complex in the object-oriented conceptual framework; other interpretations are of course doable. If you find inheritance simpler than association, for example, then the next concept to introduce after the class concept is inheritance.

Apart from using the complexity of the underlying conceptual framework as a definition of progress, we also use the "early bird" pedagogical pattern

[Bergin, 2000]: *"The course is organized so that the most important topics are taught first. Teach the most important material, the "big ideas," first (and often). When this seems impossible, teach the most important material as early as possible"*.

3.2 Goals

Coding and understanding conceptual models is done hand-in-hand with the latter leading the way. Introduction of the different language constructs are subordinate to the needs for implementing a given concept in the conceptual framework. After introducing a concept from the conceptual framework, a corresponding coding pattern is introduced. A coding pattern is a guideline for the translation from UML to code of an element from the conceptual framework.

This approach supports a spiral course layout [Bergin, 2000], reinforcing the most important concepts several times in the course. There are two criteria for the design of the spiral layout: the most common concepts of the conceptual framework are introduced first, and throughout the course, the students must be able to create working programs.

The conceptual framework is comprehensive. For CS1, we restrict the coverage to association, composition and specialization, which by far, are the most used concepts in object-oriented modelling and programming.

The starting point is a class and properties of that class and the relationship between the class and the objects created from this class. One of the properties of a class can be an association to another class. Consequently, the next topic is association. This correlates nicely to the fact that association (reference) is the most common structure between classes (objects). Composition is a special case of association, and composition is taught in the next round of the spiral. The last structure to be thoroughly covered is specialization. Specialization bridges nicely to the second half of the course where the focus is on software quality and design where specialization is often used as a way to make more flexible designs.

3.3 A Concrete Implementation of a Model-First Course

In the following subsections, we describe some of the elements of the design of the course focusing on the first half of the course where transformation from models to code dominates.

Experience. The presentation below is based on the authors' experience from more than 20 years of teaching introductory programming. The ideas have been used both in traditional university courses (5-10 ECTS) with a lecture style of teaching and 300+ students attending as well as in a classroom style of teaching. It has been used both for young students who have just entered the university without any computer science background as well as for adults in further education courses where the students have been programming in another paradigm (the imperative). It has been used for students majoring in a computer science as well as students with a liberal arts and humanities background.

Getting started. We want to give the students an everyday understanding of object-orientation and a very informal understanding of the process of creating a UML class model. We, therefore, start by illustrating the concepts using everyday life situations in a role-play. The goal for the role-play is to illustrate structure and dynamics in terms of concepts, phenomena and messages in a problem domain and classes, objects and method calls in a corresponding (class and program) model. We use UML (primarily class diagrams) to describe concepts and their properties without any formal introduction to the modelling language.

To introduce the students to basic coding, we use a graphics package [Caspersen and Christensen, 2000]. The graphics package is presented in terms of a class diagram. Hence, very early the students experience the strength of a class model as an abstract description of a program component as well as a communication tool. Basically, the UML-model provides an effective "language" for documenting and communicating about classes.

This introductory part of the course provides an external view of classes and objects. For a further discussion on these problems, see *"CS1: Getting started"* by Caspersen and Christensen.

Class. After having used classes and objects, we turn to an internal view and start writing classes. We do this by introducing the following first coding pattern: Implementation of a class. A coding pattern is a general description of (and one way of) implementation of an element of the conceptual framework. The students discuss a domain concept, select a few properties and express the domain concept using UML. We emphasize, however, that the description of concept in itself is not important. Instead, we use that fact that the students themselves create the concept as a motivation for the students. Using the coding pattern, the UML-description is systematically translated into Java code. The general coding pattern is not shown to the students. The students observe implementations of classes and little by little abstract over these different implementations of different models. The learning is from Diverging, accommodating, converging to assimilating in the four learning styles described by [Kolb, 1984].

In this phase of the course, the students learn about basic language constructs such as assignment, parameters and conditional statements. These are constructs needed for the systematic translation of model into code like classes and objects, state and behaviour, primitive types and object types, reference, parameterization, this, methods, attributes and constructors.

As described before, a spiral approach is used. This implies that only what is needed is taught, for example, in the coverage of primitive types. In this case, we only use **int** and do not worry about the other types —they will be introduced when they are needed by the exercises.

The focus is on a systematic way of programming. This implies the following three things: many examples are shown to the students, explicit use of UML and a focus on the programming process (see [Caspersen and Kölling, 2006] for details on the process). The examples used are general concepts from the students' every day life like Person, Account, Die and Date.

We use BlueJ [Kölling et al., 2003] as the programming tool. In BlueJ, the user has a kind of UML diagram, but the internal details of the classes are not shown. We, therefore, use drawings of a UML class in order to explain an abstract understanding of a class.

Since we find it important to focus on the programming process and not just the end products (the program), we heavily apply "live coding" [Hyland and Clynch, 2002]. The purpose of this is not to show the students the nice and linear way from problem to solution, but to show the students how a professional programmer attacks the problem, making the actions visible and a source of identification [Nielsen and Kvale, 1997]. For more elaboration on this, see *"Exposing the Programming Process"* by Bennedsen and Caspersen.

Association. In the model of the problem domain, the most common structure between classes is an association. We use several examples with progressive complexity to illustrate the concept and its implementation.

One class with a reference to itself. Through a number of progressive examples we illustrate that an association is a property of a class, that a class can have more than one association, and that an association is a dynamic relation.

The students extend a previous example with a recursive association. One example is that a Person can be "married_to" another Person or the "lover" of another Person. This results in the model in Figure 1.

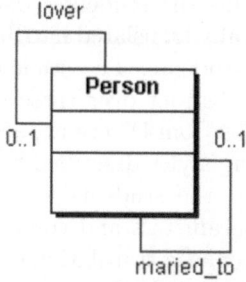

Fig. 1. One class with two associations

In order to implement associations with 0..1 cardinality the student needs to know about programming language elements (e.g., reference and the null value). It also gives the students an understanding of interaction between objects (calling methods on other objects) and reference semantics.

Another example of a recursive association is a simple adventure game where the rooms in the game are connected to other rooms in different directions. This can be modelled by the following model:

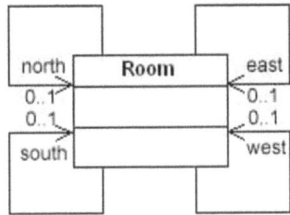

Fig. 2. One class with four recursive associations

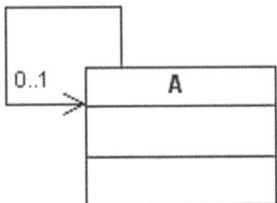

Fig. 3. General, recursive association

Again, the idea is that the students sees many implementations of the same general concept from the conceptual framework and realizes the general coding pattern:

This can be implemented by using the following coding pattern:

```
public class A {
    private A a;
    public void setA(A a) {
        this.a=a;
    }
    public A getA() {
        return A;
    }
}
```

Turning to 0..* associations imply that the student needs to know about Collections (either one of the Java standard Collections or the array type) and the need for iteration arises (the for-each loop, an `Iterator`, or an index variable and a simple loop). This is done by using a simple algorithm pattern for sweeping through a collection. One example we use to motivate collections and loops is the concepts of "friends" (a Person can have many friends):

More Classes

In order to get more interesting collaboration between classes, the next concept is associations between different classes. As a starting point we use a domain model with the following structure:

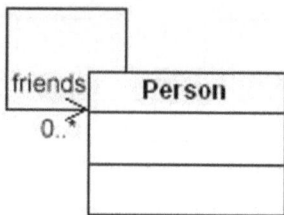

Fig. 4. A person with many friends

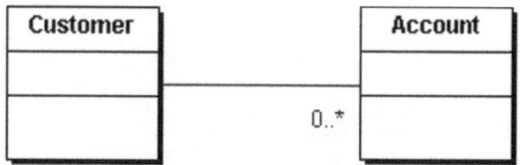

Fig. 5. One customer can have many accounts

The students quickly understand that an association between different classes, in principle, is the same as a recursive association. This is true for the implementation as well. Again, the students generalize to a generic coding pattern for 0..* associations.

3.4 Composition, Specialization and Interfaces

We treat the remaining elements of the conceptual framework, composition and specialization, in a similar way. As mentioned earlier, specialization bridges nicely to the second half of the course by focusing on software design and quality. The primary quality aspect is coupling and the main language construct by which to achieve low coupling is interfaces. Interfaces play an important role in the separation of specification and implementation: the specification of properties of a domain concept and (different) implementation(s) of these properties.

4 On the Role of Conseptual Modelling in CS1

In the following section, we will discuss some of the aspects of our integration of conceptual modelling in an introductory programming course. As mentioned in section 3.2 entitled "Goals", it is not a goal in this course that the students creates conceptual models by themselves, but that they learn to use the conceptual model as a map of the code guiding their actual programming.

4.1 Systematic Approach to Programming

The goal is to teach the students to appreciate and to achieve quality software. By good quality software we mean modifiable software (i.e., readable and understandable programs with a good structure, low coupling and high cohesion). These quality measures are by no means obvious to newcomers, and how to achieve them is even harder. We need to teach the students guidelines for achieving it and a vocabulary to talk abut their programs in order to help them build quality programs. The guidelines can be at different levels —see section 1.4 entitled "Contracts".

4.2 Providing Confidence

To program is difficult! In [McCracken et al., 2001], the authors found "shockingly low performance on simple programming problems, even among second-year, college-level students at four schools in three different countries". It requires knowledge and skills of many things such as the programming language, development tools and the capability of formulating a solution in such a way that a computer is able to understand it. Especially, the last demand implies the need for creativity when programming.

Students find the creative process very difficult. In a more traditional programming course, students are guided by standard algorithmic techniques such as searching, sorting, divide and conquer, etc. The problem is that algorithmic techniques do not help the students to create the overall structure of a solution. Thus, they do not know where and how to start because the mental gap between the problem description and an implementation in terms of algorithms is too big. Conceptual modelling gives a systematic and structured approach to programming, which provides confidence and a safe ground for addressing the programming task.

Most programming tasks are trivial and can be handled by using simple standard techniques such as the generic coding patterns described above. By focusing on standard techniques first, the need for algorithmic creativity is reduced (and a thorough treatment is postponed to CS2).

4.3 The Programming Process

The modelling approach to programming invites for an iterative process where the program is developed incrementally. Through progressive exercises, we reinforce such a process in order to imitate modern program development processes [Beck, 1999].

4.4 Abstraction

One of the important skills we want our students to possess is the capability to abstract. One way of stimulating the student's ability to abstract is to give several exercises with similar structure.

One example from the bank domain is the model shown in Figure 5. In a student administration domain we have the model as described in Figure 6.

Initially, the students see these two models as completely different, but gradually they realize they are both instantiations of the same abstract model (Figure7).

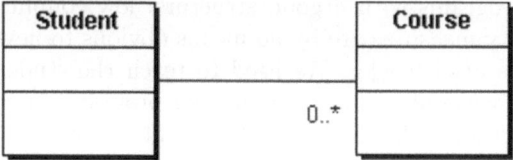

Fig. 6. A student can participate in many courses

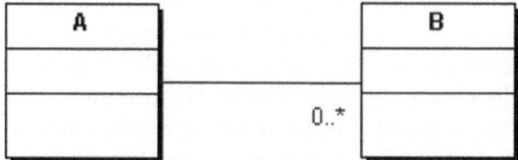

Fig. 7. Abstract to many association

From this abstract model, they can produce a corresponding generic coding pattern (Listing 1.1).

```
import java.util.*;
public class A
{   private Collection bs;
    public A()
    { bs = new ArrayList(); }
    public Collection getBs()
    { return bs; }
    public void addB(B b)
    { bs.add(b); }
    public void removeB(B b)
    { bs.remove(b); }
}
```

Listing 1.1. Generic coding pattern for 0..* association

4.5   Object-Orientation and Procedural Programming

Apart from implementing the overall static structure of a program, students need to implement the inside of the methods as well. As described in the section 1.4, "Contracts", we use several systematic approaches to this. In the introductory programming course, however, we do not teach the complete picture of systematic tools useful for implementing methods. Nor do the students themselves create class invariants or loop invariants since we supply them in an informal way (e.g., by describing the role and constraints on each attribute of the classes by using a comment or by general comments in the javadoc of the class). This shows the students how we, as experienced programmers, use this information when implementing methods. In a later course, the students will learn how to create contracts themselves at all the levels mentioned in the section 1.4, called "Contracts".

This focus on the use of contracts implies that our focus on the more traditional, procedural aspects of programming is scaled back —the students learn how to implement general sweep algorithms. But, the more subtle problems related to algorithmic problem-solving is postponed to a later course.

5   Conclusions

In our many years of experience in teaching introductory programming, we have found this approach to be useful. It gives the students structure and confidence within the program and helps them to focus on the local problems instead of focusing all over the program text. We believe that this way of structuring the course especially helps the weaker students.

The structuring and the content of the course of course depend on the learning goals for the course. One of our learning goals is that the programming process should be demystified. We have demystified the programming process by focusing on a systematic way to convert specifications to working code, thereby postponing the "design" element of the course. Thus, the students do not design, but are given the design by the lecturer. We believe that a good "reading" ability is a prerequisite for a "writing" ability. In other words, the students need to read a lot of contracts and have a good understanding of how one can implement the contract before the students create contracts themselves.

CS1: Getting Started*

Michael E. Caspersen and Henrik Bærbak Christensen

Department of Computer Science
University of Aarhus
Denmark
{mec,hbc}@daimi.au.dk

Abstract. The Logo programming language implements a virtual drawing machine —the turtle machine. The turtle machine is well-known for
giving students an intuitive understanding of fundamental, procedural
programming principles. In this chapter we present our experiences with
resurrecting the Logo turtle in a new object-oriented way and using it
in an introductory object-oriented programming course. While, at the
outset, we wanted to achieve the same qualities as the original turtle
(understanding of state, control flow, instructions), we realized that the
concept of turtles is well-suited for teaching a whole range of fundamental principles. We have successfully used turtles to give students an
intuitive understanding of central object-oriented concepts and principles
such as object, class, message passing, behaviour, object identification,
inheritance, and recursion. Finally, we have used turtles to show students
the use of abstraction in practice because the turtle package, at a late
stage in the course, becomes a handy graphics library used in a context
otherwise unrelated to the turtles.

1   Introduction

It is our firm conviction that the primary aim for an introductory programming
course is that students learn fundamental programming principles and techniques. The mastery of a programming language is, of course, necessary, but we
view it as a secondary concern. Mostly, we want to focus on fundamental principles and general techniques as early as possible, and thereafter unfold these
throughout the course.

Contrary to this, most introductory programming texts focus on the programming language. This is often described in a bottom-up fashion starting with the
simpler constructs of the language and progressing to more advanced constructs;
only subordinate to the presentation of the language constructs follows the presentation of programming techniques. However, all too often, these programming
techniques are not even explicit in textbooks.

---

* This chapter is based on Michael E. Caspersen and Henrik Bærbak Christensen.
 Here, there and everywhere — on the recurring use of turtle graphics in CS1.
 In *ACSE '00: Proceedings of the Australasian conference on Computing education*,
 Melbourne, Australia, 2000, pp. 34–40.

J. Bennedsen et al. (Eds.): Teaching of Programming, LNCS 4821, pp. 130–141, 2008.
© Springer-Verlag Berlin Heidelberg 2008

Another motivation for our approach is that most people learn more easily through the concrete towards the abstract [Brightman, 1998; Myers and McCaulley, 1985]. Seeing constructs and techniques being applied in an appealing and intuitive way provides an excellent basis for a later thorough and more abstract treatment. Thereafter, students are able to mimic these to solve similar problems. In this way, the students have some practical experience to ground the more abstract treatment that follows.

1.1 The Inverted Curriculum

Our view is not a novel one as is evident from many papers from past SIGCSE conferences [Astrachan and Reed, 1995; Decker and Hirshfeld, 1993; Hilburn, 1993; Pattis, 1993; Reek, 1995]. Bertrand Meyer [Meyer, 1997] coined the term "the inverted curriculum" (or "consumer-to-producer-strategy") meaning that important topics and concepts should be covered first by using classes solely through their abstract specifications. Only then, the students learn about the internals of classes. A simplified variant of Meyer's vision is the objects first approach, which is prevailing in many new textbooks. Still, many of these books are structured on the basis of the constructs in the programming language, and not on the basis of the language independent concepts, principles and techniques that the students are supposed to master by the end of the course.

Of course, in order to be able to focus on programming techniques and to apply these in concrete programs, it is necessary to be —at least to some extent— fluent in a programming language. However, we do not want the learning of the language to take over and to become the primary concern, especially not in the beginning of the course. What we want is to jump start the students so that they, as early as possible, can start writing interesting and challenging programs based on the fundamental principles and techniques that are our primary concern in the course: programs as physical models, objects, behaviour, classes, state, control flow, parameterisation, design by contract (specifications), inheritance, etc.

In order to facilitate a jump start of CS1, we have developed a Java package called Turtles that takes, as its starting point, the familiar turtle graphics developed by Seymour Papert and others at MIT in 1967 [Papert, 1980; diSessa and Abelson, 1981]. We use it to give an intuitive introduction to concepts such as state, control flow, and parameterisation. Somewhat to our surprise, it turned out that the Turtles package could play many more roles within CS1 than initially anticipated. In fact, it has become a recurring vehicle for introducing such diverse topics as objects, classes, object models, recursion, polymorphism and class hierarchies. Indeed, turtles popped up here, there, and everywhere.

In the current version of our introductory programming course, we are using the programming language Java, which is also the language of choice for the presentation in this chapter.

2   The Turtle Machine

The original Logo turtle machine is a virtual drawing machine that uses the metaphor of a turtle with a coloured pen moving around in a Cartesian drawing area producing drawings. The state of the turtle machine can be described as a 4-tuple: a turtle position (x, y)-coordinates, an angle, a colour, and an up/down status for the pen. Initially, a turtle is placed in the lower left corner (0, 0), the angle is zero, the colour is black, and the pen is down (Figure 1).

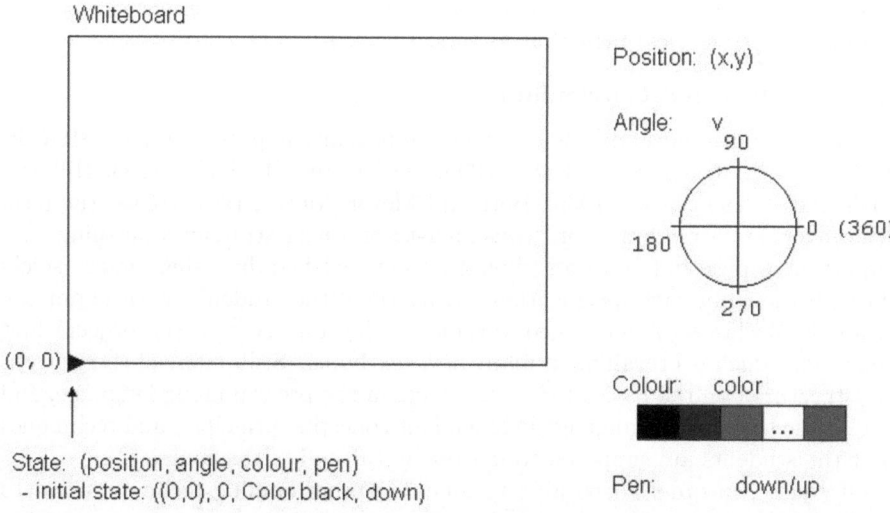

Fig. 1. Architecture of the Turtle Machine

The set of instructions for the machine is minimal —only nine instructions are used to operate the machine (see Table 1).

Table 1. Instruction set for the Turtle Machine

Command	Behaviour
move(l)	move l units in current direction
moveTo(x, y)	move to position (x, y)
turn(d)	increase the angle d degrees
turnTo(d)	set the angle to d degrees
center()	move to center
penUp()	lift the pen
penDown()	lower the pen
setColour(c)	set the pen's colour to c
clear()	clean the drawing area

3   The Turtle Machine Resurrected: Turtles

The original turtle machine sprang out of the procedural programming paradigm that views a program as a sequence of instructions carried out by some virtual machine. In contrast, the object-oriented programming paradigm views a program as a model where model elements are objects that have behaviour and that will interact with other objects. Thus —in our object-oriented CS1 course— the turtle machine has naturally been replaced by turtle objects. In our Java implementation, there is no machine that executes turtle commands. Instead, there are objects that exhibit turtle behaviour that is described by the Turtle class. The instruction set in Table 1 is replaced by (otherwise semantically equivalent) methods in the Turtle class.

This change of view and paradigm comes natural because the original metaphor of a turtle moving around on a drawing area is inherently an object-oriented model.

4   Jump Starting

At the beginning of the course we teach the concepts from the concrete towards the abstract. We start by introducing our "mascot" turtle with the odd, but short, name t. t lives in a sandbox (the large drawing area) and has a pen that leaves a trail when it moves around. t has *behaviour*: move-,turn-, and pen-behaviour. t exhibits the move-,turn-, and pen-behaviour when we pass it the message to do so (e.g., t.move(100) tells t to move 100 units forward). Before we show a computerised turtle, we actually let the audience command the lecturer around the floor in an attempt to produce a rectangle. While it reinforces the intuitive understanding of the behaviour concept, it also 'breaks the ice' between audience and lecturer as the audience for a short period is 'in control of the lecturer' as they pass messages like "Henrik, please move 2 meters" and so on. Controlling the turtle (or lecturer) also brings an intuitive understanding of the importance of the sequencing of messages passed, or the control flow. Parameterisation also follows naturally as, for instance, the 'move'-behaviour needs additional detail, namely the actual distance to travel. The computerised turtle is then described through online viewing, editing, and running of Java code by using a laptop computer connected to a projector.

We motivate loops in control flow in order to avoid textual repetition. For example, looping four times over {t.move(100); t.turn(90);} is easier than writing eight turtle messages. This quickly leads to quite interesting drawings as illustrated in Figure 2 produced by program 1.

Program 1. The "Spirille" program

```java
// 36 squares each turned an angle
// of 10 degrees from the previous
public class Spirille {

  public static void drawSpirille() {
    Turtle t = new Turtle();

    t.setColor(Color.blue);
```

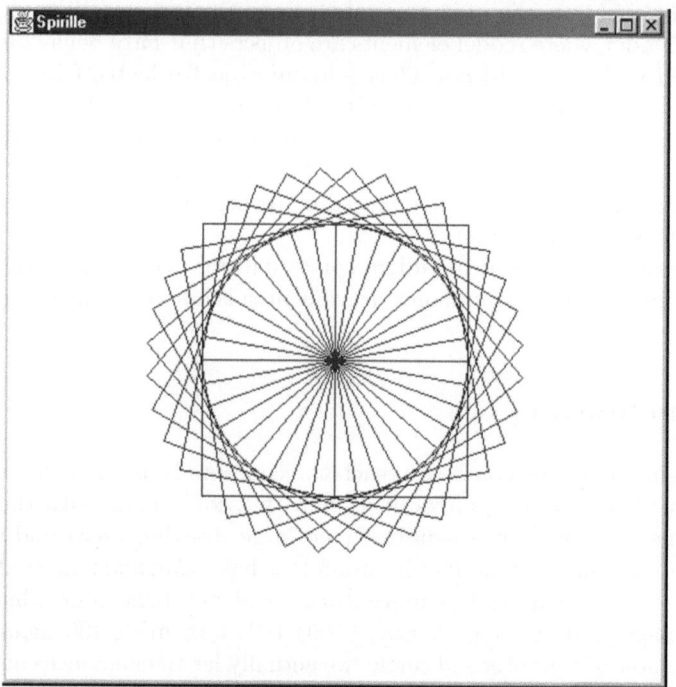

Fig. 2. The Spirille

```
t.center();
for (int i= 0; i<36; i++) {
  for (int j= 0; j<4; j++) {
    t.move(100);
    t.turn(90);
  }
  t.turn(10);
  }
}
}
```

At this point, students already have gained an intuitive first understanding of fundamental object-oriented concepts through a concrete and highly visual metaphor. The concepts include object, object identification, message passing as well as fundamental procedural concepts such as state, flow of control (including loops) and parameters. The immediate visual feedback from the program makes it easy for students to identify logical programming errors and helps the inexperienced student. At the same time, the material is still advanced enough to challenge those students that are already familiar with the basic topics. Also, the lab exercises are about making simple drawings (a flag and a house), nested drawings (pyramid seen from the top, a high-rise block, etc.) and animations (various objects that move around).

Typically, students can be divided into two of the following groups: one group of students tend to use the relative commands `turn` and `move`, whereas others are more comfortable with the absolute commands `turnTo` and `moveTo`. We discuss the different approaches in class, and in particular, we investigate the difference of using the relative and the absolute commands. This turns into a discussion on important and fundamental software engineering issues such as generality, modifiability, and reusability of programs.

5 Objects and Classes

A natural next step is to introduce two turtles into the same drawing area. This seemingly trivial addition is actually an intuitive and powerful way to introduce the students to another important range of fundamental concepts in object-orientation. This represents a trivial and natural step in an object-oriented language, but a difficult one in the original turtle machine.

Having two turtles makes the importance of object identification clear: How else can you identify the actual turtle to which a message has been sent? Another reinforced point is that the two turtles have different states though they share a common behaviour. Basically, they appear and draw in different areas of the drawing area. From this example, it is natural to discuss the benefits of categorising objects with common behaviour, and to give examples from everyday life where we classify concepts and phenomena. Introducing the notion of a (Java) class is, thus, relatively easy.

6 Class Hierarchies and Procedural Abstraction

The next step is to introduce procedural abstraction through defining new methods to draw, say, a rectangle. At first sight this seems like an overwhelming task to do in the second lecture as the only way to add a new method in Java is either to introduce it into the Turtle implementation or to extend the Turtle class and introduce the method in the subclass. The first alternative is not an option —primarily because the turtle is provided as a Java package, and secondly, because we do not want to expose the implementation with all its details of the Java graphics. But, the second option, which is to extend the Turtle class, turns out to be quite natural as described below.

6.1 Class Hierarchies

What do you do when you want your turtle to learn new "tricks", such as drawing a rectangle? You train your turtle until its behaviour extends to include the ability to draw rectangles —and your turtle becomes a skilled turtle.

Program 2. Procedural abstraction and parameterisation

```java
public class SkilledTurtle extends Turtle {

  public void rectangle(int w, int h) {
    for (int j= 0; j<4; j++) {
      t.move(100);
      t.turn(90);
    }
  }

  public static void main() {
    SkilledTurtle t= new SkilledTurtle();

    ... t.rectangle(100, 50); ...
  }
}
```

Program 3. Specialisation of turtles

```java
public class GeometryTurtle extends Turtle {
  public void rectangle(int w, int h) { ... }
  public void circle(int r) { ... }
  ...
}

public class ArchitectTurtle extends GeometryTurtle {
  public void window(int w, int h) { ... }
  public void door(int w, int h) { ... }
  public void roof(int w, int h) { ... }
  ...
}
```

By focusing on the idea of 'extending behaviour', the Java syntax for declaring subclasses seems feasible (program 2 and 3). We show the students how (program 2), and they are able to mimic the idea in exercises where turtles with new special skills are required as exemplified in program 3. We do not dwell on abstract, complex, properties of inheritance and class hierarchies. Rather, we show how this technique —grounded in an intuitive understanding of "training turtles"— can be used to solve a concrete problem. In this way, we have an excellent basis for a thorough treatment later in the course when the students have concrete experience and an intuitive understanding of inheritance. Also, the students have seen an aspect of what inheritance is actually used for. In the end, we find this is the basic purpose of the course: not merely to understand language constructs and object-oriented principles, but being able to apply them to solve recurring problems in computer science.

6.2   Procedural Abstraction and Design by Contract

Based on the metaphor of skilled turtles, the focus is turned to the problem of "training". The first skilled turtle is one that can draw rectangles, and clearly, one wants to be able to define once and for all how to draw a rectangle with width w and height h (program 2).

From the SkilledTurtle example (or similar ones), we initiate a discussion on the necessity of the last `t.turn(90)` in the rectangle method of program 2. The statement is superfluous as far as the resulting drawing is concerned, but there are obvious reasons to include the statement. One is to leave the turtle in the same state as before the call, making it easier to make composite drawings by multiple calls (like the Spirille). The students understand the point, and hopefully, valuable seeds have been sown.

On the basis of simple examples like this, we discuss important fundamental principles such as design, specifications, and the distinction of what and how. In the context of the turtles, it comes natural for the students to express sound and well established principles for procedural abstractions. Later in the course when things get more complicated, we return to this common ground and recall the principles.

The moral of the discussion is that we need to be precise about what we want a piece of software to do. The best way to express such requirements is by writing a functional specification. Hence, we introduce the notion of design by contract [Meyer, 1997], and from then on we use the technique throughout the course. This is reinforced as we provide the specification of the Turtle as JavaDoc API documentation, thereby forcing the students to become acquainted with the standard way of documenting Java classes and packages.

7   Recursion and Fractals

A traditional way to introduce recursion is to compute factorials. We find this unfortunate because it introduces the technique on a problem for which it is inefficient and an iterative solution is straightforward to express. Contrary to this, we introduce recursion for problems where the recursive solution is effective, and where iterative solutions are difficult to express elegantly.

The students are asked to write a program that can produce the list of drawings, Triangle, Penta, and Poly in Figure 3 (and the next seven figures, which are given equally odd names). However, first we demonstrate how to write methods for the first two drawings (program 4).

Program 4. Java code for triangle and penta

```java
public class TriangleTurtle {
  public void triangle(int length) {
    for (int i= 0; i<3; i++) {
      move(length);
      turn(120);
```

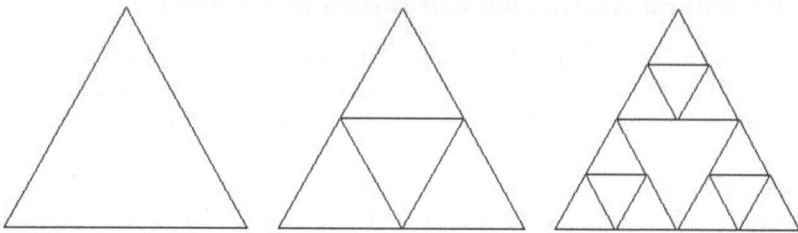

Fig. 3. superTriangles

```
    }
  }
  public void penta(int length) {
    triangle(length/2);
      move(length/2);
    triangle(length/2);
      turn(120); move(length/2); turn(-120);
    triangle(length/2);
      turn(-120); move(length/2); turn(120);
  }
}
```

As expected, the students produce eight new methods by copy-paste-and-substitute of the penta method. It works, but of course, the students get the hunch that this cannot be the proper way to do it.

Once more, we emphasise the notion of parameterisation, and we introduce the term superTriangle(n) to mean "a superTriangle of degree n". Defining superTriangle(0) to denote Triangle, superTriangle(1) to denote Penta and so forth, brings us more than half way towards the general solution. Realizing that superTriangle(-1) does not make sense and handling this special case brings us the rest of the way (program 5).

Program 5. A general (recursive) solution

```
public class TriangleTurtle {
  public void triangle(int length) { ... }

  // pre: n >= 0
  public void superTriangle(int n, int length) {
    if ( n == 0 )
      triangle(length);
    else {
      superTriangle(n-1, length/2);
        move(length/2);
      superTriangle(n-1, length/2);
```

```
        turn(120); move(length/2); turn(-120);
      superTriangle(n-1, length/2);
        turn(-120); move(length/2); turn(120);
    }
  }
}
```

The derivation is fairly easy. With little guidance, the derivation is almost exclusively done by the students. But, even more interesting is the fact that nobody mentions the notion of recursion. The solution just turns out to be recursive.

8 Turtles as a Class Library

Later in the course, when we are covering more advanced object-oriented topics such as class hierarchies, polymorphism and application frameworks, we dig out the "old" Turtles package and use it as just another class library. We also find it important for students to use class libraries and the accompanying documentation as early as possible in the undergraduate curriculum, as pointed out in [Tewari and Gitlin, 1994].

8.1 Class Hierarchies and Polymorphism

We use geometric shapes as an example of a class hierarchy. An abstract class Shape has concrete methods move and erase and an abstract method draw that is implemented in subclasses of the Shape class. Each Shape instance has an associated turtle to which it delegates the drawing tasks. In this way, the turtle becomes our graphical drawing library, effectively encapsulating the Java specific graphical toolbox (Figure 4).

There is another important point in (re-)using the Turtles package as a drawing toolbox. Abstraction is the key concept in programming, and the code that is the intense focus of design, development, and testing today (the implementation view, how) will be taken for granted next month and simply used (the specification view, what). In a similar vein, the turtle was "the problem" in the beginning of the course. Instead, now it is the solution to the problem of drawing shapes in a new and different context.

8.2 Application Frameworks

Before introducing the students to GUI-programming with AWT or Swing, we give a lesson about frameworks in general, and we exemplify by providing a simple framework for the students. The purpose of the framework, called Presenter, is to allow fast development of graphical presentations of a set of images (actually graphical components) and text, where the ordering in the set is arranged by using a familiar navigational metaphor, the compass with directions north, east, south, and west.

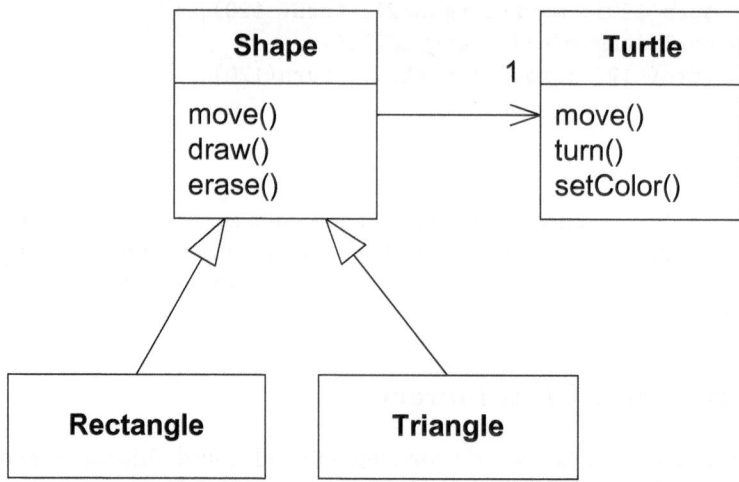

Fig. 4. A hierarchy of geometric shapes

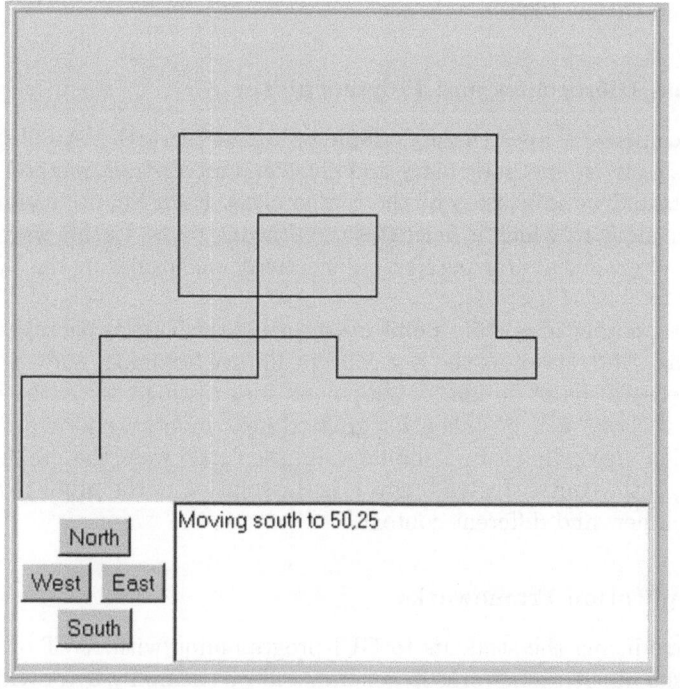

Fig. 5. A turtle in the Presenter framework

Our initial instantiation of the framework is a multimedia presentation of the tomb of Tutankhamen. By using the compass buttons, the user can move between the different chambers of the tomb, with each chamber described both in text and by a picture from the original opening of the tomb.

In an exercise, the students are asked to program a turtle controller. For instance, the buttons North, West, South and East must control the movement of the turtle as shown in Figure 5. While it shows the turtle in yet another context, the main point here is that the turtle's drawing area is actually a subclass of java.awt.Component, the basic graphical component in Java, and, therefore, the framework accepts to display the turtle drawing area. This way another important property of inheritance is demonstrated to the students. It is not so much a language construct, but a technique for solving a specific set of problems.

9   Conclusion

We have described our use of a Java package, Turtles, which is an object-oriented variant of the classical turtle machine. Early in the course, we are using the Turtles package to jump start our CS1 course by giving an intuitive introduction to classical procedural concepts in the spirit of the Logo language. We are doing this by introducing only the most necessary constructs and only by example. We do not want to provide detailed explanations that will not be understood nor remembered at this early stage.

Turtles is a great way to introduce simple as well as more advanced object-oriented concepts such as state, behaviour, object identification, inheritance, and polymorphism because the metaphor of a turtle on a drawing area is inherently an object-oriented model.

Furthermore, the Turtles package has been successfully used to illustrate abstraction at a later stage in the course. While the semantics and details of turtles were the focus and problems in the early part of the course, it is simply used as a drawing class library in the later part of the course.

The applicability of the Turtle graphics in introductory programming is acknowledged by the ACM Java Task Force, who have included a class GTurtle in the acm.graphics package of the JTF library [Roberts et al., 2006].

Though we have not conducted qualitative nor quantitative analysis of the effectiveness of our use of turtles to introduce object-oriented concepts to students, we have many indications of the positive effect. Our teaching assistants report that most students are proficient in basic object-oriented and procedural techniques early in the course, and students report using the turtles as fun and motivational. After all, this is not too bad.

Acknowledgement

We acknowledge Jens Bennedsen for stimulating discussions and collaboration during early development and use of the Turtle Machine.

Part III

Teaching Software Engineering Issues

Part III

Teaching Software Engineering Issues

Introduction to Part III
Teaching Software Engineering Issues

The previous sections of this book covered mostly topics related to early parts of programming education, such as introductory courses and teaching of object-orientation to beginners. Now, it is time to move on.

This section discusses issues that may be touched on in introductory courses, but are more commonly covered in intermediate or in advanced courses.

All three chapters in this book discuss the difficulties of —and propose some solutions to— teaching software engineering issues. Teaching software engineering in a university context is often difficult to arrange in a meaningful way. Gaining practical experience in projects approximating real world development situations is especially hard to organise.

Software engineering techniques are most important when working on large projects in teams, and when project maintenance and extension are real goals of the project. At university, students typically work in small teams on small projects, and do not need to adapt or to maintain their work after initial submission. As a result, software engineering teaching is always in danger of remaining abstract with presentations of the relevant issues in lectures, but very little chance for students to train the techniques and to experience the effects of good or bad software engineering practices.

The following chapters address many of these problems and offer ideas for solutions. All have in common that they use real applications as their context of study. They deal with issues often neglected in programming teaching, such as how to assess quality (or, in fact, how to make students think about quality in the first place, rather than just functionality) and how to arrange an organised process.

The first chapter in this section concentrates on the issues of quality, and quality assurance through testing. It demonstrates how course work can be arranged in a way that causes students to regard software quality as an important factor, and breaks the typical pattern of aiming for wide functionality to the detriment of quality. A careful treatment of testing, specifically unit testing with JUnit, is the main vehicle to achieve this goal.

The second chapter expands on this by discussing a complete development process, namely 'eXtreme Programming' (XP). It describes in detail two courses designed to use XP to teach important techniques in software engineering, and presents solutions to the large number of organisational problems that are associated with such courses. *Iterative learning* and *peer learning* are two essential elements in this approach.

Both chapters have in common a central view that it is essential for students to get their own experience with these techniques, and the effects of following them (or not following them, as the case may be). Both present practical solutions to the problem of creating concrete learning experiences that go far beyond just

J. Bennedsen et al. (Eds.): Teaching of Programming, LNCS 4821, pp. 145–146, 2008.
© Springer-Verlag Berlin Heidelberg 2008

presenting lectures. Both also emphasise the idea of varying scope of solutions instead of compromising quality.

The third chapter adds another topic to this mix as follows: the teaching of frameworks and patterns. Even though this subject matter is a fairly advanced topic, the chapter also discusses the possibility of introducing it in introductory courses.

Together, these chapters present a rich source if ideas for the teaching of modern programming with all its related challenges inherent in the development of large systems on top of large platforms in large teams.

Michael Kölling

Experiences with a Focus on Testing in Teaching[*]

Henrik Bærbak Christensen

Department of Computer Science
University of Aarhus
Denmark
hbc@daimi.au.dk

Abstract. Software of high quality is a major concern in teaching programming: simply making any program that fulfills the requirements is not enough. Yet the way teachers often state exercises tends to make the students focus more on functionality requirements and deadlines than on keeping the program quality high. This chapter discusses some concrete teaching guidelines that help in keeping the learning focus on quality and reports on our experiences in applying them. It furthermore presents an important observation relating to the use of test-driven development as a process that focus on high quality, namely that it tend to improve also the flexibility and reusability of the production code. This issue is presented and argued by a concrete development example.

1 Introduction

Education in software engineering should focus on teaching students to produce high quality software. It is striking, therefore, that topics that are aimed directly at verifying software quality, like testing and systematic review, play a very small role in curriculum standards and in the curriculum taught at many universities. Even worse, the prevailing way that teachers state and evaluate programming assignments has a negative impact on quality: though we claim to focus on quality, students are nevertheless forced to value other aspects higher in their programming effort.

Over the last five years, the author has focused on the topic *reliable software* through teaching techniques like *systematic testing and test-driven development*, as well as reconsidered the way assignments are stated and evaluated in courses in advanced object-oriented programming. The teaching context of the presented ideas is that of courses in advanced object-oriented programming in various forms at Department of Computer Science, University of Aarhus, Denmark. The courses in which the ideas have been built up and used are a 15 week, 10 ECTS, course for part-time education, and a 7 week, 5 ECTS, course for full-time students. Most of the students on the part-time education 10 ECTS

---

[*] Parts of the present chapter have been published in early form in a paper entitled Systematic Testing should not be a Topic in the Computer Science Curriculum!. In *Proceedings of 8th Annual Conference on Innovation and Technology in Computer Science Education*, Thessaloniki, Greece, 2003.

J. Bennedsen et al. (Eds.): Teaching of Programming, LNCS 4821, pp. 147–165, 2008.
© Springer-Verlag Berlin Heidelberg 2008

courses were employed in industrial software development ("old/experienced"). The students on the full-time 5 ECTS courses have been second year full-time students ("young/inexperienced"). In both courses a major focus is put on design pattern, frameworks, reliability and testing, and software architecture. The 10 ECTS course has been taught five times and the 5 ECTS course has been taught twice. Both courses have a large compulsory project consisting of a number of separate deliverables to be handed in and accepted in order to attend the final exam, which is oral. The deliverables are the results of design and programming exercises. The ideas and insights reported within the present chapter were introduced initially in the second instance of the 10 ECTS course.

The chapter is organized around two major proposals that are argued and reflected on. The first part is presenting reflections and views upon how to get the students to focus on reliability in their programming effort and sets forward a set of concrete guidelines, techniques and tools that we have used ourselves. We also present some indicative evaluation in the form of student evaluations and our own reflections. The second part reports on observations on how test-driven development pushes the design of production-code towards more flexible, framework-like designs. We present a case study that we have used in our teaching as well as for presentations in industry. This creates an interesting link between the requirement of production code to be testable and advanced programming techniques like design patterns, responsibility-driven design and frameworks.

2   Emphasize Quality!

Teaching is about telling students "the right way", is it not? Teaching is about high quality solutions to (complex) problems, whether it is databases as solution to large data sets, programming constructs for handling concurrency, or object-oriented design for handling complex design challenges, etc.

Long discussions can then be made on "what is quality?" For a good account on the different views that stakeholders have on quality, consult [Kitchenham and Pfleeger, 1996]. But, in a teaching and programming context, most would agree that quality has more to it than just providing the required functionality to the end user. Aspects like internal structure of the program, its ability to accommodate new requirements, the degree to which it is easy to understand for other programmers, and its performance with respect to speed and memory usage are just some examples of what we would like to see our students reflect upon, understand, and ideally, apply concrete techniques to achieve. For instance, coupling and cohesion are metrics that tell something about a piece of software's modifiability, a quality attribute that is often advocated as important.

The problem is that any piece of software is necessarily a balance between conflicting, quality attributes as noted by [Bass et al., 2003]. If we raise modifiability, it more often than not means that performance is lowered due to more indirections in the code. And, the quality attribute of *cost* is always affected. Making the software more modifiable, improving its performance, or making it more secure, means the cost is raised. While software cost is usually not a topic we address very specifically in programming (or design courses), cost is always there.

In education, software cost is measured in student workload!

It is our hypothesis that the reason teachers are all too often disappointed with their students' submissions is because the assignments have overlooked the effect of software cost on the other qualities we like to see.

[Beck, 1999] has stated this balancing of opposing forces as a qualitative equation:

$$S = f(p, t, s, q)$$

That is, the development of a piece of software S is a function of four parameters: p is the resources allocated (that is, the price of developing the software), t is the time allocated for developing it, s the scope (that is, the amount of functionality developed), and finally q is the quality of the resulting software. Obviously, these parameters are highly coupled. If you spend more time (increase t) on a software project, you can broaden the scope and/or improve the quality. If you put more resources (increase p) on the team you may be able to get more done in less time, etc. However, the coupling is subtle since spending too much time may actually lead to lower quality. And, just doubling the number of people on the project will in most cases not lead to a twofold increase of scope.

The point, however, is that if three of the four parameters are fixed, then very little freedom is left for adjusting the forth parameter. Industrial projects are usually defined in terms of p, s, and t because *"the software must implement features X, Y and Z; it must be delivered on June 1st; and a group of four developers will develop it"*. Thus, the only parameter left for the team to adjust is q (quality). As p, s, and t are often set optimistically, q necessarily becomes low in order for the team to survive the project.

[Beck, 1999] states that to overcome this problem of low quality we simply have to make another parameter the free parameter that development teams are able to adjust. He argues convincingly that this parameter should be s scope. That is, development teams should insist on high quality and sacrifice functionality instead when "the going gets tough." The argument is:

Software changes its own requirements.

Once end users begin to use new software, they get a lot of inspiration and insight into the relation between the software and their own work processes that spark many proposals for changes and new requirements. Therefore, XP projects work with short iterations to ensure that end users are using the software right from the start, and end users are available to consult when decisions must be made on what functionality that can be postponed to a later iteration. That is, XP projects try to fix the parameters p, t, and q, and in open negotiation with the customer, to control the project by varying the provided scope, s.

What has this to do with teaching? Our postulate is that many programming assignments in education are formulated by using the exact same parameters as industrial project. They are controlled by exactly the same parameters. p is the resources allocated: usually a single person for a small assignment or a group of, say, three people for a larger, compulsory, assignment. t is always fixed: the group must deliver at a fixed date. And, the assignments are explicit and detailed about scope, s: the amount of functionality that the resulting software system should be able to deliver.

Thus, we are in a situation where the predominant way of stating assignments contributes to the same negative impact on quality as is often observed in industrial projects. We all know that some very good students will (always) succeed, but many fall short due to similar problems as seen in industry.

2.1   Guidelines

If we want to take software quality seriously then we must organize assignments, courses, yes, even curriculum in a way where quality is encouraged. We have started "in-the-small" and have responded to the challenge by formulating three teaching guidelines that we have used to guide and to restructure our programming courses over the last couple of years.

We have taken our inspiration from Beck's claim that the proper parameter that teams must be allowed to control is scope. This leads to the first guideline:

Guideline 1: Quality takes precedence over scope. Insist on documented high quality rather than full scope in exercises.

This guideline tells us that an assignment should outline its premises in terms of the group size p, delivery date t, and required quality q, and then outline a flexible framework for the required functionality s. The latter must define minimum functional requirements for acceptance (a thoroughly tested "Hello world" program is still not good enough), and show a suitable progression of more advanced features that allows students to extend the assignment's scope. The main point is that it is legal for students to skip functional requirements as long as the functionality provided is of high quality.

The other aspect of the guideline is of course that the students' use of techniques, methods and investment of effort into quality must be documented. The exact form of documentation, of course, depends upon the quality aspect that is the focus. We discuss this in more detail below for the quality of reliability.

This guideline is strongly related to the "Fixed-Time Budget" principle advocated by Hedin, Bendix, and Magnusson and discussed in *Teaching Software Development using Extreme Programming*. As reported in the experience section, this guideline is apparently so controversial that both students as well as teachers have difficulty in accepting this as the *real* premise for an assignment.

Guideline 2: Measure quality. Make quality measurable.

Why do teachers evaluate exercises based upon the parameters of time, resources and scope? They do so for the exact same reasons that industrial salesmen and project managers do: they are easy to assess! Evaluating quality is much harder. Therefore, we need to make quality measurable and manifest to both the students and to the teachers. Again, the exact technique to use may vary depending on the nature of the quality one want to measure.

We have used two techniques to make the quality of reliability measurable. For this quality attribute, we teach systematic testing techniques and demand that students always report the principles and arguments they have used to ensure that their testing of a specific programming exercise is complete. To make the quality manifest/visible, we use the JUnit testing framework [JUnit, 2005]. We will explain JUnit in the next section.

Furthermore, we ask the students to follow the recommendation of eXtreme Programming, namely the test-driven implementation approach: *Write a test that won't run, then write the code that will make it run* [Beck and Gamma, 2005]. As reported in the experience section, this is actually the guideline that we have found most difficult to follow. Large sets of test cases are unfortunately no guaranty that a piece of software is well-tested and reliable.

Guideline 3: Progression. *Make exercises a progression.*

While we find that the argumentation above and the two previous guidelines are applicable for any quality you want to stress in student projects, this guideline is more rooted in the concrete quality, reliability and the technique used (e.g., testing) in the reported work.

Making software reliable by insisting on systematic testing is a long term investment as seen from the developers' (students') point of view. Developers pay by spending time on testing, and the customers get the benefit of better software. Unfortunately, this is not in line with human nature. Humans want to have the benefit of an investment themselves and the faster they get the benefit, the better. Thus, it is vital that teachers ensure that the students benefit from their tests. This is the only way we can hope that they will continue writing tests as a natural part of programming.

Our proposal is to formulate exercises as a progression. For example, exercise n is based upon the solution to exercise $n - 1$. This way, students are forced to maintain and extend their existing code base instead of starting from scratch every time.

In formulating the progression, it is important that the students are not aware of the precise demands that exercise $n + 1$ will pose on the solution they are working on at present. This way the students will be forced to redesign and to re-implement parts of their earlier solution in order to accommodate new requirements. It is here that systematic tests show their power as a tool for programmers. Without systematic tests, it is very difficult to ensure that design changes and re-implementations do not invalidate the functionality within the existing code base. With systematic tests, however, a sound basis is provided for refactoring the system while ensuring that it still provides the required functionality.

This guideline serves several pedagogical purposes. First, students learn that tests counteract architectural erosion of their existing code base. Second, students learn that not focusing on quality early may become very costly in the long run, as they are stuck with their previous solutions. Third, the processes they are going through resemble the industrial reality of software development much more.

2.2   Implementation

We have used the guidelines as the primary vehicle for a compulsory exercise formulated as a programming experience with a varying number of deliveries. The topic of the exercise is the board game *Backgammon* and example deliveries are:

- *Backgammon Board:* Design and implement the basic domain: board, board-locations, checkers and methods to move checkers and to determine board state.
- *Backgammon Validation:* Design and implement validation of moves; the logic to control game flow (rolling of dice, which player is in turn, how many moves are left); undo of moves; and ability to switch at runtime who controls the two players (AI or human player).
- *Backgammon Variants:* Design and refactor the code base to allow different backgammon variants to be played. Variants typically require other types of move validation (e.g., it is allowed for checkers to jump backwards), initial board position (e.g., board is initially empty), and/or how turns are controlled (e.g., throwing 2-1 gives one extra turn). An advanced requirement is to facilitate the change of variant played in mid-game (e.g., rule set change at run-time).
- *Backgammon User Interface:* Design and implement a GUI based on JHot-Draw [JHotDraw, 2005] and link it with the developed domain model to provide a full backgammon game.

Using a board game as an exercise has a number of advantages. The domain is well-defined and often known to the students. The rules of backgammon are complex and demand systematic testing techniques to ensure that move validation is correct, for example.

2.3   Experience

Next, we present some experiences gained with the guidelines. The main source is our own observations combined with feedback from students' reports and course evaluation.

Guideline 1: quality takes precedence over scope: In the specification of all deliveries, we explicitly stress that *quality takes precedence over scope.* That is, in the case that the students are running short of time, then they should choose to implement less functionality, but keep the quality high.

The means achieving high quality is systematic testing. We teach standard techniques such as equivalence testing, boundary testing, etc., and ask the students to document their testing practice. We demand that they use the JUnit testing framework, described next, to organize and to document their test cases.

Guideline 2: measure quality: We introduce [JUnit, 2005] as a testing framework to the students in the course. JUnit is a powerful, yet simple testing framework that significantly lowers the effort required to setup a testing environment. A snapshot of the JUnit framework is shown in Figure 1.

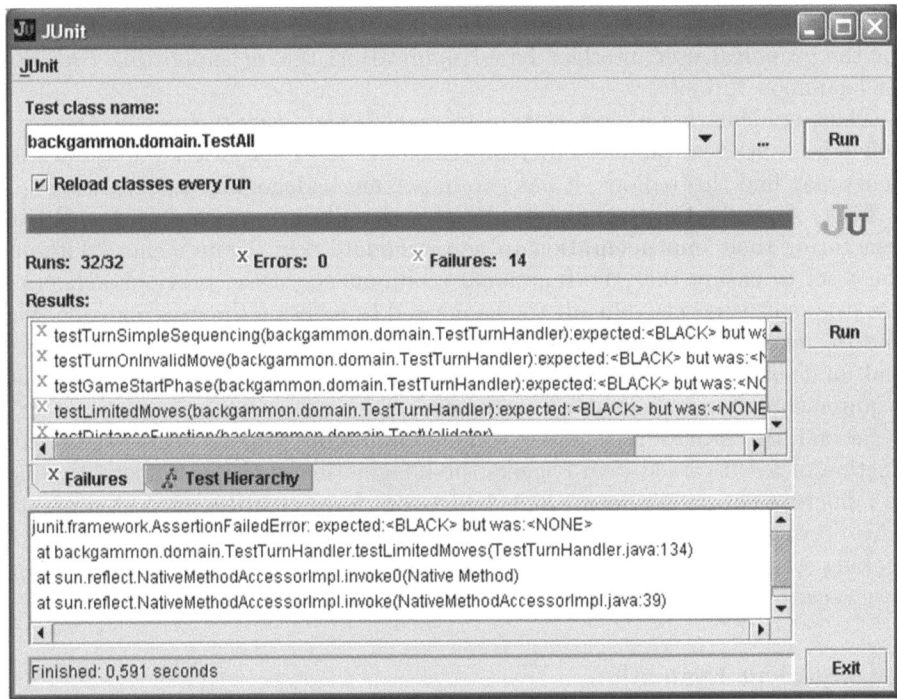

Fig. 1. JUnit testing framework

One major advantage of using JUnit is that students can focus their effort completely on programming the backgammon model in the initial deliveries: there is no need for writing "drivers" or user interfaces in order to develop and to try the model implementation. All testing and debugging can be done from within the JUnit framework. As is also apparent from Figure 1, JUnit provides very detailed information about tests that break. Here, the expected value was "BLACK", but the implementation produced "NONE" in test "testLimited-Moves". The failure occurs at line 134 in class TestTurnHandler as seen in the lower window.

JUnit can also be run as a console-based tool by writing its output to the console. This makes it a nice tool to integrate with the Apache Ant build management tool [Ant, 2005]. Ant is a Java-based replacement of traditional build tools like Make. What makes the integration interesting is that running the test suites becomes a natural part of the development process. Ant automates an "edit-compile-**test**" cycle and makes it as natural as the usual "edit-compile-run" cycle. Through this, students modify their Java source files and invoke Ant that compiles the code and runs all the tests. Thus, tests become a natural step, just as compiling.

Guideline 3: progression: A key point in having several deliveries within the same project is that students are *not* told what the requirements are in the next delivery. This way, they cannot design and implement the backgammon model in anticipation of particular, later, requirements like, for instance, our demands for the graphical user interface based upon JHotDraw or supporting concrete backgammon variants.

Thus, students are almost certain to make design decisions during the first deliveries that are invalidated by requirements of later deliveries. While the students may find this tedious, it has two important pedagogical aspects.

First, students learn that their JUnit test suits are an important help in refactoring their implementation to accommodate new requirements. Without the tests to ensure that the functional requirements of the previous deliveries are still kept, it is very difficult to change and to redesign the existing code. We find this experience important for the student because those tests are *their* tool and for *their* benefit. They are not something they reluctantly do to serve the requirements of management or customers.

Second, this situation is similar to many industrial projects where the introduction of a software system triggers the imagination of the customers, leading to numerous new requirements and changes not foreseen at the project start-up. This observation is also one of the reasons that Kent Beck argues in favour of making *scope* the free parameter for the development team: *Software changes its own requirements*.

2.4   Student Evaluation

Students have been asked to reflect on the test-driven process and their experiences with testing during their implementation effort. They have reported in required sections in their deliverables. Often, they also comment on their experience in the open-ended evaluation schema they are required to fill out at the last course lecture. Over the years, many of the comments and observations are the same and are reported here.

Many groups point out that writing tests first or early is actually a great help in understanding the functional requirements and issues such as class responsibilities and method parameters. The same observations are reported by Beck.

Many groups also find testing a benefit when they need to refactor their solution because of new insight or new functional demands. As this was a key insight (that tests are a technique for the benefit of the developers themselves just as much as for the customers), we are, of course, happy that this has been consistently reported.

Some groups report that the tests written made them reluctant towards changing interfaces as this requires the tests to be modified as well. This is, of course, a liability of having test suites.

Concerning the test-driven process itself, one particular group reported *"...especially as test and build becomes one step in the ant build script, testing feels as a natural part of the translation of the program"*. Another said that they felt that they moved forward every time their JUnit bar went green and felt that they were *"99% sure that all functions worked"*.

One thing that has struck us is how deeply the "we must satisfy all functional requirements" mindset is rooted in many people. Several groups over the years have handed in a first delivery that fulfils all functional requirements, but has almost no testing. Obviously, the students feel it more as a failure to leave out functionality than to leave out the tests, although this contradicts the explicitly stated project requirements! We must admit, though, that we ourselves suffered from the very same mindset because in the first year, we let those exercises pass. We have learned from the experience and are now very explicit towards the students that such a delivery will not pass —and they do not pass any more.

In the first year that we tried the approach, the scope demands in one of the deliverables was set way too high, and most groups reported it necessary to leave out specific requirements. Though it was not planned so, we may argue (in hindsight) this is a very direct way to convey the *quality takes precedence over scope* point to the students —and to force them to prioritize requirements.

In the graphical user interface deliverable, some groups reported a great satisfaction and even some puzzlement that *"...when we combined model and GUI, the two systems worked together right way."* Thus, the model testing effort was rewarded by a painless integration and improved modularity.

2.5   Teachers Evaluation

We have found a great additional benefit from the "quality over scope" guideline that was not obvious from the start. One problem that we are facing as teachers asks, "Is my compulsory exercise too easy or too hard?" An especially young teacher without much experience will have this problem. Requesting quality over scope lessens the burden of finding the right level because one can write an assignment that contains enough challenges even for the brightest students without overwhelming the average or the poor student. The average students make a quality implementation of 80% of the functional requirements while the bright students may achieve high quality of all requirements. Students can focus their energy more on selected requirements instead of panicking that they do not have time to get everything working.

One issue that needs further work is the question of making quality measurable. Students were required to A) report the techniques used to define test cases, and B) to provide the actual JUnit test cases. However, it was difficult to assess aspects such as coverage and how the testing systematic was transferred to test cases from the reports. One plausible path may be to integrate test coverage tools in the project, but we have not tried this yet as the courses already introduce a lot of new tools.

Another issue is that progression, by nature, stands the previous achievements. Thus, some groups that have implemented limited functionality may have a problem as the next deliverable may build on something they have not done. We have tried to counter this in two ways. The first way is to be true to XP's ideas and to simply require that they continue with the previous assignment. A second way that we have had some success with is to make the assignments very modular so the influence of limited functionality is lessened. For instance, it makes perfect sense to add a graphical user interface even though the validation of moves is not complete. Variants can also be added even though the GUI is not in place, etc. Thus, this is also a way to put focus on the benefit of loose coupling.

3   Test-Driven Development Produces Flexible Software

In this section, we will leave the abstract guidelines, and instead, will concentrate on a concrete observation regarding test-driven development and discuss an example and its use in a teaching context. Test-driven development using JUnit builds up two substantial bodies of code: the *production code* and the *test code*. The production code is software defining end user functionality and whatever supporting code that serves the software system's purpose. The test code is a large body of JUnit test cases that is expressed as subclasses of JUnit's `junit.framework.TestCase`, and often, also a set of supporting code that abstract and streamline the test code itself.

These bodies should be kept apart in the respect that in an industrial setting, the test code should not be deployed as part of the final system, but only be kept as part of the in-house development. While this is not true, of course, for the submissions by the students, it is still important to stress this point as part of good software engineering practice.

The requirement that production code is not filled with all sorts of methods and code bits that serve testing purposes is actually a big challenge. Many students (and indeed, industrial developers) do not reflect much on the problems of bloating production code. We have found that reflecting over this point and discussing solutions to it introduce changes into a design that is advantageous in terms of the underlying code's modifiability and flexibility qualities.

In essence, we have made the following observation:

> *Keeping production code clean of test code while still having strong testing control of it induces refactorings and design changes that move the production code towards framework-like designs.*

The above statement is not a scientific thesis, but stated here as a hypothesis that we encourage practitioner teachers to explore. In the following section, we will explore this statement by a small case study that we present at class and the key observations from it. Next, we will try to extract and to distill the lessons learned.

3.1   Building the Case

The context of our example is the implementation of a simple, parking ticket vending machine. You enter some coins to buy parking time and finally receive a receipt that you may put in your car so that it will be readable for any parking officer. A Danish (or rather "Aarhus") parking ticket vending machine is shown in Figure 2.

Fig. 2. An Aarhus parking ticket vending machine

We take our starting point in a very simple interface by describing the parking machine.

```
public interface ParkingMachine {
  /** Insert a single coin. The coin is represented by its value
      as an integer.
      Precondition: Only values of 1, 2, 5, 10, and 20 are valid,
      representing Danish coins.
      @return true if coin was accepted, false otherwise
  */
  public boolean insertCoin( int coinValue )
```

```
/** Return the number of minutes of parking time the so
    far inserted amount entitles you to.
    @param number of minutes parking time.
*/
public int readDisplay();

/** Return receipt for parking time bought.
    @return a receipt.
*/
public Receipt pushBuyButton();
}
```

The pricing model is described separately:

7 minutes of parking time cost 1 kr.

The initial challenge is to produce a reliable implementation of this - remember that the context is test-driven development.

This is quite a straightforward exercise. Test-driven development says: develop the test cases first. Equivalence testing techniques guide us in developing the test cases: one for each valid value of the input parameter `coinValue` and at least one invalid value. This leads to a number of JUnit test cases:

```
public void testInsert() {
  assertTrue( pm.insertCoin(1) );
  assertEquals( 7*1, pm.readDisplay() );

  assertTrue( pm.insertCoin(2) );
  assertEquals( 7*(1+2), pm.readDisplay() );

  assertTrue( pm.insertCoin(5) );
  assertEquals( 7*(1+2+5), pm.readDisplay() );

  ...
  assertFalse( pm.insertCoin(253) );
}
```

where pm is a valid parking machine object that has been initialized in the test setup.
A reasonable implementation may look like:

```
public boolean insertCoin( int coinValue ) {
  switch ( coinValue ) {
  case 1:
  case 2:
  case 5:
  case 10:
  case 20:
    time += 7* coinValue;
    return true;
  }
  return false;
}
```

At this point all is nice and well. We have defined a set of test cases by using systematic techniques, an implementation and verified its reliability by running the tests. The production code and test code is fully separated and no test specific code has entered the production code.

But, "software changes its own requirements", so the happy customer asks for a new pricing model:

− For the first hour every 7 minutes of parking time cost 1 kr.
− For the second hour every 6 minutes cost 1 kr.
− For the third hour onwards every 5 minutes cost 1 kr.

On face value, we have just wasted a lot of effort. Not only is our implementation wrong and has to be recoded, but even worse is that we have written almost more code lines in a test case that no longer reflects a functional requirement and the effort invested seems even more wasted. "Damn..."

3.2   The Challenge

A challenge that we state in class in this situation is the following:

> **Challenge:** *Is it possible to redesign the production code so that both pricing models may coexist and a choice can be made of which one to use at run-time?*

This challenge might at first seem like it is balancing between being purely academic and being utter nonsense. Hopefully, the following argument will show that the challenge serves well to establish a good principle of value to students. The students are left time for considering proposals for the challenge, and we next go through a number of proposals:

− Brute-force `if`. "Decisions are handled by if."
− Polymorphism. "Inheritance is a code reuse construct."
− Refactor responsibilities. "Favour object composition." [Gamma et al., 1994]

3.3   Proposals

Brute-force. `if` Many students cling to the idea that decisions in software are always dealt with by using conditional statements. A straightforward sketch may look like:

```
public static int LINEAR_MODEL = 1;
public static int PROGRESSION_MODEL = 2;
int priceModel;
public boolean insertCoin( int coinValue ) {
  if ( priceModel == LINEAR_MODEL ) {
    switch ( coinValue ) {
      .. .. ..
  } else if ( priceModel == PROGRESSION_MODEL ) {
      .. .. ..
  }
}
```

Let us analyze cost/benefit. The benefit is, of course, that we meet the requirement of the odd challenge, but there are a lot of liabilities. First, the most problematic issue is that we have now bloated the production code with additional structure that makes it somewhat harder to read (that it contains "dead code" must be expected as it is part of the requirement.) Second, another major issue is that the contract for the parking machine has been bloated, so now we have to ensure somehow that the `priceModel` is set. This includes two things: A precondition that the value is properly set before invoking `insertCoin`, and next, that the client has an interface for doing so. Finally, we may argue that we now have a minor performance penalty, but we consider this a minor issue.

In conclusion, the odd challenge is answered by a somewhat absurd implementation. In the C languages the notorious `#ifdef` could be introduced, but it is basically the same proposal except that no performance penalty is paid.

Polymorphism. A more elegant solution is seen in Figure 3 where we subclass the parking machine implementation and simply override whatever method that performs the price calculation.

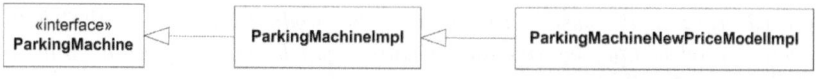

Fig. 3. A polymorphic proposal

This proposal is, in many respects, much better than the one above. First, the changes to the price calculation are encapsulated in its own class, and thus improving overview and understandability of the code. Another benefit is that there is no pollution of the parking machine interface since the decision of what price model to use is made in the test code in the instantiation phase. Still, one may argue that we have bloated the production code with another class.

The proposal has a severe main liability though. In essence, the stated requirement is that of *variability* in the design. Namely, the pricing model is a *variability point* and something that is likely to change relatively often. In the polymorphic design, we have "spent" the inheritance relation on a single dimension of variability. This is problematic, especially in single implementation inheritance languages like Java, because what happens when we introduce another dimension of variability? Consider a new requirement that the payment method should also include the possibility to pay over your mobile phone account (which is actually possible with the Aarhus parking vending machines). Clearly, the two dimensions of variability are independent. Thus, one polymorph solution is sketched in Figure 4 where the subclass introducing mobile phone payment overrides the original implementation, and thus inherits the original pricing model. One could also inherit from the `ParkingMachineNewPriceModelImpl` leading to a subclass that we may denote `ParkingMachineNewPriceModelMobilePaymentImpl`, but as the naming scheme already indicates, there is something really problematic going on.

As the number of possible variations increase over a set of variation dimensions, this solution simply runs into a combinatorial explosion of subclasses. You

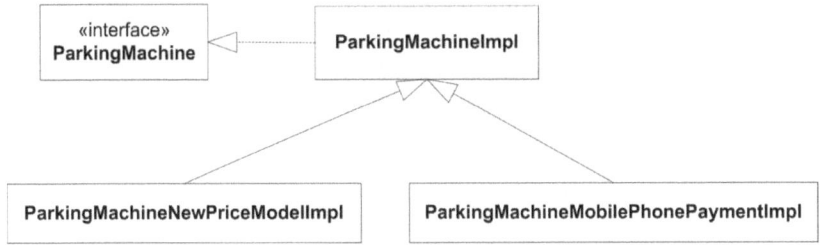

Fig. 4. Introducing another dimension of variability

would need to make separate subclasses to handle (new price model + mobile payment), (old price model + coin payment), (old price model + VISA card payment), etc.

Again, in the case of a concrete parking machine example this may seem like a lesser problem, but it should be viewed as an example of how new requirements often arise and combinations are envisioned once customers are exposed to software: "Software changes its own requirements..."

Factor out responsibilities. The final proposal discussed is to reflect upon the factorization of responsibilities in the parking machine. Looking closer, the parking machine abstraction actually covered a number of responsibilities:

- Acceptance of payment
- Calculation of payment based on price model
- Printing the parking ticket

Then, why are the all handled by a single abstraction? Thus, let us refactor the design in such a way that the price model calculation is embodied in its own object. "There should be an object responsible for the price calculation", and to let the parking machine delegate to this object.

A proposal is depicted in Figure 5.

Fig. 5. A delegation based proposal

As evident from the chosen naming, this is actually an application of the strategy pattern. But, the proposal is not derived by looking in a design pattern book for a solution. Rather, it is derived simply because we need to control the price calculation and a natural way is to factor out responsibilities in a separate object. The GoF book states it as *consider what should be variable in your design* in their introduction.

So, what are the benefits and liabilities? We again fulfil the requirement of coexisting price models. We have encapsulated the changes to the price calculation in its own class improving overview and understandability of the code and have improved the design compared to the polymorphic solution because the PricingStrategy interface is clearer and better focused on its responsibility. This way, there is less chance of mixing payment and price calculation code. One may argue that this proposal also requires a change of the parking machine contract because a parking machine object must be told which pricing model to use, typically in a constructor or a set method, but we consider this a small price tag for the improvements made. Of course, we also experience the typical introduction of more classes/interfaces that follows delegation based designs. But, this liability is again countered by a more focused responsibility of each. The test code can easily select the price model to test.

The real power of the solution lies in its flexibility, as it adheres to one of the principles of reusable designs defined by the GoF book [Gamma et al., 1994]: "Favour object composition over class inheritance".

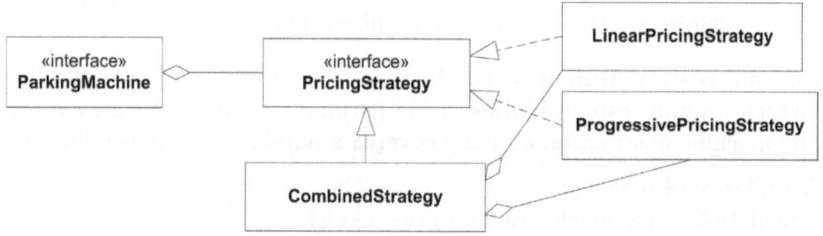

Fig. 6. Composition of pricing models

For instance, consider the following changed requirement: *"For the weekends we like to use the linear pricing model and for working days the progressive pricing model."* This is easily made in this proposal as sketched in Figure 6. Here a new subclass, CombinedStrategy, simply instantiate and delegate to instances of the already well-tested classes, and the code in the CombinedStrategy object itself boils down to a single switch:

```
public class CombinedStrategy implements PricingStrategy {
  ...
  public int calculateParkingTime ( int totalInserted );
    if ( [weekend?] ) {
      return linearStrategy . calculateParkingTime (
                                totalInserted );
    } else {
      return progressiveStrategy . calculateParkingTime (
                                totalInserted );
    }
  }
}
```

This design has an important, additional benefit from the reliability point of view. It is an old principle that says it is better to *add code than modify code* because additions does not require regression testing or, even worse, rewriting a lot of tests. This design follows this principle and provides a good case for introducing or once again emphasizing this principle.

The final important point is the strength of delegation based designs for handling variance over multiple dimensions, which is shown by considering variability of payment forms: coins, mobile phone accounts, VISA card, etc. How does this design cope?

Again, we simply revisit the list of responsibilities and note that we can "turn the machine once again" and encapsulate the payment responsibility in a separate object leading to a design like the one depicted in Figure 7.

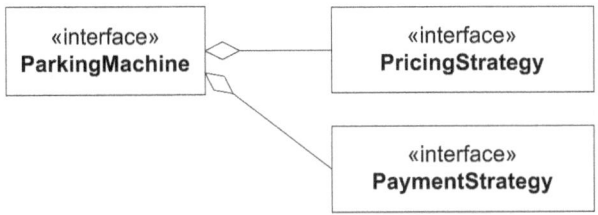

Fig. 7. Variation in several dimensions

The same, simple principles are used and now we see that any of the dimensions may be varied independently of each other, and no explosion of implementation classes occur. "Mixing the cocktail" of price model and payment method is simply a matter of instantiating the proper strategy objects and ensuring that the parking machine uses these.

3.4   Revisiting the Challenge

How does the latter solution relate to the challenge —and what lessons can be learned regarding tests and software development? The discussion so far has been focused on the positive aspects with regards to aspects of reusability and flexibility in the design. But, looking over the design process of meeting the challenge, we may note the following observations:

The first thought when the changed price model requirement arose was "Damn, now we can throw away both code and the unit test!" Thus mental energy and its manifestation, code and tests, was simply wasted.

Then came the somewhat odd challenge of coexisting price models. Now, we can recast the challenge and understand it as a test-driven refactoring technique.

1. The coexistence criteria has made us keep the original, working, unit tests validating the correct behaviour of the parking machine with the linear price model. No unit tests are wasted and the mental effort invested has been kept.

2. The coexistence criteria has made us come up with an improved design where responsibilities are factored out in well-focused interfaces and implementing classes.

3. The changed design requires a refactoring. And the validity of the refactoring process *is guarantied by the original linear price model unit tests!* That is, the PricingStrategy interface is introduced, and the linear pricing model code moved to an implementing class LinearPriceStrategy. Thus, this refactoring is behaviour preserving and is tested by the test cases that we have already written. Thus, from being a wasted effort, the unit cases have turned into an important asset in the refactoring process.

4. Based upon the validated, refactored design, unit tests as well as implementation for the progressive price model can now be introduced in the normal test driven manner.

We have seen this principle in action in many different situations. Basically, it boils down to extreme inertia towards wasting solid test cases. So, if there is a way to keep the tests by making the production code more flexible then it should be considered.

The observations made are supported by similar observations made by others. One outcome of the test-driven approach has been *mock objects*. Mock objects were invented to completely isolate objects under test. Instead of the object undergoing test communicating with real environment objects (like database connections, sockets, random generators, etc.), these objects are replaced by mock objects that are merely simulating behaviour under complete control of the test code. Thus, to use mock objects, behaviour must be clearly factored out and handles provided to allow testing code to change which objects are combined. In essence, it is the same force at play. Basically, the wish to keep production code testable and clean of testing code drives the design towards more flexibility.

3.5   Student Observations

One of the war stories we have is from the compulsory exercise in Backgammon. One of the deliveries has, as its main objective, a systematic testing of validation of backgammon moves while another's main objective is to refactor the design to allow the player to choose from different backgammon variants to be played. In essence, this turns the production code into a backgammon framework.

An observation made by many student groups is that testing move validation is very cumbersome unless the backgammon board has the ability to be preset into a certain configuration of checkers. To illustrate this point, consider testing proper validation of the end game situation where checkers are moved out of the board. To get the board in a state where this can be tested, all checkers must be in the so-called inner table, but getting it into this state by making individual moves will result in several pages of move code. Thus, it is obviously better to be able to define a board configuration.

This challenge is actually very similar to the parking machine challenge, and we see the exact same proposals. These include the brute-force "introduce a set method", subclassing where the subclass defines another initial configuration of checkers, and a few groups that actually tried to factor our responsibility of setting up the board that we analyzed previously. Thus, the board receives a "SetupStrategy" object in its constructor that tells how the initial configuration should be. And so, the unit test for validation will typically provide the board with a particular setup that immediately ensures that the board is in the state relevant for the particular test.

Now, the point is that in the backgammon framework exercise, one of the variants that students are required to consider is "Tapa". In Tapa the initial setup is that all checkers are off the board and then must be put into play, much as with the game of Ludo. The students then realize that they have already introduced this framework hotspot.

4   Summary

In this chapter we have presented guidelines, techniques, ideas, and observations. They all revolve around the importance of producing reliable and high quality software —a topic we find very important in teaching software engineering. Our main technique for ensuring reliability has been testing and test-driven development, but we acknowledge that there are many other approaches to strengthening reliability that we have not pursued. Still, we find it important to present students from a well-known and proven technique. Furthermore, we have found that test-driven development couples nicely with other aspects of advanced programming in a supporting manner.

We cannot provide scientific evidence or measurements to support our hypotheses, except for what we find valid and logical argumentation. Our main purpose is to present the ideas to the teaching community to be tried out and tested. We would be most happy with any feedback if the reader decides to implement some or all of the recommendations.

5   Additional Reading

A very good and practical-oriented book about test-driven development is *Test-Driven Development By Example* by Kent Beck [Beck, 2003]. Beck also has a short discussion on why test-driven development tends to produce framework-like designs. The eXtreme Programming paradigm is outlined in *Extreme Programming Explained, Embrace Change* that is now in its second edition [Beck, 1999,Beck and Andres, 2004]. For a fine introduction on how mock objects happen, consult *How Mock Objects happened* by Freeman [Freeman, 2005].

Teaching Software Development Using Extreme Programming

Görel Hedin, Lars Bendix, and Boris Magnusson

Department of Computer Science, Lund University,
Box 118, S-221 00 Lund, Sweden
{gorel,bendix,boris}@cs.lth.se

Abstract. Software development is a complex area and extensive practice and reflection is required in order to obtain a good understanding of the different tasks involved in going from idea to deliverable software. To help in providing this understanding, we have developed a team programming course based on extreme programming and a coaching course. We discuss how these courses affect the curriculum, the design of the courses, and our experience from running them for four years, involving over 100 students per year. We also discuss how we have used the extreme programming approach to support the learning cycle through the use of iterative learning, peer learning and a fixed-time budget.

1 Introduction

The area of software development is complex, involving many different inter-related tasks. Knowledge is needed at many different levels from programming languages and tools to good design, productive methodology and social skills. We have found the eXtreme Programming methodology (XP) [Beck, 1999a] to be very helpful in teaching these complex interrelated topics. We have developed two courses based on XP: *Team Programming using XP* (the "XP course") and *Coaching of Programming Teams* (the "Coaching course"). The XP course provides the students with basic useful skills that cover the whole spectrum of software development from ideas to working software. The course has two main goals. The first one is to give a basic understanding of the main concepts in software engineering, grounded in the students' own experience. This serves as a foundation for being able to understand more specialized software engineering topics, like configuration management, requirements handling, testing, and so on. Secondly, the course gives the students a productive and useful methodology that they can use themselves in subsequent course projects. The primary goal of the Coaching course is to learn skills useful when leading and coaching programming teams. Additional goals include a deeper understanding of the XP methodology including software architecture. The students in this course serve as coaches of the teams in the XP course.

The students are following a 4.5 year program in Computer Science and Computer Engineering. After graduation, the students often start to work in companies developing advanced technical equipment with embedded computers. The

J. Bennedsen et al. (Eds.): Teaching of Programming, LNCS 4821, pp. 166–189, 2008.

program is designed to give them detailed knowledge and skills central to subjects in software development, and sufficient overview in other subjects like physics and automatic control so they can interact with other engineers in these fields.

Other, early adopters of XP for university courses have often focused on teaching XP late in the curriculum, and/or for a small number of students [Keefe and Dick, 2004, Wilson, 2001, Müller and Tichy, 2001]. In contrast, our XP course is given early in the curriculum, already during the second year, and we have around 100 students per year. A key to making it possible to run the course for this number of students is the use of the students from the Coaching course to serve as project leaders and coaches of the XP teams. We have described our courses in previous papers [Hedin et al., 2003b, Hedin et al., 2003a, Hedin et al., 2005]. In this chapter, we give an updated description of our courses and focus on the pedagogical experiences.

The rest of this chapter is organized as follows. In Section 2, we discuss our view on the curriculum concerning software development where we place our extreme programming courses, and how that affects other courses. In Sections 3 and 4, we explain the detailed design of the two courses and how they interact. Section 5 discusses three important pedagogical principles that we use in our courses to enhance learning: iterative learning, peer learning and fixed-time budget. Section 6 discusses some concrete experience we have from giving the courses. Section 7 discusses related work and Section 8 concludes the chapter.

2   Curriculum Design

Focusing on the part of the curriculum in Computer Science that concerns software development and programming, we have identified three levels that match different levels of maturity of the students:

- Programming individually
- Programming in a team
- Software development in an organization

The courses at the first level are designed to teach students the fundamentals of programming that consist of mastering a programming language, elements of algorithm and data-structures, and so on (see Figure 1). The focus here is on their skills as individual programmers, and even if there are situations where they work in pairs, we do not teach any systematic methodology for that (yet).

The second level, programming in a team, is setting the focus on how to organize the work when you are a team (approximately 8 to 10 people) working together on software development. Here, we introduce students to one particular methodology, extreme programming, that is designed specifically for that situation. The course is driven by a fairly large project that motivates the introduction of a software development methodology. In addition to enhancing their skills in programming and design, they learn about planning, interacting with customers, testing, releases and delivery. They also learn several new tools such as JUnit, Eclipse and CVS.

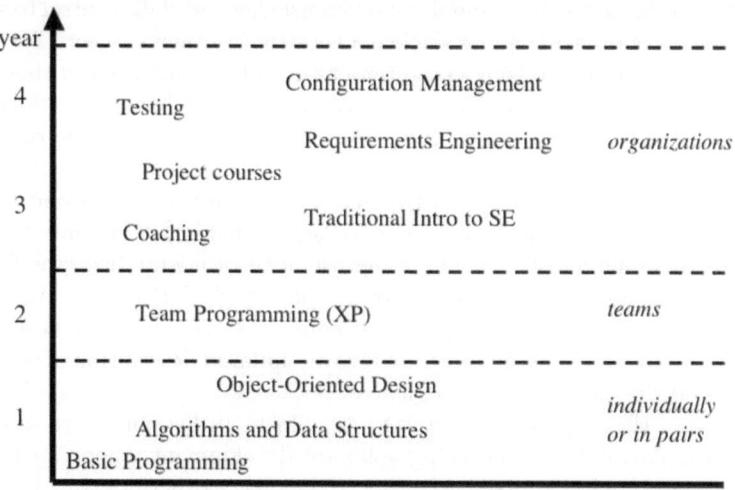

Fig. 1. The courses in each of the three levels

At the third level, software development in an organization, the focus is on even larger settings of 100 or more developers in which the traditional material of Software Engineering is taught. The idea is that by having the experience of actually working in a team with software development, they are better prepared to study the problems that appear in a larger setting than if they only had experience from programming on an individual basis. Here, our curriculum offers an overview software engineering course and several focused courses in subjects such as configuration management, requirements and testing.

Before we developed the extreme programming courses, we had a traditional software development project course that introduced the traditional software engineering concepts and illustrated them by letting the students run a waterfall style project. We experienced many problems with that course. When reading the theory, they had no experience to relate to, making the subject abstract and uninteresting to them. The waterfall document-driven methodology used in the project was overkill for the small projects we could have in a teaching situation. In practice, a few students did all the work because that was simpler and quicker for them than to cooperate through the methods we taught. These problems made us rethink the curriculum and the courses, and the result was the three-stage model that we use now.

3   The XP Course

The XP course gives 6 ECTS and is taken by more than 100 students each year. It is placed in the second year of the CS program and the prerequisites are courses In Programming, Algorithms and Data Structures, as well as Object-oriented Modelling and Design.

The course has two main learning goals. First, to obtain a basic understanding of key concepts in software engineering like requirements handling, architecture and design, configuration management, test, and deployment that are grounded in the student's own experience. Second, students will learn a number of important techniques in software development that are embodied in the extreme programming methodology. Perhaps, most importantly, time-boxed planning, small-step development, automated testing, refactoring and pair programming will be learned. In addition to the main learning goals, the students learn to work in a team and they become more proficient in programming.

The course has many scheduled hours for the students: 22 hours during the theory part and 64 hours during the project part. However, because of the use of teaching assistants in the theory part and the use of teaching assistants and student coaches in the project part, the faculty resources needed are reasonable. Table 1 summarizes the number of in-class teaching hours used.

Table 1. Teaching efforts - XP course

Type of personnel (role)	Description	In-class hours for t teams	In-class hours for 10 teams (100 students)
Senior faculty (lectures)	7*2h lectures + 1*2h concluding lecture	16	16
Teaching assistants (lab supervisors)	4*2h labs (serving 2 teams simultaneously)	4*t	40
Teaching assistants (customer in project)	6*2h customer at planning session (serving 2 teams simultaneously) + 6*4h at development sessions (serving 4 teams simultaneously)	12*t	120

Normal preparation hours are needed for the lectures and laboratory supervision, whereas the customer role requires much less preparation. Additional teaching costs include a one-hour exam, administration of the course, administering "focus practices" and handling absence (i.e., keeping track of students that are ill, come in late, etc.) and taking appropriate actions. The costs above do not include the creation of stories for the product since we have reused approximately the same set over the 4 instances in which the course has been given.

3.1   Course Structure

At Lund Institute of Technology (the Faculty of Engineering at Lund University), each year is divided into four reading periods of eight weeks each —seven weeks of teaching and one week of exams. Most courses are concentrated into one reading period, but some courses extend to two consecutive reading periods. Both the XP course and the Coaching course extend to two reading periods and run in parallel. They both have a theory part in the first reading period and a project part in the second reading period, as can be seen from Figure 2. We spread them over two periods because the project part requires a preceding theory part for the students to actually do the project. Since we do not use the exam weeks, the effective duration of the courses is 14 weeks. We have tied the XP course and the Coaching course together to allow the students on the Coaching course to practise on the XP projects as well as to use the coaching students as a teaching resource. This setup has been run for four years now.

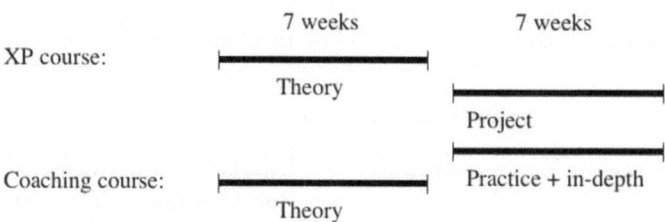

Fig. 2. The XP course and the Coaching course run in parallel

3.2   The Theory Part

The theory part of the XP course is run in a traditional manner with lectures and laboratories. There are seven 2-hour lectures (given weekly) and four 2-hour compulsory laboratories to support the topics taught in the lectures. A short, written exam concludes this part in order to mark the transition and to gain admission to the project part.

Lectures. The main purpose of the lectures is to introduce the students to software development in general and to make sure that they will understand the values and practices of XP and how they differ from more traditional development methods.

The first lecture is a general introduction to the course and to software development methods. XP [Beck, 1999b] is mentioned as one of many possible ways of developing software. The different phases of the lifecycle in traditional development methods are explained and related to XP.

The second lecture gives an overview of XP and its philosophy and values. It motivates the canonical practices of XP [Beck, 1999b] and relates them to different phases and tasks of traditional development methods.

The third lecture is entirely dedicated to Software Configuration Management, which is a topic that is not explicitly covered by XP. But, it is heavily needed in the practices of Collective Code Ownership, Continuous Integration, Frequent Releases, Planning Game and Refactoring.

Lecture four goes into details with the practices of Test First and Pair Programming. The unit and acceptance tests are motivated and related to more traditional ways of doing tests. Likewise, it is carefully explained why XP insists on writing tests first and code later. Pair Programming is motivated in being a multi-activity that is profitable from an economical point of view. It is not just one person watching another person write code. Rather, it is code review while the code is written along with design discussions, test writing and much more.

Lecture five is on design and software architecture. The students have already taken a course in object-oriented modelling and design, but have experience mainly from the design of small toy examples. The lecture introduces and motivates the XP practices of Simple Design and Refactoring. The focus is on how to grow a design by using these practices, and stressing the importance for architectures to be able to grow and to change over time.

The sixth lecture is about the Planning Game practice. It details and motivates the practice and gives guidance for estimation of the stories that the customer will write. Furthermore, it also discusses the different roles in XP and their rights and responsibilities, and stresses the fact that when time, resources and quality are fixed, then the only parameter left to negotiate is scope.

The final lecture is not really a lecture, but two 1-hour sessions. The first hour is a short written exam with the purpose of checking whether the students have sufficient understanding of XP values and practices to be allowed onto the projects. Most students are happy that we have this check as it assures them that the other students in their project team have certain, minimum competences. The second hour is an introduction to the project explaining the problem domain and the general product that they are expected to develop.

Laboratories. There are four compulsory 2-hour laboratories, each done in groups of 20 students, which is the number we can accommodate in our lab rooms when they work in pairs. The purpose of the laboratories is two-fold —to anchor the topics that they have been taught in the lectures, and to introduce the tools that they will have to use and master in the project part.

The first laboratory is an eXtreme Hour [ExtremeHour, 2007] held in an ordinary classroom (rather than in a computer lab). The students are taken through a couple of iterations of an XP project in two hours to get an impression of the tasks, roles and "phases". In two hours it is not possible to write any code, so students draw on paper and integrate on the blackboard the pieces of the product that they have to develop (a mousetrap, a bicycle or a lawn mower). Some of the students play the role of customers writing stories, and the others play the role of developers. After each "phase" (story writing, estimation, etc.), there is a short discussion where the laboratory instructor stresses the important parts and points out where they have deviated.

The second laboratory is on Software Configuration Management using CVS [Berliner, 1990]. The students work in pairs and are given small exercises to solve. They work in two separate windows on the same computer so that they can see what happens in the other person's window. They work their way through a series of "updates" and "commits" to get a grip of the basic commands of CVS and what happens when two people have to coordinate their parallel work. This laboratory supports directly the XP practices Collective Code Ownership and Continuous Integration.

The third laboratory is introducing Eclipse [Eclipse, 2007] and JUnit [Beck and Gamma, 2007]. Practicing Pair Programming, they have to implement a number of small and simple tasks by using the Test First practice and the tool JUnit to automate the unit tests. Obviously, they have to continue to use CVS and the way of working that was introduced in the previous laboratory.

The fourth laboratory focuses on the practice of Refactoring and explores the facilities in Eclipse that support Refactoring. They continue to program in pairs and use CVS and JUnit.

Literature. The current primary course literature is the "Extreme Programming Pocket Guide" [chromatic, 2003]. This book works well as a summary and reference guide for XP, but is very terse, and does not give much background or examples. As a supplement, we give the students lecture notes, laboratory material, and a few articles such as Beck's original article about XP [Beck, 1999a], a chapter from Babich's book on configuration management [Babich, 1986], and a chapter on architecture in XP from Wake's book on XP [Wake, 2001].

In the first two years of giving the course, we used the book "Extreme Programming Installed" [Jeffries et al., 2000]. This book offers a lot of good, concrete advice for the different activities involved, and is well worth reading through. But, it is aimed primarily at developers in industry, and is a bit verbose and unstructured to work well as a textbook for a university course.

We have also considered using the second edition of Kent Beck's book on XP [Beck and Andres, 2004]. However, we find the book to be too theoretic and too abstract for the students to gain sufficient help about the practices that they have to carry out. For a teacher, on the other hand, it is literally a goldmine of background and in-depth information about XP and its philosophy.

3.3   The Project Part

Once the theory part is over, the students that pass the exam are assigned randomly to teams of 8 to 10 students for the project part. Each team has two coaches (students taking the Coaching course) and one customer (a faculty member). The project goes through six development iterations, each consisting of a two-hour planning session, four hours of individual work ("spike time") and an eight-hour development session. At the end of the seventh week, the different teams evaluate each other's products.

The product. The product in all our course instances has been an application that can be used to time and to produce result lists for Enduro races (off-road motorcycle races). Important basic requirements include the handling of several different types of races. The product can be extended to include various kinds of functionality like on-line registration, real-time publication of results in HTML-format and a client-server solution.

Planning sessions. At each planning session, we give the teams new user stories. We try to give them a sufficient amount of new stories so that no team can implement them all. This motivates estimation and prioritization of the stories. The new stories (and remaining un-implemented stories from the previous iteration) are presented to the team by the coaches acting on behalf of the customer. The team then discusses the impact the new stories will have on the system and estimates how much time it will take to implement each story. If a story is unclear, or if they have questions, they can consult the customer, who has to service two teams in parallel. After the estimation of the stories, the customer does and motivates a prioritization of which stories will go into the present iteration, and which stories will be postponed to coming iterations. The amount of prioritized stories is based on the amount of stories that the team in question implemented during the previous iteration. The customer also indicates which of the postponed stories are most important, just in case the team happens to implement more than planned. During the planning session the team also discovers that they need to look deeper into some things before the upcoming development session. These tasks are defined and assigned to people to do as individual work before the upcoming development session.

Individual work. Between the planning session and the development session, each student is asked to do 4 hours of individual work. At the planning meeting, the team decides exactly what should be done and by whom. Often, this time is used for *spikes* (i.e., explorations into new programming solutions). In ordinary XP, spikes are often used during planning meetings in order to determine if a particular solution is feasible, and in order to estimate stories and tasks. However, because of our downscaled version of XP, there is no time for programming during our 2-hour planning meetings. Much of the individual work is done as spikes on finding and using Java libraries. Another use of the individual work is to study some particular topic. For example, at the first planning meeting, many teams allocate 1 to 2 hours for each student to read through the Java coding conventions. Other examples include refactorings. While most refactoring takes place during the development sessions, it is sometimes discovered during the planning meeting that some global changes to the architecture are needed. Such refactorings are often scheduled as individual work (usually by two students pairing up), and can then be done without getting into merge conflicts during the ordinary development. Note that our term "individual work" relates to the fact that this work does not occur at a scheduled place and time because the students decide themselves exactly when and where they do it. The students may well work in pairs or small groups for their individual work, if they prefer that.

Development sessions. For the development sessions, the team is together in the computer lab from 8 AM to 5 PM with a one-hour lunch break, just like a normal working day. Because of the size and number of our labs, usually two teams need to share a lab room. Other students also use these labs at other times, so the rooms are not "owned" by the team. That would have been desirable, but something we cannot afford. Most teams start with a short stand-up meeting where team members communicate the results of their individual work and the team goes through the tasks that have to be done, assigns tasks to people and pair up. The coaches are with the team most of the time during the development session. The customer calls on the team regularly to see how things are going, or is called upon if the team has questions or something to show to the customer.

Reflection. After each iteration (a planning session followed by a development session), each participant in the team is asked to reflect on what went well, and how that can be anchored in the team for the coming iteration(s). It is also asked about what went wrong, and what can be done to improve on that for the following iteration(s). At the planning session, the team starts by discussing the reflections and take measures to fix and/or anchor things. During the first few years, this was done very informally, and we found that it did not work as well as we wanted it to. As a consequence, we have introduced explicit teaching focus for each of the iterations in order to focus the reflection on just a few, selected XP practices. There is more about teaching focus in Section 5.

The customer. In vanilla XP, the customer should be on-site and constantly available to the developers for discussions and questions while preferably located in the same room. This is a goal that is usually hard to achieve in any project since the customer will have other things to do as well, and cannot be physically in the team room at all times. Also in our case, it would be too costly for us to have one customer (faculty member) for each team, located in the same room during the whole development session. Instead, we use one customer to cover four teams. The customer visits the team at least twice per development session and twice per planning session. The customer is also available on mobile phone and email and can visit a team on request. For some questions, the coach can serve as a customer proxy, but more importantly the coach has the responsibility to foster an active communication between the developers and the customers. The coach will encourage the developers to keep track of their questions to the customer and to take the initiative to contact the customer.

There are two occasions when the customer can become a bottleneck: during the planning session and at release time. We have solved that by scheduling the planning sessions for the teams so that each customer only has to service two teams at a time. For the releases, the customer has 15 to 20 minutes scheduled for each team, where he or she installs the release and makes sure that the most basic things work in the presence of the team. A more thorough evaluation is then done at a later time.

Releases. From the start of the project, the teams know that there are three scheduled releases: after iterations 2, 4 and 6. This is the customer's initial plan and wishes, but it never works out so. The first release is always a disaster and the customer is not satisfied, so he or she requests a new release after iteration 3 and postpones the subsequent releases to iterations 5 and 6. As part of the release, the customer requests a user's manual. This is scheduled as an ordinary story with updating tasks for each new release. Late in the project, the customer also introduces a story for producing technical documentation for the system with the goal being to allow a future team to pick up the product and to develop it further. Although this actually does not happen in the course, a partner team is assigned to evaluate these releases. So, the last two releases actually have two "customers": the partner team and the usual customer.

Examination and product evaluation. There is no written exam at the end of the project, and we pass all students that have taken active part in the project. We do have, however, a peer evaluation at the end. The partner team that receives the last two releases does a presentation of the application and an evaluation of the code, tests, and documentation of the other team's project from the point of view of how difficult it will be to continue development. We encourage teams to do a critical, but constructive, evaluation. To motivate the teams further we have a race around the campus lake where each team has to use its own application to time the race and produce a result list. The winner is the team that first produces a correct result list. This year we also had additional prices (and praises) for the team that had the best code (using a set of informal metrics).

4   The Coaching Course

The Coaching course gives 9 ECTS, and is taken by more than 20 students each year. The duration and overall structure is the same as for the XP course: 7 weeks of theory followed by 7 weeks of project. In addition, the students do an in-depth study of a topic of their own choice (related to XP and/or coaching), often using the team(s) as material for their study. The Coaching course is placed in the third year of our CS curriculum and the main pre-requisite is that the student has taken the XP course, and has shown coaching potential. In addition to technical competences (e.g., in programming), we value skills like the ability to take responsibility and to take initiatives. We receive this "soft" information by asking the old coaches, and/or by doing interviews with the applying students.

The primary goal of the Coaching course is to teach skills that are useful when leading and coaching programming teams. Additional goals include a deeper understanding of the XP methodology, including software architecture.

The course has many scheduled hours for the students: 14 hours during the theory part and 78 hours during the project part. However, most of the project hours are mainly unsupervised with faculty members only visiting a short amount of time. The faculty resources needed are, therefore, reasonable. Table 2 summarizes the teaching efforts.

Normal preparation hours are needed for the lectures, whereas the coach meetings require less preparation. Additional costs include course administration. In practice, we have had slightly larger costs because we have often had 2 to 3 faculty members at the coach meetings. This is partly because we have had different individuals responsible for focus practices and story creation, but also because

Table 2. Teaching efforts - coaching course

Type of personnel	Description
Senior faculty	Lectures: 7*2h
Senior faculty	Supervision of coach meetings: 7*2h
Senior faculty	In-depth studies: Feedback on preliminary abstracts + Feedback on preliminary versions + 4h final seminar.

we have been interested in the course development as such. In the long run, it should be sufficient with one faculty member taking care of the coach meetings.

4.1   The Theory Part

The theory part consists of weekly 2-hour lectures, but they are more like discussion seminars than ordinary lectures. The lectures are mandatory and between the lectures, the students are given small homework assignments to be handed in the day before the next lecture. A typical assignment is to read a couple of articles and to write a brief personal reflection on the content. For example, this could include summing up issues they appreciated, issues they did not appreciate (and why not), and issues that they found unclear. Other assignments can be to write a brief 1 to 2 page essay reflecting on their own experience concerning some particular XP practice. A lecture typically starts with a discussion on last week's assignment, and then, some new theory is introduced, usually interleaved with discussion exercises. The literature used consists mostly of articles and an ever-growing use of in-depth studies by previous coaching students. We also use a book on XP, either [Jeffries et al., 2000] or [chromatic, 2003], depending on what they have from their own XP course.

Lectures. The content of the theory part has gone through quite a number of changes over the years. The first time we gave the course, the coaching students did not have any experience from XP, and the theory part, therefore, focused on XP as such. The course was then given as a graduate course that complemented with some handpicked, talented, undergraduate students. In subsequent years, when the course became part of the normal undergraduate curriculum, we have taught a combination of technical skills like configuration management and testing techniques, and more soft skills like coaching skills and team building. Over the years, we have put in a little more theory about soft skills, replacing some of the technical content. This is partly a result of the students asking for this information, and partly because we, as professors, have learned more about these issues. After all, as professors in computer science, our primary competence is in the technical area. In the latest instance of the course, we had the following topics for the lectures:

The first lecture is a general *course introduction* and repetition of XP. The students have the opportunity to reflect on and to discuss their own experience from working on an XP project. The second lecture focuses on *software configuration management* (SCM). SCM is an important part of coordinating the work of a group of people, but it is also more than that. It is the control and tracking of changes and the production and quality assurance of releases. From their own XP project they have some practical knowledge, but mostly from the coordination point of view. In the SCM seminar, we give the future coaches a broader "theoretic" background by introducing a number of sub-practices for SCM on agile teams [Asklund et al., 2004].

The third lecture is on *patterns and anti-patterns* as tools for documenting experience. Much of the literature on agile programming is written as formal or informal patterns. For example, there are a number of early XP-like practices described as pattern languages [Cunningham, 1996, Beedle et al., 2000, Foote and Yoder, 2000]. The "bad smells" of Fowler [Fowler and Beck, 1999] are a kind of anti design patterns, and the testing patterns of Beck sum up important experience and advice for test-driven development [Beck, 2002]. Some students use the pattern format for documenting experience in their in-depth studies.

Lecture four is on *architecture*, focusing on the agile practices that help form the architecture, and in particular, the Initial Iteration and Metaphor. Some typical architectural styles are also discussed like layers, pipes-and-filters, etc. In the project, the coaches have the responsibility for making sure that the architecture is discussed and evolved by the team.

Lecture five is dedicated to *testing, tracking, and planning* on XP projects. Test First is difficult to learn for many of the XP students, and it is important to give the coaches some extra training on this topic. Tracking and planning is important for the coaches, as they are responsible for supervising the planning sessions.

Lecture six covers *general coaching and team building practices*. This topic is usually a strong request from the coaching students as this is an area in which they often feel very insecure about, and in particular, before the project has started. Topics briefly covered include team building, business coaching, the FIRO model of group dynamics and project retrospectives.

The last lecture focuses on *XP coaching practices* that we have developed ourselves during the years we have held these courses. In addition to our own material [Hedin et al., 2003a, Hedin et al., 2005], we use some in-depth studies that previous coaches have written about their experiences as coaches.

4.2   The Project Part

During the project part, the coaches work in pairs to coach one of the teams from the XP course. They coach their team through six iterations, each consisting of a 2-hour coach meeting (where all coaches meet and get guidance from faculty), a 2-hour planning session and an 8-hour development session. Before the project starts, the coaches develop an initial "zero'th iteration" of the product to provide a starting point for their team. These activities are described in more detail below.

Zero'th iteration. It is the responsibility of the coaches to create an initial version of their team's system. This "zero'th iteration" should be executable, but implement no full stories. The goal is to provide an initial simple architecture where several pairs can start directly to work on different parts. Typically, the system will be very small, faking some simple functionality and containing only a few classes. The basic infrastructure should be in place and the system should be checked into a CVS repository. It also should contain some simple test case, allowing the team to start with a "green bar".

Coach meeting. All coaches meet for two hours a week in order to discuss what happened at the last iteration, and to get advice for how to act during the next iteration. Problems are aired and possible solutions are shared. Discussion is done both in plenum and in smaller groups. They are given an example agenda for the planning meetings as well as advice on what is important to focus on during the next iteration. The coming iteration's stories are also presented by the super-customer (with the "ordinary" customers also being present).

Planning session. The coaches have the responsibility for preparing and leading the planning session for their team. In addition to the usual XP Planning Game with story estimation and discussion with the customer, the planning session is used for a brief reflection on what happened in the previous iteration in relation to the focus practices. The coaches summarize this information from their team and send it on to us. The coaches also make sure that individual work is defined and assigned during the planning session.

Development session. During the development session, the coaches actively coach the developers in the team according to practices we have developed for the coaches [Hedin et al., 2003a]. The coaches have to monitor closely what is going on, both technically with the product and concerning how the team follows the methodology. The coaches are encouraged to Pair Program on and off with the developers in order to foster a good way of performing the XP practices. We have found that a very important aspect is to help the team to start functioning as a team and to communicate directly with each other in order to get help from each other.

Because the coaches take a variety of other courses, they often have schedule conflicts with other classes, and we do not require them to be present at all times during the development sessions. Normally, they are present for 6 hours and sometimes only for 4 hours per development session.

4.3   In-Depth Study

During the course, the coaching students do in-depth studies on a topic of their choice, but related to XP or coaching. There are very diverse topics from very technical ones, like looking at different refactoring or testing tools, to softer topics like trying to formulate their own coaching practices. The topics of the in-depth studies are formulated already during the theory part of the course, but the bulk of the work is carried out during the project part. The reports from these studies are peer reviewed among the students and are presented and discussed during an additional coach meeting towards the end of the course.

5   Pedagogical Considerations

Software development requires very many different skills at many different levels, from simple mundane things like the syntax of a programming language and tool commands to high-level design expertise and organizational and communication skills. All these ingredients are needed to develop software successfully. In order to not overwhelm the students, we think that an iterative learning environment is absolutely essential. It is necessary for the students to get the chance to do concrete work according to their current understanding and to get the possibility to reflect and to get feedback from others in order to improve their understanding and their skills, following Kolb's learning cycle [Kolb, 1984] for experiential learning.

The use of XP provides excellent opportunities for learning in this way. In our experience there are three important pedagogical principles that in particular support the learning cycle: iterative learning, peer learning and fixed time budget. We will now discuss these in more detail.

5.1   Iterative Learning

At the start of the project, the students have read about XP in theory, and although they have some practical experience with some of the practices from the laboratories, they have on the whole a passive and superficial understanding of the techniques. For example, they know that they should write tests and automate them, but they have not practised this skill very much, and usually have only vague ideas about how the Test First practice actually works. The course design with six complete project iterations gives them many chances to reflect on how the practices work, to get feedback from their coaches and peers, and to improve during the project.

Although the 12 canonical XP practices seem fairly simple in principle, they take time to understand and to master fully. In order to not get overwhelmed by trying to learn everything at once, we have introduced the technique of *focus practices*. The idea is that while we instruct the students to try their best at following all the XP practices, we ask them to focus in particular on 4 of them during each iteration. They are asked to refresh the theory for these practices before they go to the development session. And, they are asked to discuss and to reflect on their experience from these practices at the subsequent planning session and to suggest ways of improving. We ask the coaches to summarize these discussions and each week, we compile a summary and post it on the web.

In the latest instance of the course, we used the following focus practices for iterations 1-6:

I1: Planning Game, Pair Programming, Test First, Continuous Integration

I2: Frequent Releases, Collective Code, Coding Standards, Customer On Team
I3: Refactoring, Simple Design, Frequent Releases, Common Vocabulary
I4: Continuous Integration, Refactoring, Customer On Team, Pair Programming
I5: Collective Code, Planning Game, Sustainable Pace, Test First
I6: Refactoring, Frequent Releases, Coding Standards, Simple Design

Below, we give some motivation for these choices.

Iteration 1: Getting Started. The focus practices during Iteration 1 are intended to help get a first shot at some of the most fundamental parts of XP, in particular Test First and Continuous Integration. The most important part of the Planning Game at this point is to get the experience from working with and completing small stories. An important part of Pair Programming in the beginning of the project is to try to switch frequently so that the team members get to know each other quicker and so that everybody learns to feel comfortable with switching partners.

Iteration 2: The First Release. During iteration 2, the most important focus practice is Frequent Releases. The teams are asked to release their product three times during the six-week project period. So, it is important that they get the release process to work smoothly. In fact, this is so important and difficult that they have this as a focus practice three times during iterations 2, 3, and 6. After iteration 2, they usually understand the benefit of automating as much as possible of the release process, and of having a checklist (i. e., a release process) that is kept up to date. Other aspects of the release process usually take more time to appreciate. One aspect is the benefits of having automated acceptance tests to make sure that previously implemented stories still work. Another aspect is the importance of doing a test deployment to make sure that the release is complete and that the installation instructions are intelligible.

It would have been easy to provide the teams with a "to-do" list for the releases, and to ask them to follow it. But, it seems that they gain a better understanding of how to work with the releases by simply asking them to do one, and to see the consequences of doing various mistakes. By reflecting on what worked and what did not, the students often invent improvements themselves. Naturally, if they do not come up with suitable improvements then they can receive advice from their coaches in a situation where they realise that they have a problem and can appreciate the advice.

This technique of making mistakes, reflecting and learning also usually works very well with the focus practice of Continuous Integration during iteration 1. If students integrate untested code, their team mates will very soon find out, and the team usually comes up with a technique to prevent this from happening in the future. If some students wait too long with integrating, they learn that they are punished by getting large merge conflicts.

Iteration 3: Code Quality. During iteration 3, the focus practices have the common theme of design quality (in addition to the repeated focus on Frequent Releases). This is a very difficult area where students need lots of practice, where they can learn a lot from each other, and where they can benefit a lot from mixing theory with practice. For example, paying attention to various bad smells as part of reading about Refactoring and Simple Design gives them an interest for finding smells in their own code.

Iterations 4-6: Repeating the Focus Practices. During iterations 4 to 6, most of the focus practices are repeated. This allows the students to reflect once more on each of the practices in a context where they are more experienced.

5.2   Peer Learning

Gaining experience by doing mistakes, reflecting and learning, is a slow process. Peer learning provides a shortcut to gaining experience, and XP gives excellent opportunities for peer learning. The most obvious way is through Pair Programming. The way Pair Programming is carried out in XP, by using a driver and a partner, provides an excellent way of supporting peer learning. This is because two minds are focused on the same task and verbalizing their thoughts, which helps both in understanding how the other person reasons and solves problems. It also helps in clarifying your own thinking.

The Pair Programming practice helps to share experience and knowledge at all levels from simple things like syntax and tool commands to advanced design decisions and work practices. In the course, we try to provide opportunities for a large amount of peer learning by various measures.

Random teams. The teams are put together in a random fashion. Usually, the students initially say that they would prefer to form teams with their friends, but after the project, they agree that they probably learned a lot more by being part of a random team. Many students comment that the use of random teams makes the project feel more realistic.

Frequent partner switch. We encourage the pairs to frequently switch roles of driver and partner and to frequently switch partners. In the learning situation, in particular in the beginning, it is beneficial to have some artificial scheme for this, because switching does not come naturally to most students. The teams themselves decide on the switching policy, and many teams come up with a policy like switching partners at lunch time, regardless if the current stories are finished or not. It is a goal that everyone should have Pair Programmed at least once with everyone else in the team.

Large teams. We use fairly large teams of 8 to 12 developers. In most other project courses, the students work in much smaller teams, typically of 2 to 4 persons. With experienced people, smaller teams of 4 probably perform more effectively than larger teams because it takes time to communicate and to agree within a larger team. Plus, it may be difficult to find sufficiently independent tasks, thus leading to more merging work than for a smaller team. However, the larger team size promotes peer learning simply in that the collected body of knowledge is larger. In the learning situation, the "drawbacks" of larger teams can actually be a benefit. For example, more merging problems are provoked in a larger team than in normal development, allowing the team to learn how to handle merging in a shorter time.

Reflection. The many, short iterations allow frequent reflection and the possibility to hear about other team mates' experiences.

Coach as pair programmer. Some practices are very difficult to teach and much easier to learn by a hands-on Pair Programming session together with an experienced partner. One good example of this is working in small steps. We give the students the theory that says that you should keep your code working, and to implement in small steps that get you back to the working situation as soon as possible. This is easy to say, but seems difficult for many students actually to practise. They need to see how it is done before they can try to do it themselves. To this end we encourage the coaches to Pair Program with the team members. Pair Programming is another practice that seems difficult to learn for some students. The coach can influence the developers by setting an example of how to communicate, how to switch roles, etc.

5.3   Fixed Time Budget

Our course differs from most other university courses in that it uses a fixed time budget for studies, rather than the usual requirements/examination set up. The functional requirements for the project product are given in the form of user stories, but it is not required that the teams implement all of them. The number of implemented stories is very easy to measure, but measuring work process quality and code quality is very difficult. The fixed time budget helps the students to give priority to quality over quantity in their work. This is similar to the objectives presented in *Experineces with a Focus on Testing in Teaching*. One could argue that if we do not require the students to complete a certain number of stories, why would they do anything at all? But in our experience there is an automatic strive to complete many stories. By having a fixed time budget we can counter this tendency so the students do take time improving their work process and the code quality as well. For many of the work practices of XP, the students appreciate the theory, but need to be pushed to actually try them out. They fear that following the practices might make them spend more time per story. The use of a fixed-time budget has the consequence that they can try out the practices without fearing that they will need to spend more total time on the project. For example, they are guaranteed not to be punished for trying out the practices. They risk nothing and can gain a lot.

Work in small steps. One of the most important aspects of XP is the idea to work in small steps like making small improvements of functionality and/or code quality, and obtaining working code (that runs and passes all the tests) after each small step. This means that even if you have the idea for a complete solution to a large problem in your head, you should break it down and implement it piecemeal. This is counterintuitive to many students who think this piecemeal way of working will mean more total work because you will change your code several times. By working on a fixed-time budget the students can try out the technique without the fear of spending more total time on the project.

Tests. It is often difficult to motivate the students to write a sufficient amount of tests and to use test-driven development. They are naturally optimistic and think that their code will work without tests, and that it is easier to write the tests after writing the code. Again, by having a fixed-time budget, it is possible to make them try out test-driven development. They do not run the risk of having to invest more time in the project if test-driven development does not work out. We as customers/teachers take that risk and that makes us much more credible.

Refactoring. Many students' first reaction to refactoring is that it is a good idea, but that it takes time away from implementation of new stories. It may be difficult to find the right engineering balance to do sufficient refactoring for keeping the code easy to understand and to change. The fixed-time budget allows the students to do refactoring without having to worry about getting behind schedule.

Changed/added stories. It is a natural part of real-life software development that requirements are added and changed during a project. Because of the fixed time budget, the students do not get angry or feel cheated when the customer asks them to implement things not asked for initially, or to change stories that were given earlier that would make it necessary for them to change what they have already implemented.

Work process experiments and improvements. The basic work process is given by XP, but there are many detailed issues that the teams refine over time during the project. Because of the fixed time budget, they can spend time on such refinement, and not only on product development. For example, we give them basic training on CVS for sharing the code base. Some of the teams experiment with branches in order to make release handling simpler. For example, when a release is due for a certain iteration, they can split off a release branch at noon. Half of the team can focus on packing up the release or test deploying it, etc., and the rest of the team can continue with development. After the release is complete, the branches can be merged again, maybe during the iteration if there is time, or at the next iteration. Because of the fixed-time budget, the idea of branches can be tried out without fear of having to spend more total time.

6   Challenges and Experience

There are many challenges when giving a course that is so different from usual university courses. How should the product be selected? What is there to consider when writing stories in an educational setting? What are the administrative considerations? How can we evaluate the students? How can we deal with uncooperative students? What is the economy for the course? What are the effects on the rest of the curriculum? In this section we report on our experience from these issues.

6.1 Selecting the Product

Since the students are learning XP, we want them to work in a controlled environment where other participants (coaches and customers) have expertise in XP. We also want to have control over the stories in order to make sure our pedagogical goals are met. For this reason, we decided to not try to involve external customers, but to act ourselves (faculty) as customers. Some important guidelines for selecting the product and designing the stories that we have arrived at are the following: make the first iteration easy, ask for meaningful releases, provoke architectural change, supply enough stories, provide both easy and difficult stories, do not make the product too "fun", and do not select products that require innovation.

Make the first iteration easy. During the first iteration, everything is new to the students. They are using a work process they are unfamiliar with, their starting point in development is a product skeleton that they have not written themselves, they are not very used to the tools, and they do not know each other very well. It is very important that they get to succeed at this first iteration, completing stories and feeling that they have made progress with the product. For this reason, we supply simple and clear stories that are easy to implement. The stories are described in more detail than later on, and we even break down the stories into tasks for them. We make sure that the first stories are reasonably independent of each other so that it is easy for them to work in parallel. Later on in the project, the code base is so large that it is usually not a problem to work in parallel, but in the beginning some thought has to be given to this aspect. It is also important that the stories are sufficiently small so that they are able to complete several of them during the iteration. We try to adjust the size of the stories so that around 2 to 4 programming pair hours are sufficient for implementing them. It is a goal that all developers are able to commit at least one story or task (and merge with others) during the first iteration.

In the zero'th iteration of the Enduro project, the coaches have constructed an executable program with approximately the following skeleton functionality. There is a registration program and a sorting program. The registration program has a very simple graphical user interface where driver numbers can be entered. The registration also prints some (faked) data to a file. The sorting program reads some simple data from an input file and produces (faked) data to an output file. The stories supplied for the first iteration are the following:

- Enhance the sorting program so that it can read files with both start and finish registrations, merge the results, and write out a result file.
- Enhance the sorting program so that the total time for a driver is computed, and written to the result file.
- Design a file for keeping track of extra information about the drivers (e.g., which club they belong to, what kind of bike they are riding). Merge this information into the result file of the sorting program.
- Enhance the sorting program to find possible anomalies (e.g., missing start or finish time, too many start or finish times, unreasonably short total time

that is shorter than some constant, say 15 minutes). Some of these anomalies could be due to mistakes during registration (e.g., entering the wrong driver number).

– Enhance the registration program so that the registration of driver results in a file with driver numbers and associated registration times.
– Enhance the graphical user interface of the registration program so that you can see the latest registrations.

The first story is central in that it needs to be finished before three of the other stories can be completed. To aid in parallel work, several pairs can work on different tasks for the first story. Pairs can also start working on the other stories, and test them partially by using unit tests.

Ask for meaningful releases. In the second iteration, the students should provide a first release of their system. We ask them to produce a system that can handle a kind of very simple Enduro race. There are some stories that are central to implement for this release and a number of stories that are nice to have, but not absolutely necessary for being able to run the race. This focus on using the system for a particular kind of race provides a nice, meaningful focus for the release. Since the students usually have problems with their first release, an important part of the third iteration is to provide an updated release where they have fixed the major problems that were discovered by the customer.

The focus for the second release (in the fifth iteration) is in supporting also more advanced kinds of races. At the end of the course, the students use their own systems in a real race (where the sport is pair walking rather than Enduro motor cycling), and for the last release (sixth iteration); the focus is on fine-tuning the usage and error-handling mechanisms of their system. Note that in all these releases, we do not ask for a specific set of stories. Rather, we have a specific scenario for the intended use of the system, and then the customer negotiates the stories to implement with the team.

Provoke architectural change. For the first iterations, we want the development to go smoothly. But, we also want the students to experience the fact that more radical changes to their software are possible. The simple race for the first release calls for some rather simple data structures in their programs. But, for the second release when we call for support for more advanced kinds of races, their core data structures need to be substantially updated and/or changed. On purpose, we have selected the priority of the stories so that they will need to rework their core data structures, and thus, they will have to exercise the refactoring practice in a natural way. Maybe this is not always easy to do for all products, but we find it a nice property of our current set up.

Supply enough stories. The teams work at different paces. Some teams complete many stories, others fewer. It is important to have a product where it is easy to scale up the number of stories. The Enduro project has this property. There are many different kinds of races that can be supported, and it is easy to build more functionality into the system. These include support for web-based advance registration of drivers, fancy result files, client-server connections of machines that do registrations and sorting, in order to produce intermediate results, and many kinds of error checking. It is also easy to provide both easy and more difficult stories. There is a need for both simple stories that are easy to complete to feel that the project moves forward, and more difficult challenging stories that make the project interesting to the more capable students.

Do not make the product too much fun. Some of our students complain that the Enduro system is a boring product and they would like to work on something more fun, like a game, or a chat program, or similar. We sympathize with that wish, but we are hesitant to select a product that has too much appeal to it. We think this might distract the students from the process so that they focus too much on just delivering more functionality. At least, this is a good excuse to those students that think that the product is boring. Many of the students, in fact, comment that they think it is a good product because it is realistic.

Do not pick products that require innovation. Another risk with selecting a game or a chat program is that this would be an area which is very open to innovation, leading to a situation where the students would probably come with many suggestions for stories and would challenge the priorities set by the customer. Of course, there is nothing wrong with such innovative products in general. But, in teaching XP and basic software engineering concepts, we think it is better to have clearly separated roles of customer and developer where the customer is the domain expert. For the Enduro project one of the faculty is such a domain expert, and this helps very much in finding meaningful releases and in prioritizing the stories. Because there is an existing reality where the system should work, it is easy to clarify the requirements, simply by checking against reality.

6.2   Administrative Experience

Examination. The course has only the grades pass/fail. The main reason why we do not give finer-grained grades is because the important things that they learn —like code quality, work process skills, teamwork skills, etc.— are difficult to measure. In particular, it is difficult to measure the individual performance of the students.

In order to pass, the students should show up and work actively on all planning meetings and development sessions, and do their homework in the form of spikes. In order to motivate the students to perform as well as they can, we mainly rely on group pressure. Sometimes, there are students that are lazy or uncooperative and some policing is needed. We do the policing in steps. First, the coach tries to solve the problem by talking to the student in private or by bringing up the problem on a general level within the team. If this does not help, we involve faculty and ask the student do some extra work (hand in assignments) to compensate the team for lack of activity. Failure to improve behavior may ultimately lead to the student failing the course.

Course economy. Teaching work processes requires heavy coaching and assisting the students in their reflection and helping them to improve. The course would have been much too costly to run by using faculty only especially when considering that we have over 100 students each year. The key to making it work economically is to rely on student coaches. This turns out as a win-win situation: the XP students are in general very satisfied with their coaches, and the coaches find their course very interesting and worthwhile. Furthermore, we have reused the same project for several years. It is not easy to find projects with the right characteristics from a learning point of view (see 6.1). Likewise, it is quite a job to think out and to write stories and acceptance tests for a project that has also a teaching purpose.

Plagiarism. How do we avoid plagiarism? If we reuse the same problem year after year, what stops teams from copying projects from previous years? First of all, we would point out that our impression is that our students get drawn in by the project and take great pride in trying to do their best. So the last thing they think about is copying from others. In the case that they should try to copy a previous project, we feel confident that the tight collaboration with the coaches (who sometimes even pair program with their team) and the customer (who sometimes sits and watches them spike forward a demo) would make it impossible to hide. It will be far less work for the team to do the code themselves than to try to find and to copy relevant code. To rip an old repository and to "play" the same line of development as the team that made the original repository is possible, but only in theory. Old repositories are not freely available, but it would be possible to obtain one if you really wanted. However, our customers behave inconsistently when they have to decide what stories should go into the next iteration and the priority of them. So, even for teams with the same base set of stories implemented, the customer would request slightly different sets of stories for the next iteration. However, our students do talk to students from other teams and exchange problems and ideas/solutions. In fact, it is something that we directly —and indirectly through the coaches— encourage them to do. The desire is for them to spread knowledge not just within the team, but also between the teams. Our general impression is that the students take so much pride in trying to work out problems themselves, that they have to be actively encouraged to "seek help" when they get stuck. We have seen several cases of pairs and teams that go on for too long solving a problem before they admit that they are stuck and need help.

Effects on the curriculum. The change of the team programming course to be based on XP has the potential of positively affecting many other subsequent courses. First of all, the students should get general access to the tools they have learnt, so they can continue to use CVS, JUnit and Eclipse. In particular, for CVS they need help in setting up repositories since this is something they usually cannot do themselves from their unprivileged accounts. Subsequent courses can also make use of their skills (e.g., requiring them to split their work into stories, requiring them to provide a zero'th executable iteration, requiring them to turn in resulting systems with working test cases, etc). The introduction of XP can also affect the courses at the introductory level. In particular, the practices of test first and pair programming can be pushed down to this level.

7   Related Work

There are several reports from trying out XP or parts of XP in courses. Most of these are very positive towards using XP in education, and confirm our experience that XP provides an excellent learning environment by being so highly iterative, and allowing the students to build experience gradually and learn by doing [Wilson, 2001, Noll, 2002, Becker-Pechau et al., 2003, Mugridge et al., 2003, Steimann et al., 2003, Bergin et al., 2004]. Many of them point out the importance of active coaching and reflection, but we have not seen other courses making use of student coaches. In most other cases, the classes have been small, and faculty have been used for coaching.

There are different approaches to placing XP in the curriculum. Some place it already in the freshman year [Becker-Pechau et al., 2003], whereas others view it as an advanced topic and have tried it out in graduate or upper-level undergraduate courses [Müller and Tichy, 2001, Lappo, 2002]. Some argue for a hybrid approach because students should learn the more traditional techniques as well as the agile ones [Shukla and Williams, 2002]. We think that XP is very beneficial to teach as is, and in the beginning of the curriculum, in the first or second year. It exposes the students to the complete spectrum of software development activities and gives them a set of very useful skills that they can refine and build on in subsequent courses. Not the least in capstone projects, or in software engineering courses that teach more traditional methodologies. A problem with introducing XP late (e.g., in a capstone project) can be that the students have already developed traditional habits that need to be changed, and that they need to be very heavily coached in order to not revert to those practices [Keefe and Dick, 2004]. Interestingly, it is suggested by Lappo that it is a good idea to let students run projects with no method, or with the Waterfall method, in order to really appreciate the XP method [Lappo, 2002]. We agree that there is truth to this, but a waste for the students to have to run complete projects in that primitive way.

Our approach —and the use of XP in teaching in general— has much in common with the use of Problem-Based Learning (PBL) as done by Nuutila et al. (see *Learning Programming with the PBL Method — Experiences on PBL Cases and Tutoring*). Their tutor is our coach, their domain expert is our customer, and they use older students as tutors and us as coaches. Their seven-step method has the phases of Opening Session, Study Period and Closing Session, much resembling our Planning Game, Spike Time and Development Session. Our XP course, however, differs in having only one single case with which the students actually gain practical experience. They develop a real, working product together in a team by living all the practical, technical and social problems that they will eventually meet after they graduate. Finally, we agree with their observation that certain basic skills have to be in place first. It is in accordance with our experience and placing of the XP course.

8   Conclusions

Software development is a complex area, and success depends on many different skills including programming skills, organizational skills and people skills. Many of these skills require extensive practice in order to get a good understanding of the whole picture and the complex interrelations between different tasks. We have argued for a three step curriculum design to teach software development, starting with individual programming, continuing with team programming, and thereby, preparing for more specialized, third-level topics of software development. In this chapter, we have focused on the middle step of team programming by using XP, which gives a thorough foundation for further work and studies. This supplies the students with a scaled-down, but complete experience of real-life software development.

Given the complex nature of software development, we have found three important pedagogical principles that we find very beneficial in order to teach the subject: iterative learning, peer learning and fixed time budget. *Iterative learning* allows the students to try out their skills, get feedback on what worked and what did not, and to have many chances to improve. It allows the students to focus on different things in different iterations in order to not get overwhelmed with the complexity of the subject. *Peer learning* is utilized to a very high degree by keeping the team together whenever they do production work, by pair programming and reflection meetings, and by using student coaches. The use of random and fairly large teams (around 10 developers) substantially increases the collected body of tacit knowledge that the team can share and benefit from. The *fixed time budget* is very important for providing a good learning environment. It allows the students to give priority to quality and iterative improvement of both the developed product and their own skills, in contrast to implementing a set of functional requirements in as short time as possible. An important aspect of the fixed time budget is that it gives a realistic experience, more similar to a real-life project than what can be obtained in the traditional requirements/examination set up of a course.

Acknowledgements

We are very grateful to the many students in both the XP courses and the Coaching courses. They have provided us with many insights and ideas for improvements that have helped us to continually refine the courses over the past four years.

Frameworks in Teaching*

Michael E. Caspersen and Henrik Bærbak Christensen

Department of Computer Science
University of Aarhus
Denmark
{mec,hbc}@daimi.au.dk

Abstract. Software reuse is important in modern software engineering
to ensure high quality software while keeping cost down. Software reuse
is therefore an important topic in teaching. This chapter discusses issues
relating to teaching object-oriented frameworks that represent a central
technique for software reuse. We present concrete techniques for teaching
the topic at both introductory and advanced programming level and
convey our experiences. At the introductory level we discuss a simple
yet powerful framework, Presenter, that serves as a first introduction
to programming using frameworks as well as a gentle introduction to
the more complex topic of graphical user interface frameworks like Java
AWT and Swing. At the advanced level we discuss a complex framework,
JHotDraw, that both serves to demonstrate concepts and techniques used
in complex frameworks, as well as demonstrate how design patterns are
combined in object-oriented frameworks.

1 Introduction

Over the last decade or two we have seen a dramatic change in the way software is developed. Earlier, the basis upon which software was developed was
basically the operating system, the programming language, and whatever libraries came along with the language. An archetypical example is C, its `stdio,`
`stdlib`, and `math` libraries. Most of these libraries are merely the binding between the programming language and the operating system. Consequently, and
quite obviously, our teaching reflected this hard fact. Topics like programming
languages and operating systems were unavoidable subjects in the curriculum,
and of course, emphasis was also put on the more abstract structures that were
needed to heighten the level of abstraction above the individual statement level:
algorithms, data structures, abstract data types, parallel programming, etc. Basically, crafting a program meant filling in the blank space between `Program`
`MyProgram; Begin` and `End`.

---

* The content of the present chapter is an extension of material previously published at
  conferences and workshops. * Frameworks: Putting Design Patterns into Perspective,
  published at ITiCSE 2004. * The Need for Killer Examples for Object-Oriented
  Frameworks, workshop paper at the "Killer Examples" workshop, OOPSLA 2003.
  * Frameworks in CS1 - a Different Way of Introducing Event-driven Programming,
  published at ITiCSE 2002.

J. Bennedsen et al. (Eds.): Teaching of Programming, LNCS 4821, pp. 190–205, 2008.

Software development today is in many ways radically different. The previous two chapters addressed some of the new challenges by concentrating on specific aspects of the modern development process, namely testing and a team process (eXtreme Programming). In this chapter, we discuss a different, but important aspect of modern development practices: software reuse [Jacobson et al., 1997, Karlsson, 1995].

Software reuse is an important aspect because building software from scratch that matches modern requirements in terms of usability, reliability, connectivity, and demands for complex functionality is simply not feasible. (By "from scratch" we mean using only the programming language and the functionality provided by the operating system.) Application developers today can draw on a wealth of reliable software frameworks that allow them to focus on the domain of their customers. Examples are numerous: Enterprise Java Beans, Microsoft .NET, Java Swing and Remote Method Invocation, CORBA, ODBC, and complemented by frameworks in particular domains like tele-communication, game development, finance, insurance, etc. Thus, software development today is just as much a practice of *finding and reusing* software as it is of *building* software. Being a successful developer today is no longer just a question of being a good programmer, but just as much a question of understanding complex interaction patterns in third party frameworks and being able to design in accordance with their guidelines.

This changes the skill set that we need to teach students, or rather, that we need to teach new skills in addition to the old ones. Writing even a simple program that has a graphical user interface in Java Swing is radically different from the old "fill in the blank space between **begin** and **end**" agenda. The event-based protocol in Swing (and any modern GUI framework) is conceptually an inverted control scheme that requires students to understand the complex interplay between framework code and their own code. Usually, this coupling is accomplished by design patterns like, for instance, observer. Thus, development today is a *reuse business* and we should accordingly prepare our students for this from the very beginning. An object-oriented framework is one of the very few concepts that have realized the long searched vision of software reuse. Sadly, however, most teaching books still lack a proper treatment of the fundamental concepts and techniques of frameworks.

Over the last six years the authors have taught numerous introductory as well as advanced courses in object-oriented programming. In these courses, we have spent time to introduce, to use and to theorize about frameworks at different levels of abstraction. In this chapter, we present ideas and experience from this work. The chapter is divided into two major parts. The first part deals with frameworks in introductory teaching and revolves around the Presenter framework that we have developed specifically for teaching framework concepts. The second part deals with frameworks in advanced object-oriented programming courses. Here, the JHotDraw framework, developed by Gamma and Eggenschwiler is presented and discussed.

The concrete teaching context where the ideas have developed is three courses at the Department of Computer Science, University of Aarhus, Denmark. Two of these are 10 ECTS, 15 week long courses for at part-time education, while the third is a 5 ECTS, 7 week long course for full-time students. The students in our department's part-time education can be characterised as professional software developers in industry. Typically, the students are experienced, but initially not familiar with the object-oriented paradigm.

The introductory course is structured as "objects first" with a strong emphasis on modelling as described in *CS1: Getting Started*. The environment used is the BlueJ environment (*Using BlueJ to Introduce Programming*). The Presenter framework is introduced in the second half of the course.

The advanced courses are a 10 ECTS as well as a 5 ECTS course. In both courses a major focus is put on design patterns, frameworks, reliability and testing, and software architecture. The 10 ECTS course has been taught five times and the 5 ECTS course twice. Both courses have a large compulsory project consisting of a number of separate deliverables to be handed and accepted in order to attend the final oral exam. The deliverables are solutions to design and programming exercises. The JHotDraw framework is introduced early in both courses.

2   Pedagogical Points

While our main motivation for teaching frameworks has been the obvious need to teach students about the techniques that govern modern software development, we have found additional pedagogical aspects that make the topic worthwhile to spend time on.

1. *Student motivation.* A framework defines the skeleton of an application that can be customized by an application developer. This changes the focus radically. If students must program everything from scratch, then the workload and complexity simply rule out making programs that in any respect compare to the sophisticated and appealing programs that they are used to from their home PC. Prime numbers printed in a shell are not that spectacular. However, a framework provided by the teacher can provide the "bells and whistles" that makes the effort invested by the student look more appealing or "professional". Talking business language, the "return on investment" is simply greater for the student. This point is valid no matter what the level of the course is: introductory, advanced or PhD level.

2. *Gentler learning curve.* Many aspects of modern programming are arguably very complex. The Java Swing framework for developing graphical user interfaces is overwhelming in terms of the number of classes and in terms of the techniques involved like inversion of control and design patterns. Framework theory can provide students with the concepts that allow them to keep their sense of direction in this wilderness.

3. *Object-oriented concepts.* Good object-oriented frameworks are unique examples of just how strong a paradigm object orientation is. Looking behind

the scenes of good frameworks shows how careful modelling of domain concepts and the use of interfaces, polymorphism, and delegation make a piece of software highly flexible. This also demonstrates the power of low coupling and high cohesion. Thus, it is a good case study to learn from.

4. *Complexity.* Kristen Nygaard, one of the fathers of object-orientation, often emphasized that object orientation's main strength lies in its ability to tackle complex problems. Therefore, we must provide students with problems of some complexity in order to motivate object-orientation.

3 Frameworks: What Are They?

Before we go into details about the frameworks we have used in teaching, it may be worthwhile to spend a few moments on the concept of frameworks. According to Merriam-Webster's Collegiate Dictionary, the word "framework" means the following:

 i basic conceptual structure (as of ideas)
 ii a skeletal, openwork, or structural frame

This general definition fits nicely with frameworks in software engineering. Several authors in the computer science community have provided definitions that address the software aspects as follows:

− A framework is: a) a reusable design of an application or subsystem, b) represented by a set of abstract classes and the way objects in these classes collaborate. (Johnson, OOPSLA 97)
− A framework is a set of cooperating classes that make up a reusable design for a specific class of software. (GoF, p. 26)
− A framework is the skeleton of an application that can be customized by an application developer. (Fayad)
− A framework defines a high-level language with which applications within a domain are created through specialization. (Pree)
− A framework is an architectural pattern that provides an extensible template for applications within a domain. (Booch, Rumbaugh, & Jacobson)

If we look closer at these definitions, there is a core of recurring themes:

− *Skeleton / design / high-level language:* The framework delivers application behavior at a high level of abstraction. This is much in line with the general definition of a framework as a basic conceptual structure.
− *Application/class of software:* A framework provides functionality in a well-defined domain —frameworks address specific domains like graphical user interfaces, gaming, insurance, tele-communication, etc.
− *Cooperating / collaborating classes:* A framework defines the interaction patterns between a set of well-defined components/objects. To use the framework the developers have to understand these interaction patterns and must program in accordance with it.

- *Customize/abstract classes/reusable/specialize:* A framework is flexible so that you can tailor it to a concrete context —as long as this context lies within the domain of the framework.
- *Classes/implementation/skeleton:* A framework provides reuse of code as well as reuse of design.

4   Introducing Frameworks: Presenter

In this first part, we present our experience with introducing frameworks in the introductory course. As argued in the chapter introduction we find that software reuse should be introduced early and reinforced often. However, frameworks are a complex topic and basic programming skills are necessary. We, therefore, introduce a simple framework, Presenter, late in the introductory course. While it is late in the introductory course, it is still early in the curriculum. Presenter also serves a concrete purpose, namely, to provide a gentle introduction to Java's graphical user interface framework by lowering the learning curve and providing students with an understanding of this large and complex framework.

In this section, we describe the introductory framework of Presenter, and the exercises associated with it. We discuss how the terminology introduced by the simple framework is used in our introduction to Java AWT as representative of modern, object-oriented graphical user interface frameworks.

4.1   A Two-Step Learning Process

We have adopted a *two-step* learning process for introducing graphical user interface frameworks.

In the first step, we teach the students a basic understanding of the principles underlying frameworks by using a concrete, simple, yet flexible framework example called Presenter. Presenter has nevertheless the following fundamental characteristics of a framework:

- *Inversion of control:* The framework defines the control flow and collaboration patterns of the objects in the final application, instead of the usual "driver" program that the students write themselves.
- *Hotspots:* The provided framework is abstract and needs to be specialized to the particular domain of the final application. Abstract classes that must be subclassed define the hotspots of our concrete framework.

In the second step, we introduce Java AWT to the students through the context and terminology introduced by the first step —what are the hotspots of AWT and how do we tailor them to our needs? The main point is that AWT/Swing is large and complicated and, thus, confusing to the beginner. And, students must master the underlying concepts and principles in order not to be overwhelmed by the sheer number of classes and methods.

4.2   First Step: Presenter Framework

Our requirements of the framework were the following aspects: It should illustrate the basic principles of frameworks (inversion of control and hotspots); it should be simple for students to use; it should be flexible in the sense that a number of sensible instantiations should be possible; it should be fun, challenging and visual.

We did not find a framework that fitted all these requirements, and therefore, set out to build our own. The result is a *presenter framework*. The presenter framework facilitates construction of multi-media presentations of a domain where the compass-directions are a suitable metaphor for user navigation. So far, "multi-media" is limited to images and text, but it would be straightforward to extend it to movies and sound.

In our *first step* lecture we introduce the presenter framework through a specific instantiation, namely, a multi-media presentation of the tomb of Tutankhamen, the pharaoh whose tomb was miraculously found rather intact in 1922 by [Carter et al., 1985]. Figure 1 shows a screen snapshot of the Tutankhamen tomb presentation. The presenter framework is an applet, thus the presentation and later, the student exercises can be run in a web browser. Using the four buttons marked with the compass directions, the user can navigate around the chambers of the tomb. In each chamber, the user is presented with a picture taken during the original opening of the tomb along with some explanatory text.

In class the concrete instantiation —moving around a tomb with pictures from the original opening— usually grabs the imagination of the students.

The Tutankhamen's tomb instantiation also allows us to underline an important software engineering principle such as separating model/domain code and user interaction code. We build a small object-oriented model of the domain with classes: *chamber* (having exits, an image and a description) and *visitor* (having an association with a specific chamber and a `move` method). Thus, we can concentrate on the model code and on the user interface code in turns that are relatively independent of each other.

Design. The presenter framework provides the application programmer with a simple interface (in practice, the interface is split into two, as described in the next section):

```
public abstract class ImagePresenter
   extends java.applet.Applet
{
   public void showImage(String filename)
   {...}
   public void showText(String text) {...}

   public abstract void northButtonPressed();
   public abstract void eastButtonPressed();
   public abstract void southButtonPressed();
   public abstract void westButtonPressed();
}
```

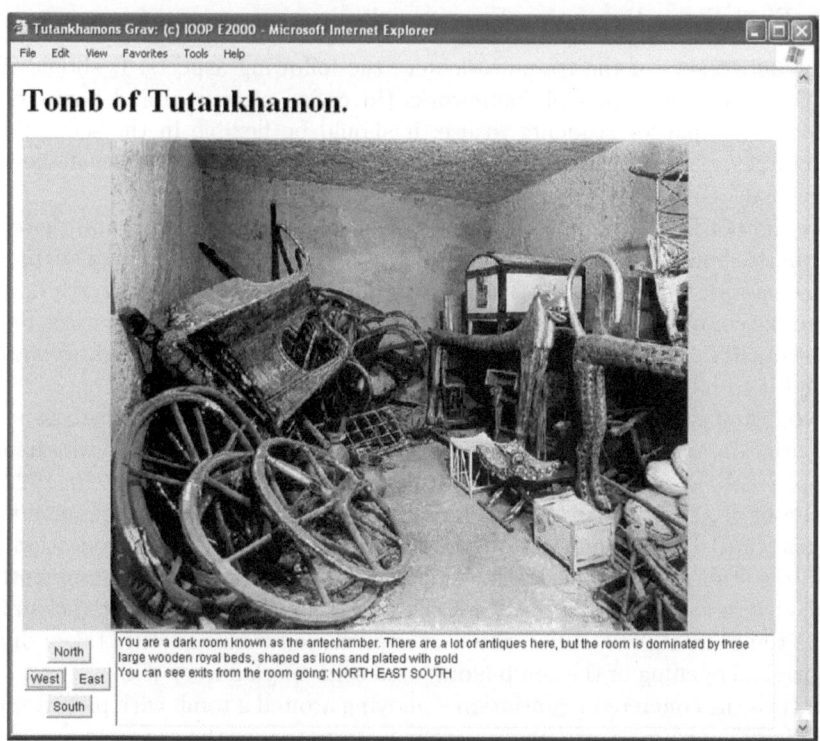

Fig. 1. The presenter framework instantiated to present a guided tour of Tutankhamen's tomb

An instance of `ImagePresenter` is an applet that provides the graphical user interface: a large area for displaying images, a smaller one for displaying text and the four compass direction buttons that respond to user clicks.

The `showImage` and `showText` methods are methods that provide services for the application programmer. Thus, instantiating the tomb presentation is a matter of overriding the `ButtonPressed()` methods, for example:

```
public void northButtonPressed() {
  visitor.move(NORTH);
}
```

Here, the move method of visitor must test for an exit leading north and invoke the `showImage` and `showText` methods with appropriate parameters.

The new technique the students must adopt is that in order to provide application specific functionality that reacts on user interaction, they have to subclass the abstract `ImagePresenter` to define the actions to perform when the user presses the buttons on the user interface. This raises discussions of the central points of frameworks as outlined below.

Inversion of control. In their previous programming experience from example code and exercises, there are always a number of interacting objects and a single 'driver' that does the setup and defines the main control flow. Now the control flow is dictated and controlled by the presenter framework instead. The application code comes into play only when the overridden `ButtonPressed()` methods are called. This is a simple variant of event-driven programming and illustrates the inversion of control principle.

Hotspots. Frameworks define core functionality, control flow and object collaboration patterns. Application programmers refine frameworks to specific domains by adding code at well-defined points denoted hotspots (also called hooks or variability points). Hotspots can be defined using a number of the following different techniques: callback methods, objects that implement interfaces, subclassing, etc. We have adopted the subclassing technique as we find it the simplest, and as it also demonstrates yet another use of polymorphism and specialisation.

4.3   Elaboration

We found that the framework could be used in more contexts by introducing a higher level of abstraction: A presenter that does not demand that the central graphical area is an image. Thus, we split the framework into a `Presenter` class and a more specific subclass `ImagePresenter`, the latter being the one used for the tomb instantiation. The `Presenter` only demands that the graphical centre component is a Java AWT component and provides an abstract factory method [Gamma et al., 1994] for subclasses to define the concrete instance.

Thus, the framework classes are:

```
public abstract class Presenter
   extends java.applet.Applet
   implements ActionListener
{
   public abstract java.awt.Component createCenterComponent();
   public void showText(String text) {...}
   public abstract void northButtonPressed();
   public abstract void eastButtonPressed();
   public abstract void southButtonPressed();
   public abstract void westButtonPressed();
   ...
}

public abstract class ImagePresenter extends Presenter
{
   public void showImage(String filename){...}
   public Component createCenterComponent() {
     [return a Canvas instance that can display images]
   }
}
```

4.4   Student Exercises

Several simple instantiations can be made from the Presenter and the ImageP-resenter frameworks.

The first exercise is to make a virtual tour of a museum or gallery. A layout of a number of locations in a gallery is defined and a painting is associated with each location. The buttons can be used to move around the gallery and to see the various paintings. This exercise is deliberately similar to the tomb instantiation. In another exercise, only the "north" and "south" buttons are used to run through a list of images, essentially making the presenter a slide-show application.

The basic directional navigation metaphor also lends itself naturally to ad-venture games. We have an extension of the framework to include the ability to show two scrollable lists of images with one on either side of the center image. The application programmer can then program these so that one list represents an inventory of objects (images) carried by the user and the other list represents

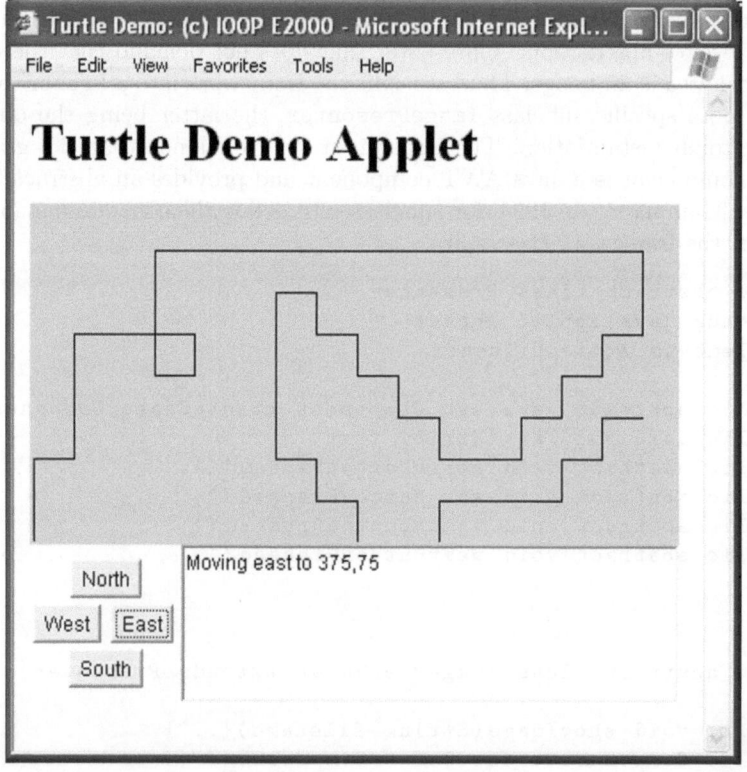

Fig. 2. The presenter framework instantiated to demonstrate turtle graphics

an inventory of objects in the visited location. A click-event on an image in a list is a hotspot of the framework that the student can refine to mean that objects are moved between the two inventories.

Other exercises are based on the *Presenter* class that takes any `java.awt.Component` as its center component. Our introductory course has often used an object-oriented variant of turtle graphics to introduce people to programming and object-oriented thinking, as outlined in *CS1: Getting Stared*. We, therefore, ask the students to make a demonstration of the turtle where the turtle moves some distance in the direction corresponding to the compass direction that the user clicks. A snapshot of the turtle instantiation is shown in Fig. 2.

In summary, although the provided functionality of the framework is limited and simple, there are a number of interesting exercises based upon the framework that force the students to negotiate the basic principles of inversion of control and refining hotspots.

4.5 Second Step: Java AWT

The *second step* in the learning process is introducing a real GUI framework. We restrict ourselves to AWT instead of Swing. The principles are the same, but Swing contains even more detail that may blur the picture for the students.

Here, we used the principles and concepts introduced by the Presenter framework to describe and to explain AWT. Students have seen the inversion of control principle in action, so the fundamental event-driven architecture of AWT is now reinforced. They have seen the principle of refining hotspots and we can now concentrate on the particular technique used in AWT for doing this refinement. Of course, the technique used in AWT is somewhat more complex as developers have to register listeners that receive event objects. But, the aim is the same, which is to create the coupling between model code and the framework.

4.6 Experience

While we have made many changes to the course material over the years, the `Presenter` framework has remained a stable part. As the framework has been used ever since we started teaching this course, we have no comparative evaluations of the advantages and drawbacks of our approach compared to other ways of introducing graphical user interfaces. However, we have some feedback primarily from discussing with students. Although they are not rigid scientific evaluations, they do illustrate aspects of the approach.

The students generally value the approach. The exercises are reported as "fun" and not too hard. The also value the visual appearance and interactive nature of their programs. Finally, they generally report that the framework terminology they have learned is used to ease and to enhance their understanding of the much more complicated AWT.

5   Advanced Frameworks: JHotDraw

In this second part, we discuss ideas and experiences with teaching frameworks in advanced programming courses. The context is two different, but similar courses. Both address issues such as advanced programming constructs, design patterns, testing and other aspects of advanced programming. In these courses much more emphasis is put on frameworks in itself.

Object-oriented frameworks make heavy use of design patterns. Then, a progression and spiraling between patterns and frameworks allows two different aspects of large scale programming to illuminate each other.

Our observations and experience are from using a particular framework known as *JHotDraw*, which was originally designed by Thomas Eggenschwiler and Eric Gamma. We believe that other well-engineered frameworks may serve to illustrate pedagogical points concerning design patterns and framework design. However, we will focus on JHotDraw as we have been using it in our teaching.

5.1   Patterns and Frameworks

In the course, we first present a set of design patterns individually with accompanying exercises. The set consists of patterns that are found in the JHotDraw framework. We then turn to the subject of frameworks. Gamma et al. define a framework as *a set of cooperating classes that make up a reusable design for a specific class of software* [Gamma et al., 1994].

Frameworks are complex software systems, both structurally and behaviorally. [JHotDraw, 2005] is an example of a medium-sized framework for developing

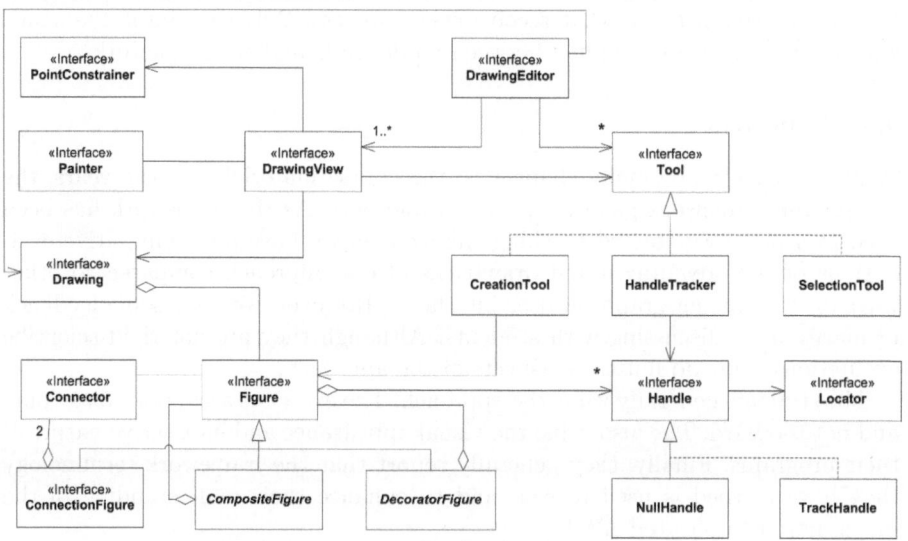

Fig. 3. Central abstractions in JHotDraw using the UML class diagram notation

2-D semantic drawing editors. Several demonstration programs are available that build Pert-diagram editors, UML class diagram editors [Kaiser, 2001], and ordinary 2D graphical figure editors based upon the framework. JHotDraw 5.1 consists of more than 180 classes. A UML class diagram only showing the central abstractions is shown in Figure 3. This is a design of much higher complexity than any single design pattern.

We present Figure 3 in class and ask the students the following question: *How on earth are we going to understand this system? Are there any road-maps that will help us to know what is going on?* The answers to these questions are, "Yes, there is an underlying road-map that allows us to understand the system —and design-patterns define this road-map". JHotDraw is basically a model-view-controller architecture with some additions. The diagram in Figure 4 shows the same structural diagram, but with the indication of which parts of the diagram plays what role in the MVC patterns, along with other important patterns.

Thus, knowledge of the MVC patterns is the key to understanding both the structural as well as dynamical aspects of JHotDraw. For instance, MVC states that the view(s) should redraw when being notified about state changes in the model component. This behavioral structure is evident in JHotDraw where the central model abstraction, interface `Drawing`, maintains a list of `DrawingChangeListeners` that are notified whenever the drawing model component is changed. The central view component, `DrawingView`, is of course a `DrawingChangeListeners`.

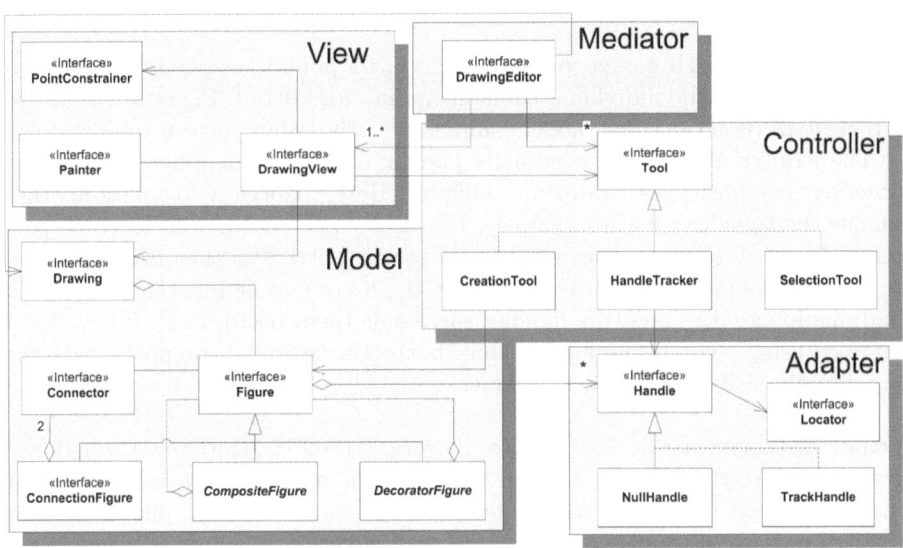

Fig. 4. Classification of abstractions

MVC is an example of the Observer pattern. We will use the terminology defined in GoF [Gamma et al., 1994]: the *subject* is the object that contains the state information while an *observer* is an object that must keep its own internal state synchronised.

Subject as observer. The observer pattern is central in JHotDraw. JHotDraw is a semantic drawing editor. Therefore, graphical figures that have semantic bindings to each other are supported. As a simple example consider the association line connecting two classes in a UML diagram: moving one class has implications for the association line that must be updated and redrawn to keep the two class figures connected. Any JHotDraw graphical object is a `Figure` instance and this interface also plays the role of subject in the observer pattern, maintaining a list of `FigureChangeListener` objects that are notified upon state changes. This supports the aforementioned association line's redrawing as it can subscribe to position changes in the two classes it connects. The nice catch is that the `Drawing` instance also simply subscribes to figure changes in all figures that it contains so that it knows when to fire change events to its views. Thus, `Drawing` is an example of a "double observer pattern". It plays the role of subject with respect to `DrawingViews`, and at the same time, the role of observer with respect to `Figures`. This is elegant, simple to program, and ensures graphical consistency.

In a teaching setting it allows us to show how powerful the Observer pattern really is. It is also to emphasize that the terms 'subject' and 'observer' are really roles in the observer pattern, and not just class implementations to be copied from a pattern book.

Abstractions having several roles. This latter point is even more emphasised when we look at the individual components in more detail. Figure 5 shows the structure of the JHotDraw model component with design pattern roles added.

The `Figure` abstraction is actually playing a role in four different patterns: observer, composite, decorator and adapter. Here, JHotDraw displays another unique, pedagogical, feature, namely, that it brings "visual" life to these patterns. Figure 5 shows an ordinary `TextFigure`, but below that is a decorated text figure having a border. On the right there are two figures that are moved and manipulated as one (the handles surrounds them both), as they have been grouped using a composite figure. Thus, both decorator and composite patterns are directly visible at the user interface.

Other patterns used. The adapter pattern is used in JHotDraw through the use of handles when the rectangular boxes appear when a figure is selected. For instance, a text figure has, when selected, a special handle that allows the font size to be changed simply by dragging it (not shown). Thus, mouse move events are converted into invocations of the text figure's `setFontSize` method, which is an example of the adapter pattern.

JHotDraw uses the idea of graphical *tools* to define the operations to perform on the drawing surface. The tool palette is the set of buttons on the left hand side

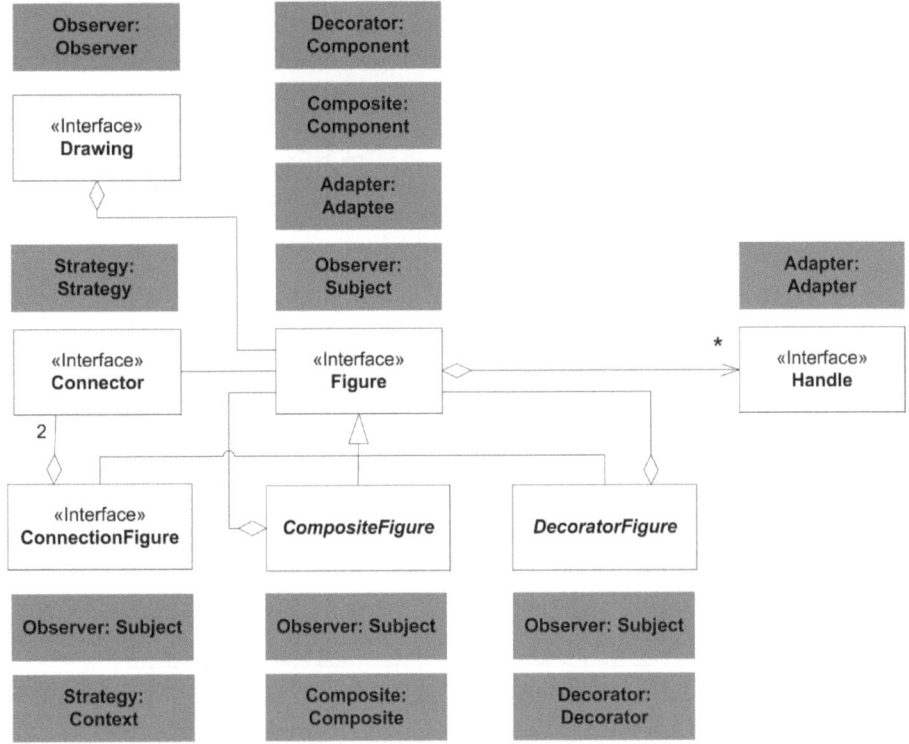

Fig. 5. Roles of each abstraction in the model component

of Figure 6 Tools may be selected to instantiate a rectangle, a text, or some other figure. And, other tools can be selected to connect figures, to add a border, etc.

The tools act as the controller component of MVC, but by looking closer, other patterns appear. The selection tool internally uses a state pattern to define the actual operation to perform based upon what is clicked (e.g., a figure [move], its handles [resize], or the background [rubber-band selection]).

Framework hotspots. An important question that we pose to the students is, "Why have the developers introduced all these complex interactions?" If you study the event sequence for a simple mouse drag, you find that the request is delegated through three or four objects before a figure is actually manipulated.

The answer is that each delegated method call presents a well defined spot to intervene: a *hotspot*. That is, framework programmers can define new types of tools and/or handles that customize the framework to his or her particular needs. They also can ask the framework to delegate to/through these custom-made objects instead. This is of course the key point in a framework, but it also demonstrates the fundamental power of using delegation [Grand, 1998].

Fig. 6. Patterns show up visually

5.2   Pedagogical Discussion

We have outlined a number of important aspects of design patterns that are easily missed by students unless they are demonstrated in a context such as the following: that a single class may participate in many different patterns or even play different roles within the same pattern; that patterns are often combined; and that framework hotspots may be defined by delegation-based patterns. We have used JHotDraw as an example because it is well-engineered, flexible, and uses patterns strictly "by the book". Other well-engineered frameworks may serve just as well to convey these pedagogical points. However, JHotDraw has the advantage of being visual and, therefore, some patterns, like composite, adapter, decorator and observer can directly visible "in action".

Our experience with this approach is generally positive. It is clear at the exams that students have understood the role aspect of patterns. However, the framework is not very well-documented and its complexity thus introduces a steep learning curve. For short courses it would be interesting to identify smaller frameworks with less steep learning curves that still illustrate the pedagogical points identified.

6   Summary

We have presented two concrete frameworks, Presenter and JHotDraw, and discussed their role in a teaching context. Presenter is used in introductory teaching to introduce basic framework concepts and as a stepping stone to learn about Java GUI frameworks. JHotDraw is used in advanced programming courses to study and to illustrate the interplay between design patterns, frameworks and delegation-based designs.

The topic of frameworks is an addition to an already long list of topics to address in introductory and advanced programming courses, and obviously having it in a course means other topics must be skipped or addressed to a lesser extent. In our opinion, however, frameworks should have a stronger role in teaching curriculums. First of all, they represent a successful approach to software reuse and are already in widespread use in industry. Thus, there is certainly a need for a solid introduction to the concepts and techniques in teaching. Second, frameworks represent a good opportunity to reinforce learning of design patterns and delegation-based designs, and to gain a deeper insight into the nature of patterns. The teaching thus naturally forms a spiral approach.

It is our hope that the presented frameworks and the presented experiences with them in teaching will contribute to make the topic of frameworks more common in programming courses.

Part IV

Assessment

Introduction to Part IV
Assessment

The last section of this book is concerned with another difficult element of programming teaching at educational institutions, that of assessment.

Assessing programming-related courses has always been difficult. The difficulties are caused by a wide variety of reasons because some are intrinsic to the subject and some are caused by aspects of the course.

One of the common difficulties is that typical exam forms —written or oral exams— are necessarily far removed from actual, realistic programming situations, and thus, they test quite a different set of skills than those defined in the intended learning outcomes of our courses. Other problems are caused by scale. Programming courses often have a large number of students, and testing them accurately and fairly with an acceptable work load for examiners is not easy.

However, the issue is wider than just determining a mark. Aspects such as providing feedback and motivating students throughout the course are closely related.

In this section, we present two chapters. The first one takes a wide view, not only covering assessment itself, but a whole range of related issues. It describes in detail two related courses for teaching data structures and algorithms. The courses are carefully designed to address a whole range of motivation and assessment issues. A central aspect of this design is to make students more active with all the positive effects that flow from this if it succeeds. It also addresses, at the same time, the issue of managing a very large course (more than 500 students), providing feedback to such a number of students, and dealing with inhomogeneous groups of students (computer science majors and non-majors). Readers may find inspiration here for a range of different areas of course design.

The second chapter in this section is concerned more specifically with assessing programming skills in a manner that is simultaneously realistic, fine-grained and fair. A common problem in designing these assessments is that programming, in its true form, is an activity typically undertaken in teams with various resources at hand over a significant period of time. Examinations, on the other hand, are often done in a very short span of time (a few hours) by individuals without access to outside resources. Thus, the question of whether such an exam really tests the skills that students need to have for programming activities seems justified.

This chapter describes an examination form that combines programming projects and oral exams. As a result, it achieves many of the benefits of either form of its own, while avoiding many of the problems. Especially, it provides a reasonable and realistic programming context while still achieving fine-grained, individual assessment with acceptable cost effectiveness.

For all teachers whose teaching includes assessment, the material in these two final chapters may spark some useful ideas that could help to improve their own courses.

Michael Kölling

J. Bennedsen et al. (Eds.): Teaching of Programming, LNCS 4821, p. 209, 2008.
© Springer-Verlag Berlin Heidelberg 2008

Active Learning and Examination Methods in a Data Structures and Algorithms Course

Lauri Malmi and Ari Korhonen

Department of Computer Science and Engineering
Helsinki University of Technology, Finland
{lma,archie}@cs.hut.fi

Abstract. In this chapter, the implementation of two courses on data structures and algorithms at the Helsinki University of Technology is presented. The courses are based on the constructivist learning paradigm in which the students participate actively and feedback is provided on their performance despite the very large number of enrolled students each year. Moreover, an Internet-based learning environment is an integral part of the larger course because it provides an opportunity to apply active learning methods. Examples of the active learning methods are algorithm simulations exercises and analysis of algorithms for small-scale problems. In addition, students design algorithms and solutions for non-trivial practical applications. Moreover, in the more advanced course they carry out a small-scale research project to determine the empirical efficiency of given algorithms and the corresponding data structures.

1 Introduction

Data structures and algorithms are core disciplines in computer science. Knowledge about their properties, efficiency and applicability to different practical cases is needed in all software projects. Therefore, one or more courses in this field are an integral part of any computer science curriculum.

In this chapter, we describe how the education of data structures and algorithms has been organized at the Helsinki University of Technology (HUT). In many universities, Computer Science (CS) education starts with a basic programming course followed by another programming course dealing with data structures and algorithms. In our case, however, the first programming course (CS1) taught in Java is followed by the Data Structures and Algorithms course (DSA) that is not programming oriented, but operates more on conceptual and analytical levels. However, the implementation of algorithms is carried out in several different exercises in subsequent intermediate and advanced programming courses. Especially, we have a special project course (Laboratory Course in Software Technology, LST) where the focus is on empirical performance evaluation of algorithms and data structures. Thus, algorithms and data structures are in focus on both of these two consecutive courses DSA and LST. DSA is intended both for CS major and CS minor students while LST is for CS majors

J. Bennedsen et al. (Eds.): Teaching of Programming, LNCS 4821, pp. 210–227, 2008.

only. About 600 students are enrolled yearly in DSA, and some 150 of them are CS majors that have the option to take LST as well.

In order to cope with such a large number of students, we have developed several tools and solutions that aid us to make the students active and to provide feedback to them. First, telematic tools are heavily used in communication with and among the students [Korhonen and Malmi, 2002]. Second, we have designed and implemented a dedicated software system called TRAKLA2 for supporting interactive learning in a visual environment and providing automatic feedback on individually tailored exercises [Malmi et al., 2004]. Third, several different working methods are used to make the students more active including open and closed labs, team work, design projects, experimental projects and writing a scientific article. In addition, students are encouraged to give feedback to each other in terms of peer reviewing, which is also an important exercise on argumentation skills. We argue that such active learning methods lead to very good learning results as well as positive feedback from the students.

This chapter is structured as follows. First, we introduce the background and present the organization of the courses at HUT as well as the learning goals. Second, we discuss the didactic principles involved in designing the courses and the role of different working methods in the whole. Third, we present the learning environment tailored to the course. Finally, we discuss the observations made, and challenges we anticipate to meet in the future.

2   Background

The Helsinki University of Technology is the largest technical university in Finland, with some 1300 new students enrolling each year. About 150 of these are enrolled in the degree programs of Computer Science and Engineering. However, several other degree programs (Telecommunications technology, Information networks and Geomatics) have included a considerable number of CS courses in their syllabus. Moreover, for most of the other engineering curricula, at least one programming course is compulsory, but many students voluntarily take more CS courses. As a result, each year about 1000 students enroll in the Introductory Programming course and about 500 to 600 on the Data Structures and Algorithms course. Thus, even though not all of the students in the other engineering curricula take Data Structures and Algorithms, a considerably large number of students do. The Introductory Programming course (5 ECTS credits) is taught in Java, and gives only a brief introduction to data structures and algorithms by introducing the Java Collection framework.

The next course is Data structures and Algorithms (5 ECTS credits) followed by intermediate and advanced programming courses. Data Structures and Algorithms are studied further in the course on Design and Analysis of Algorithms (5 ECTS credits) as well as on the Laboratory Course in Software Technology comprising of an experimental project (3-8 ECTS credits). Thereafter, there are some advanced courses directed to those CS majors that orientate themselves to Software systems or Theoretical computer science.

In this chapter, we consider only the basic Data Structures and Algorithms course (denoted by DSA) and the subsequent Laboratory Course in Software Technology (LST). DSA is compulsory for both CS minors and CS majors. LST, however, is meant for CS majors only, but not all CS majors take it. Basically, it is directed to the students who are specializing in Software Technology.

2.1   Didactic Overview

The didactic design of the courses is a result of active development of the courses since the early 1990s. In their current form, there are many connections with constructivist learning theory [Phillips, 2000]. The following issues are considered very important. The themes are revised in the courses from the different perspectives.

Topic coverage. DSA gives students a broad overview of the field covering topics such as basic data structures, priority queues, sorting algorithms, search trees, hashing methods, and graph algorithms. The course discusses the topics at a *conceptual level* instead of implementation level (i.e., the focus is on the principles of the working of algorithms instead on their implementation in a programming language). Such an approach has also been proposed by [Aharoni, 2000]. All the exercises perform at this level as well. Exercises in which the students must implement something are left purposefully to the LST course, or to the subsequent intermediate programming courses. This is due to the fact that it is the only way we can cover deeply enough such a broad range of topics in DSA [Hyvönen and Malmi, 1993].

Algorithm analysis. The students must understand the principles of algorithm analysis and, very importantly, the limitations of the formal algorithm analysis that affects the interpretation of the analytical results. DSA introduces these topics for both CS majors and CS minors. CS minors, however, concentrate more on understanding the analytical notation and following the derivations of the results, whereas CS majors solve practical exercises to perform the actual analysis, as well.

Design skills. The students should be able to apply their acquired knowledge to design solutions to realistic problems by combining or modifying the basic algorithms they have learned. Learning a set of basic algorithms is not enough, however. In addition, they must be able to analyze their solutions analytically (DSA) as well as empirically (LST). It is crucial to understand that many problems can be solved by combining basic algorithms or by modifying them to better suit the situation. Thus, they must apply their knowledge to design solutions to new and non-trivial problems.

Argumentation. Students should understand and be able to argue how various algorithms apply to different types of problems and applications. In essence, this means that they must also understand the limitations of analytical results and what kind of effects data ordering and storage structures have on the performance of an algorithm. For example, they should be able to argue why basic hashing methods are efficient in static applications where the key set does not change, whereas there may be performance problems in very dynamic applications. Or they should give arguments why range queries fit well for search trees, but not for hashing methods. Finally, they must be able to analyze their own design and to argue its pros and cons.

Reporting. LST for CS majors teaches how to analyze performance issues in terms of experimental methods. This requires that they must exercise research on some specific topic covered in the course. In addition, they should learn to present the results in a scientific way. Moreover, in DSA, the CS minors do a project during which they write a report describing a solution for a realistic design problem.

Active learning methods and collaboration. Both courses are based on the idea of making students busy during the whole course. This means that they must exercise the new issues just learned. Collaboration is also considered important and, for example, peer reviewing is used to construct new ideas and to exercise critical thinking among students. Moreover, feedback and guidance is given in all phases to keep this process going, and the learning environment is designed to support these goals whenever possible.

3   Implementation of Courses

In this section, we present the implementation of the courses for achieving the goals presented in the previous section. Most of the text concerns DSA since this is the cornerstone of the whole syllabus. LST broadens out the topic by teaching the empirical evaluation of the data structures and algorithms as well as some working methods that are regularly used in research.

3.1   DSA

DSA applies several different teaching and working methods, which are discussed here separately. Basically the course can be divided into three concurrent activities that support each other: lectures, exercises done individually, and a team project that is done in collaboration. These activities are supported by providing course support material not only in terms of text book, but from several other sources, as well. Moreover, all the activities including the final examination have their role to play in course grading in order to motivate students to study throughout the course. The timeline for the course is represented in Table 1.

Lectures are used to give an overview of the contents of the course, to introduce the key concepts and their relations, and to explain important and difficult topics. Each major topic such as principles of algorithm analysis, basic data structures, priority queues, sorting algorithms, search trees, hashing methods

Table 1. Timeline for the DSA course. There are 13 weeks lectures and the course ends at the final examination in week 15. There are two kinds of home exercises: TRAKLA2 exercises (denoted by $T_1 \leq i \leq 5$) and analytical exercises ($A_1 \leq i \leq 7$). These must be submitted mainly biweekly. The subindex i denotes the session number. The design project is divided in four phases: specification, design phase, peer review and revision.

Week	1	2	3	4	5	6	7	8	9	10	11	12	13	14	15
Lectures															Exam
Exercises	A_1	A_2	T_1	A_3	T_2			A_4	T_3	A_5	T_4	A_6	T_5	A_7	
Design project			Specification					Design phase			Peer review		Revision		

and graph algorithms are discussed in a couple of lectures. Moreover, many problems are discussed during the lectures by pointing out some obvious applications of various algorithms in order to raise the motivation and attention of the students. However, lectures do not cover the whole course syllabus in detail. Some subtopics are purposefully left for self study. In many lessons, we utilize a technique that we call *lecture exercises*. In these exercises, the teacher first explains the basic idea of an algorithm by drawing a conceptual diagram on the blackboard or utilizing a visualization tool. Thereafter, the students are given a simple problem, in which they have to apply the algorithm to a new data set. They solve the problem on pen and paper either alone or in small groups. After this, the lecturer explains the answer and discusses it with the students if necessary. By immediately exercising the topic, the students are supposed to be more active and to learn the basic idea better than just listening to the lecture. These exercises, however, are voluntary and have no effect on course grade.

Moreover, students have access to a printed lecture summary prepared by the instructor. Thus, they can easily take notes during the lectures without writing everything down. In addition, text books are used as a supplementary material that covers the details more thoroughly than the lecture summary.

3.2   Algorithm Simulation Exercises

The cornerstones of the DSA course are the visual algorithm simulation exercises in which students simulate the working of the algorithms covered in the course. By simulation we mean that they must show —in terms of conceptual diagrams— how the algorithm changes given initial data structures during its execution. These exercises are part of the compulsory exercises done individually.

A typical exercise would be: *Insert the following keys in this order into an initially empty AVL tree: H A F K U Z V D L M. Draw the tree after each insertion*". In practice, these exercises are fully computerized so that students can change the contents (i.e., keys and references) of data structures visualized on the screen by drag-and-drop operations supported by the TRAKLA2 environment [Korhonen et al., 2003]. Thus, in the rest of the chapter, we refer such algorithm simulation exercises as *TRAKLA2 exercises*. An example exercise is seen in Figure 1. The student should drag and drop the keys from the array into the appropriate positions in the red-black tree and perform rotations when needed.

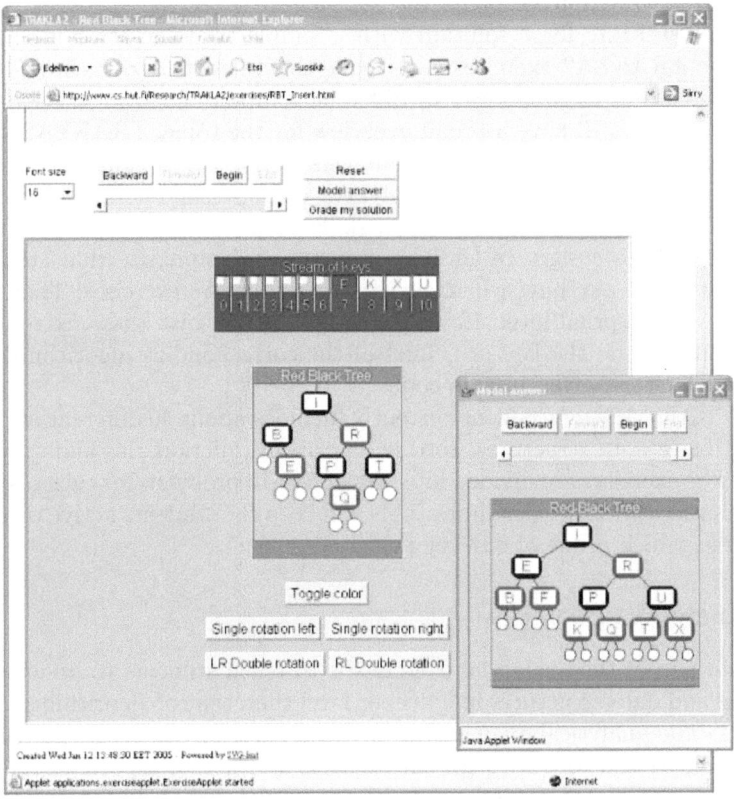

Fig. 1. TRAKLA2 applet. The exercise window comprises the data structures and push buttons. The model solution window is open in the front.

Most exercises have also pseudo code of the algorithm attached, which allows students to consider the code when solving the exercise. Such code is also helpful in identifying the version of the algorithm that should be simulated, e.g., whether the pivot in the basic Quicksort algorithm is taken from the left or the right end of the array.

Each student is given the same exercise, but a unique initial data structure to work with. The sequence of performed operations is recorded and the submitted answer is assessed automatically by comparing it to the model sequence generated by a real implemented algorithm. The student receives immediate feedback on his/her solution that indicates the number of correct steps out of the maximum number of steps compared with the model solution. In addition, they can review the model solution that is represented as an algorithm animation in order to ponder why they did not get full points. Moreover, they are allowed to solve the exercise again and to resubmit a solution. However, each time they reset an exercise they get a new instance of it with a new initial data set. In general, the number of resubmissions can be unlimited because they cannot continue with the same data set. Furthermore, the solution space of the exercises is far too large to allow brute force solution with a simple trial-and-error method. The aim of the TRAKLA2 exercises is to make the students active throughout the course to study a large number of different solutions for computational problems. Thus, they will have a broad overview for the topic. TRAKLA2 exercises include algorithm analysis as well, but this is not the primary function. The other course activities —such as analytical exercises and course project— are supposed to cover the more high level skills such as proficiency in argumentation and software design. In addition, we need to emphasize that students do not need to code anything when solving the simulation exercises. They operate purely at a conceptual level. However, to be able to solve these exercises, they have to understand the key principles of the corresponding algorithms, and be able to understand given pseudo codes.

The TRAKLA2 environment currently includes about 40 different assignment covering basic data structures, sorting algorithms, dictionaries and graph algorithms. The exercises are divided into sets of 5 to 10 problems for each session and are emphasized by strict deadlines. This will keep the students active throughout the course, which is one of our key principles.

3.3   Analytical Exercises

The main aim of the analytical exercises is to teach students to understand algorithms and data structures in a deeper level than that of algorithm simulation exercises. The analytical exercises are written exercises that ask the student to solve problems and to work with the analysis and design aspects of the course. The topics include, for example, algorithm analysis (e.g., big-oh notation), writing simple new algorithms and applications (e.g., heap to heapsort).

As with most of the other courses with a practical component, the analytical exercises are compulsory, but only for CS majors. CS minors are encouraged to do these exercises in small groups, but these have no effect to the overall course grade. For CS majors, typically around 40% of the maximum points are required to pass the exercises. Also, the students want the exercises to be like this, even though failure to obtain a satisfactory grade causes one to fail the whole course. In the feedback questionnaire at the end of the course, hardly any student desires the exercises to be voluntary. It should be noted, however, that about 15% of the students do not respond to this questionnaire since they have dropped the course earlier. Unfortunately, we do not have any statistics that cover also the opinion of this minority.

Analytical exercises are individual assignments and must be submitted in hard copy weekly or biweekly. They can be submitted in a classroom session, in which the model solutions are presented by the peers. Several different methods have been applied, but the basic principle is to make the whole student group actively participate in the session. Typically, in the beginning of the session, the students indicate the exercises they have solved. The number of solved exercises has an influence on the course grade. The teaching assistant will randomly choose a student to present his solution. However, such methods in which the teaching assistant directly presents the model solutions and the students passively follow or copy the correct answers are deliberately avoided. This latter method is only applied in advanced exercises that are beyond the course syllabus, but deserve to be demonstrated for the students.

In most of the assignments, the student is asked to construct and to analyze the data structures and algorithms that the course covers. The construction is done by using written explanations and pseudo code. There are no programming exercises. We want to direct students to work more on the design and analytical aspects of the topic rather than struggling with implementation details. This is due to the fact that the course extent is only 5 ECTS credits. Even a very small programming exercise typically requires too much overhead for the student (setting up a programming environment, writing main program, creating test cases, and so on) so that they actually concentrate more on unimportant details instead of the algorithm itself. That kind of activity is better suited in the syllabus of other courses.

As a whole, the analytical exercises practice the design as well as argumentation skills of students. The argumentation skills are rehearsed both in written form and orally because (some) students need to present their solution orally and the others should follow the presentation and assistant's comments on the solution.

3.4   Design Project

DSA for the CS minors includes a compulsory design project. For the CS majors, it is voluntary. In this project, students have to design a solution (though not implement it) for a realistic non-trivial problem in groups of 2 to 3 persons. In this task, they have to apply their knowledge about basic algorithms to solve a new problem by combining or modifying the existing algorithms. In addition, they have to analyze their solution and state its pros and cons. The problems have been set up so that no obvious solution is available. Instead, the students have to identify possible tradeoffs caused by contradictory requirements. Some example problems used in the project include designing a web search engine, or a public traffic information system capable of answering queries such as, "Give me the buses I should take to get from position A to B as fast as possible in Helsinki metropolitan area at 2 PM".

The design project has the following phases:

Specification. Students have to refine the purposefully loosely specified problem, and to sketch the key components of the solution. The course staff reviews the reports to identify groups that are likely to get into difficulties, for example, due to misunderstandings in the specification.

Design phase. This is the most important phase where students design the principles of a working solution, write a description of it, analyze its performance and give arguments of the pros and cons of their solution. All this is written into a single document.

Peer review. An essential part of the work of a designer is to present one's ideas in a clear and understandable form. To support this, the student groups review the works of 3 to 5 other groups. Thus, each group gives feedback on several other solutions, and correspondingly receives feedback on their work from several other groups. The review reports are assessed by course staff to guarantee that the feedback level is appropriate (even though correctness of the feedback is not assessed).

Technically, peer reviewing has been implemented in a number of different ways during the past years. For example, students have submitted their reports as web pages that have been processed with scripts to send them to appropriate review groups, or everything has been carried out in a course management system. The chosen method has not affected the learning goal of this phase.

Revision. After receiving the feedback, the students can revise their solution and submit it to the final evaluation that is performed by the course staff. The design project has the following advantages. First, the students get a broader view for the problem domain after they have seen the solutions of their peers. Second, they realize the difficulty of expressing thoughts in written form and how important it is. This is due to the peer reviewing process in which they have to read the solutions from other groups as well as try to express their own design. Thus, they have to carefully investigate whether the proposed solutions work or not (i.e., they have to exercise critical thinking and evaluation).

It is obvious that the method requires some collaboration and design skills. However, the assignment is designed so that a single data structure or algorithm is not sufficient to solve the problem. Thus, the group has to combine several topics to come up with a feasible solution. For instance, the public traffic information system example requires that the group applies at least one search structure to map the street addresses to nodes in the traffic network as well as graph algorithms to find out the shortest path. However, it is up to the group to argue which specific data structures and algorithms to apply. Thus, also argumentation and reporting skills are practiced. The hardest part seems to be the analysis of the solution. Only very few groups are capable of analyzing their own solution properly.

3.5 Final Examination

The final examination (a written examination at the end of the course) requires synthesis of the different parts of the course content similar to the design project. Typically a final examination comprises 4 to 5 separate problems or exercises. These kind of assignments could be "Compare the given sorting algorithms" (based on some criteria) or "Analyze the pros and cons of the Quicksort algorithm". However, one or two simulation exercises are included as well in order to encourage to solving the TRAKLA2 exercises. In addition, we have questions concerning terminology, definitions and mathematical analysis of data structures and algorithms.

3.6   Three Different Perspectives to the Course Material

There are a lot of books on the subject, but none of them are required in the course. However, getting access to some text book is recommended for students in order to have this first point of view to the overall topic. There is a list of books and chapters to read while solving the exercises and preparing to the examination. All of the books cover most of the broad topic, however, none of the books cover all of the details. Thus, typically, one book is sufficient, but some additional material is necessary. Actually, we want to encourage the students to actively seek for information, but still to be selective. Lectures do not follow any particular textbook. Thus, the lectures and the material covered in lectures give the second point of view to the topic. This material includes lecture notes, assignments solved and discussed during lectures as well as, for example, the newsgroup discussions and additional material delivered through the course home page. This material gives an emphasis to the subtopics that are most relevant according to the lecturer.

The third point of view that stresses only the focal points in this course is given by the exercises and assignments. A lot of material is involved with these practical components. The TRAKLA2 environment, for example, includes an electronic text book covering the same topics as the lecture notes. The exercises are linked to this supplementary material. However, the world wide web is today an inexhaustible source of information that the students employ while solving the exercises, thus, making it very hard to exactly define the scope of the course material. Of course, we must pay extra attention to this in order to provide exercises that really necessitate learning in each situation. For example, exercises that are easy to solve simply by copying the answer from the web or peers are not that suitable for homework exercises, but can be applied, for example, in lectures as a supplementary material. Thus, while making students busy, we must take care to ensure that the activity is meaningful.

3.7   Grading

The main point in grading is that all activities in the course have some effect on the final course grade, and thus, encouraging students to do all parts well. The grading scheme has varied during the years, but typically each subpart of the course is given a separate grade (0 - 5) where 0 means failed and 5 is the best grade. A typical example of the rule for calculating the final grade is that algorithm simulation exercises weigh 30%, analytical exercises or design project weigh 30% and the final examination 40% of the final grade.

The grade of the simulation exercises is related directly to the number of points achieved (i.e. with less than 50% one fails, 50-60% gives grade 1, 60-70% grade 2, etc). Thus, 90% out of maximum is required for the highest grade (5) of the exercises. However, typically as much as half of the students achieve the best grade, and about 2/3 of them achieve at least grade 4. The reason for this is that the automatic assessment system allows students to resubmit their answers to get better points. Since the grading policy is encouraging (the weight of these exercises is up to 30%), most students heavily apply this feature.

In analytical exercises, the points received and the grade has a similar mapping to that with simulation exercises. However, the typical points received from these exercises are far away from those with simulation exercises. This is also true with the final examination, and thus, the overall course grades are not as good as the simulation exercises would imply. Thus, we can see the final examination to be only a small part of the overall "examination" of the course that comprises not only this, but also the other practical components on the course. In addition, students cannot rely on the "last night's wonder" by preparing only for the final examination. Instead, they have to work all the time during the course.

3.8   LST

The Laboratory Course of Software Technology is a separate course to acquire practical experience in addition to the more theoretical courses. In this course, the student groups (2 to 3 persons) carry out a small-scale experimental research project, during which they compare the performance of a number of algorithms solving the same problem. For example, they compare the efficiency of various sorting algorithms, dictionaries or priority queues. Most topics also include such algorithms and data structures that are not discussed in DSA. It is also possible to choose a topic in which the performances of other things, such as database systems, or programming languages are evaluated. However, most students prefer algorithmic assignments.

From a didactic point of view, this experimental project course has two aims. First, the students learn more thoroughly a number of algorithms as they really need to implement them and to observe their behavior with different input data sets. Second, they learn about scientific working methods due to the experimental research setup. In addition, they learn how to report such an experiment in a scientific paper. Finally, the experimental work introduces them to the difficulties and pitfalls of experimental algorithm analysis under the proper guidance of the teacher already in their second or third year studies.

The course is divided into several phases following a strict schedule, and the results of the phases are reported when writing an article step by step. The timeline for the LST course is represented in Table 2. Each phase is discussed more thoroughly below.

Literature survey. Students start the project by carrying out a literature survey on their topic. This means finding out a set of references that include the descriptions of any analytical and possibly experimental results (if available) about the algorithms at hand. If the topic is non-algorithmic, they look for corresponding information, for example, about benchmark results of database systems. Typically, some initial sources of information such as textbook chapters, are given within the topic, but the students should find more references. They are encouraged to look for initial scientific papers for the topic. This phase requires providing hints and guidelines for them, since at this phase of their studies their skills are often limited to using only textbooks and Internet search engines. They should be guided to use, for example, ACM Digital library or IEEE Xplore. As

Table 2. Timeline for the LST course. There are 4 lectures, which are lectured at the very beginning of the course within the first 4 weeks. The project starts with literature survey and test plans that are reported in weeks 6 and 7, respectively. The test plan can be revised based on the feedback, but it is not reviewed anymore as such. After planning, the project group implements the algorithms and data structures to be analyzed and runs the planned tests. The report is filled in on the results and the first submission is made. This version is peer reviewed before the final submission. The best reports are selected to be presented in the conference at the very end of the course.

Week	1	2	3	4	5	6	7	8	9	10	11	12	13	14
Lectures	x	x	x	x										
Liter. survey			x	x	x	x								
Test plan			x	x	x	x	x							
Implementation							x	x	x					
Analysis & report								x	x	x		x		
Peer review											x			
Conference														x

a report of their work they write an introduction to the article describing the research problem and a summary of findings in relevant literature (1 to 2 pages in total). The report must be written using the LATEX system because it is a very important tool used in writing scientific papers, and students should learn about it.

Test plan. In the next phase, the students prepare a test plan for their research. This includes analysing the research problem as follows: what are their goals while comparing the performance of the algorithms and systems experimentally. They need to identify what kind of input data they will be using. Will they use data from real world case examples or should they define an input data model with a number of parameters and factors? In addition, they need to give arguments for their decisions, to define the values for the parameters and to define the tests in details. This means that for each test they must define what will be the values of parameters and what factors will they use or what kind of available real data they plan to use. Moreover, they should present initial assumptions or hypotheses about the results they could get based on their literature study. It is quite possible that they need to perform some initial tests to reduce the parameter space and correspondingly the number of tests to be carried out. A typical example of such work is experimenting whether to use a recursive or a non-recursive version of an algorithm (i.e., to determine if there are significant differences in the performances).

There are two other important parts of the test plan that need to be defined, as well. First, they must select the test environment (computer, operating system, programming language, use of possible libraries, compiler versions, etc.). In some topics, they need to run the tests on two or more computer systems. Second, they must define, how the results will be evaluated statistically, and what kind of criteria for gaining statistical reliability is needed. This is a challenge, too, since in a typical computer system, the distribution of the run times of test runs with equal initial data is not normally distributed.

Finally, the test plan is written as the second section of the article. The plan is evaluated and criticized by the teacher after which the students may refine it.

Implementation. The third phase in the project is implementation. All algorithms, input data generators, result handling, etc. are implemented. Or correspondingly, for example, database systems are installed and tuned for the tests. They test the programs and carry out the experiments. To gain enough statistical reliability, the tests typically have to be repeated many times. As the number of separate tests is typically counted in tens or even hundreds, this phase requires considerably time such as even several days of cpu time.

Analyzing and writing results. After the test results are available, the group writes a separate results section in their article, or fulfills the test plan with the results. They must present the results in numbers or using appropriate graphs and tables. Moreover, they need to include discussion about the reliability of results, and how well they correspond to the analytical results from the literature or their initial hypotheses. It is very typical in this phase that they encounter anomalies between their results and expectations. In actual research, such anomalies should be explained, but in the course most groups have difficulties here. The course does not, however, require that all anomalies need to be explained in details since this could mean a whole set of extra tests to understand the phenomenon more profoundly. Such work would be out of scope of the course, and could require excessive work. The more important factor is that they recognize such anomalies, and thus, learn about the challenges of experimental research work.

At the end of this phase, the students need to finalize the article by writing the abstract and summary. If needed, they can restructure their paper to make it more coherent. This paper, typically 10 to 15 pages long, is submitted to the course staff.

Peer review. To simulate the scientific process of submitting and publishing papers, the course proceeds into a peer review phase. Each group will review two papers prepared by other groups in the course. One of these is about the same topic that the group has had itself (if possible), and the other one is about some other topic. The course staff provides guidelines for the peer review that resembles typical review guidelines of a conference or journal article.

Each group submits their feedback to the initial authors of the papers, as well as to the course staff. The staff checks the feedback so that it is written in an appropriate style and level. The correctness of the feedback, however, is not evaluated. Finally, each group can use the feedback to revise their paper and to prepare a final version of their paper to the course staff for grading.

Conference. In the final phase the course staff acts as a program committee so that each paper will be evaluated by two staff members. The best 4 to 6 papers will be selected to be presented in the course final conference, which is open for other staff members and students as well. The presentations simulate an ordinary scientific conference session. The teacher in charge acts as a chair for the session, and each paper has 20 minutes for presentation and 5 minutes for discussion. The papers accepted for the conference receive a bonus in their course grade. In addition, the best papers are published as on-line proceedings in the web.

Final notes. The aim is that the students closely simulate the actual process of preparing a scientific paper. In addition, they face the challenges of experimental research. This experience fits well in their second or third year studies. They get to know what real research could be.

From the point of view of learning data structures and algorithms, the course promotes learning on the topic in two important ways. First, implementing a set of algorithms deepens the understanding of their working in details. Second, the students learn that the analytical results available in text books do not necessarily say enough about the actual performance of algorithms. Analytical results mostly deal with worst case behaviour, whereas experimental research gives light to what happens with small and medium case data sets. In many cases, the students also encounter the effect of hierarchical memories (caches and TLBs) on the performance of algorithms.

Finally, as in the DSA course, each important part of the course has an effect on the final course grade: literature study (15%), test plan (15%), peer review (10%) and the final report (60%). In addition, a 10% bonus is given to the groups chosen for the course conference.

4   Discussion

The courses described in this chapter have been organized so that the learning process of the students proceeds in phases. Lectures provide the motivation and the orientation basis for the course contents. Key topics are also discussed and exercised in them. In the practical exercises, the students have to apply information of all basic algorithms more thoroughly. After learning them they can apply the algorithms and data structures as tools for solving more advanced design problems or analytical exercises. In addition, they have to practice analysis and argumentation, which is an important skill. In the LST course, this process is continued with a true exercise in scientific work. Thus, as in the constructivist learning paradigm, we consider it essential that the students are active in their learning process. The key role of the teacher is to set up the assignments and to provide guidance and feedback for the students.

4.1   DSA and Bloom's Taxonomy

Bloom's taxonomy [Bloom, 1956] gives an interesting perspective to the DSA course design. If we consider the course objectives and implementations, we observe that both CS minors and CS majors cover all six levels in the taxonomy, but with different emphasis. For both of them, it is essential to learn the general terminology of programming, data structures and algorithms, as well as understand the meaning of the concepts (levels 1-2). The CS minors probably do not need to implement many algorithms in their future work, but are more likely to apply library routines (level 3). However, they have to be able to discuss with software professionals, to understand design documents, and to consider various options to implement programs. The experience gained in the design exercise supports achieving this goal. The CS minors have to apply their knowledge on the pseudo code and graphical design level, to analyse and to evaluate their own as well as others' designs, and thus also cover issues at levels 4-6.

CS majors, on the other hand, apply their knowledge more at a theoretical level. The written exercises in DSA cover Bloom levels 3-5. CS majors do implementation exercises (level 3) in subsequent programming courses and/or in LST course. In addition, they are pushed to study the working of an algorithm deeper when they design their experiments, make hypothesis on the expected results, and try to explain the observed anomalies as well as make the mapping with the theoretical results (covering Bloom levels 4-6). Thus, they achieve considerably deeper understanding on the properties of the algorithms compared with the CS minors.

4.2   Grading Policy Effect in DSA

We made a longitudinal study on the exercise results of years 1993-2004 [Malmi et al., 2005, Malmi et al., 2002], during which two different systems, TRAKLA [Korhonen and Malmi, 2000] (1993-2003) and TRAKLA2 (2003-) were used. A number of new features were added to the tools during these years. Moreover, the grading and resubmission policies of the course changed several times. The effects of the changes can be seen in Figures 2 and 3. The students are divided into the following four categories:

Failed. Students that achieved less than 50% of the maximum points and failed the exercise part.

Passed. Students that received at least 50%, but less than (a) 80% or (b) 90% of the maximum points and passed the exercises.

Max grade. Students that received at least (a) 80% or (b) 90% of the maximum points and received the maximum grade for the exercises.

Full points. Students that solved all the exercises correctly.

The figure is split into two parts due to the grading policy that was different in (2) 1993-1997 from that used in (3) 1998-2004. Thus, the two last categories are slightly different as well. Until 1997, the final examination determined the final grade. In the third and fourth category, however, one received +1 for the final grade except in the case when the student failed (grade 0) or already achieved the best grade 5. After 1998, however, the grading policy was changed and the simulation exercises accounted for 30%, the analytical exercises 30%, and the examination 40% for the final course grade. The simulation exercises were graded as follows: 50-60% of the exercise points corresponded to grade 1, 60-70% to grade 2, etc. Thus, at least 90% of the maximum points were required for the best grade, which is 5. This change in grading policy caused a tremendous improvement in the exercise results. A completely new, but still considerably large group of students appeared. This consisted of those who received full points from all of the exercises. In 2004, we fully adopted TRAKLA2, which allowed an unlimited number of resubmissions, but each one with different new initial data. Then, 30% of the students achieved 100% of the exercise points, even though 90% was enough for the highest grade. We do not have, at the moment, a clear understanding of this somewhat surprising phenomenon, but that the system itself encourages students to aim to get all exercises correctly solved.

The TRAKLA2 environment has become exceedingly valuable for us. As the results in Figures imply, most students get a fair or good understanding of the basic algorithms when solving the simulation exercises. Since all exercises are checked automatically, we can direct the human teacher resources to guiding and to assessing the more demanding analytic and design exercises. Since the assignments are personal, and thus no plagiarism is possible, we do not actually

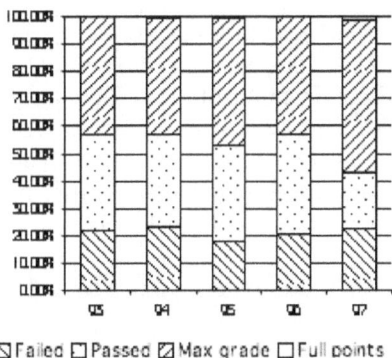

Fig. 2. Distribution of exercise grades in years 1993-1997

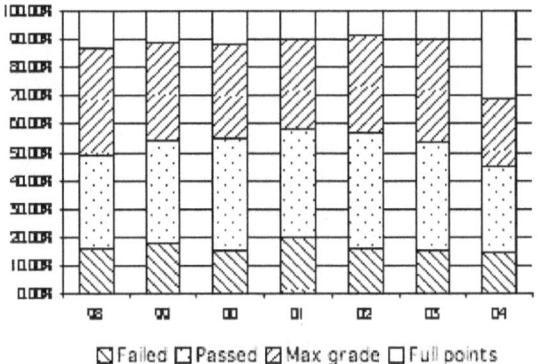

Fig. 3. Distribution of exercise grades in years 1998-2004

need to check this level of knowledge very much in the final examination either. Of course, it is possible that some students fail to learn the topics since someone else is solving the exercises for him/her. To our experience this happens rarely, and these students face the obvious difficulties of passing the more advanced exercises and the final examination.

There is, however, one problem that we are aware of. For some algorithms, especially for the graph algorithms, the conceptual level diagram manipulation seems to be at too high of an abstraction level and the connection to the implementation level code remains somewhat obscure for many students. Our goal, therefore, is to create new kinds of exercises where this connection becomes more obvious. Programming one or two of the algorithms would be a good solution, but has the problem of being quite laborious. Using some code visualization tool could achieve the same goal with less work from the students. The current simple solution is to include pseudo code of each algorithm on the exercise page so that students can study it during their solution process.

4.3 Collaboration between Students

Today, many courses have a collaboration policy in which the objective is to maximize the learning experience, in other words, the gain in knowledge and the problem solving skills. This same issue is addressed also in the next chapter of this book, but from a different point of view. The problem is plagiarism, which can efficiently ruin the learning experience. Obviously, one cannot learn by copying someone else's solutions. On the other hand, forbidding discussion of course material may deprive the opportunity to learn from peers. Thus, the dividing line between these two extremes needs to be defined in terms of collaboration policy.

We encourage comparing notes on exercises with fellow students to the extent that it leads to a better understanding of the problem and the solution. The collaboration can extend to discussion and problem solving, but not to any submissions. However, we also encourage students to spend a substantial amount of time to do the exercises by themselves. The decisive question is whether the student can learn more or less by working together or alone.

Certain assignments require different kinds of guidance in this respect. Programming exercises typically require strict restrictions on collaboration as they are very easy to copy from a peer. On the other hand, the individually tailored exercises in TRAKLA2 system, for example, seem to motivate the students to have a meaningful collaboration. The students can freely discuss any solutions, but finally, each student has to submit his or her own answer. Working in small groups also seems to reduce the number of plagiarism cases, as we have not encountered plagiarism in the design exercise. We have not researched this positive behavior in detail. However, we suppose that there are several reasons behind this.

First, in a group students can tackle the difficulties together and support each other, whereas in a time pressure a lonely student is much more likely to end up into a dead end, where he/she sees no other solution than getting a ready solution from somewhere. In addition, design tasks are open assignments where there is no single correct answer, which is more often the case with closed assignments, such as in simple mathematical calculus, for example. With open tasks, getting caught for plagiarism is much more probable since by default, designs differ from each other. Whereas, in closed tasks it is expectable that many students could end up in similar solutions. Finally, making a decision to cheat jointly in a group is much harder than making it alone. We, therefore, believe that the plagiarism problem can be solved, at least partially, by paying attention to the teaching methods and the character of tasks. However, preventing plagiarism totally is intrinsically an impossible task for an instructor, because forcing students to solve all assignments in a controlled environment is not meaningful in practice. Therefore, the only way to really prevent plagiarism is to motivate the students —in some way or the other— to take the responsibility of their own learning.

Mini Project Programming Exams

Kurt Nørmark, Lone Leth Thomsen, and Kristian Torp

Department of Computer Science, Aalborg University, Denmark
{normark,lone,torp}@cs.aau.dk

Abstract. A number of different types of final programming exams used
or considered at the Department of Computer Science, Aalborg University, are identified and analyzed. Based on this analysis, a new type of
programming exam is introduced called a Mini Project Programming
(MIP) exam. MIP is a group-based programming assignment that is intended as a medium-scale programming effort followed by a final oral
exam. MIP is characterized and compared to existing types of final programming exams by use of a number of independent criteria. The chapter motivates the MIP approach and reports on our experience over four
years. The MIP exam is a compromise between (1) a long problem-based
project exam and (2) a short oral or written programming exam. It is
concluded that the strengths of MIP are the high degree of realism in the
exam assignment and comprehensiveness relative to the course syllabus.
The main challenge of MIP is how to detect fraud.

1 Introduction

Programming is a core discipline in computer science and software engineering.
It is important, therefore, to have exams that test the programming skills of the
students. To test these skills, a number of different exam forms are used ranging
from oral to written, from 20 minutes to 6 hours duration and from pencil to
computer.

We find that there are several problems with the existing programming exam
forms. First, the existing exam forms are not realistic seen in relation to the
way programming is practiced in a real-world setting. As a particular problem,
the students are not constructing complete programs, but typically only program fractions. Second, most exam forms cover only a few central topics from
the course syllabus. Finally, the exams often require many resources from the
teachers who conduct the exam.

In this chapter we describe a new kind of final programming exam called
Mini Project Programming (MIP) exam. The MIP approach is designed to avoid
the problems discussed above while retaining the good features of the existing
exams. MIP is a take-home exam where groups of 2 to 4 students must design
and implement a complete program for a specific task. The source code and a
short design document are handed in for evaluation. The students demonstrate
the program and defend it at an oral group exam.

J. Bennedsen et al. (Eds.): Teaching of Programming, LNCS 4821, pp. 228–242, 2008.

MIP is the final exam following a four ECTS credits course in object-oriented programming (OOP). The OOP course is a CS1 course. It consists of 15 four-hour modules spread over approximately 10 weeks in a half-year semester. Each module consists of two hours of lecture and two hours of programming exercises. The Java programming language is used in the course along with the tools BlueJ, Eclipse or Emacs. Between 80 and 120 students follow the course. Attending the lectures is non-compulsory. The students do the exercises in groups of up to seven students. Each group has its own room. The lecturer and 2 to 3 teaching assistants circulate between the group rooms to assist the students during the exercises. No exercises are handed in for grading.

The MIP exam has been used for four years as the exam form at the second and the third semesters at Aalborg University. Compared to the previously used exam forms, we have found that the MIP exam is more realistic. In addition, we have found that the MIP exam requires approximately the same number of resources as an oral exam; however, the MIP exam requires fewer resources than a written exam. Despite it being a group exam, we have found it possible to evaluate the programming skills of students individually in a satisfactory way. We have only detected a few cases of fraud. Still, it is an open issue how to make the MIP exam fraud safe.

The chapter is organized as follows. In the next section, we list and discuss the central criteria for a final programming exam. This is followed by a section that characterizes the existing exam forms used or considered at the Department of Computer Science, Aalborg University according to these criteria. The next two sections describe the MIP exam and list our experiences with it. This is followed by a comparison of the MIP exam to other programming exams based on our criteria. The last section concludes the chapter.

2   Final Programming Exam Criteria

The most important criteria for a final programming exam are listed and discussed in the following. It is assumed that the exam is taken after following a programming course of 2 to 5 ECTS credits. The criteria are designed to be independent of each other. In order to explain the span of the criteria, we describe the lowest and highest score for each of them.

Realism. The exam should be realistic both in its formulation and in relation to the tools that the students are allowed to use for solving the exam assignments. In particular, the exam should be realistic seen from the perspective of what the students can expect to meet later on in a job context. Also, the exam should be realistic in size of the problem solved, coding styles used, test methodology and documentation requirements. The lowest score for this criterion is a pure, theoretical exam. The highest score is an exam based on a real-world problem. Notice that the programming exams discussed in this chapter are not intended to be realistic in relation to software reusability. The students are expected to use abstractions from the standard libraries, but it is not intended that the students reuse entire or partial solutions to the exam assignment.

Construction. The exam emphasizes the actual program. The students must show that they can use the programming language to create a program of high quality. In addition, it is emphasized that the program is executable, and that it can be demonstrated to fulfill the exam requirements. The lowest score for this criterion is the exam where the students only read programs written by the evaluators. The highest score is where the students write runnable and demonstrable programs.

Preparation. Before the actual exam the students are able to obtain a good understanding of how the exam is conducted and what the requirements are for passing the exam. The lowest score is that the students have no advance knowledge of the nature of the exam. The highest score is that the students are well-informed about the nature of the exam, for instance via preparation by using exams from previous years.

Comprehensiveness. In the students' preparation and implementation of the exam assignments, they should meet and cover the central topics of the course syllabus. The lowest score for this criterion is that the exam only focuses on a single central topic. The highest score is that the exam focuses on all central topics as defined in the course syllabus.

Cost-effectiveness. It must be possible for the evaluators to grade the solution to the exam assignments in an effective manner. In addition, the hardware, software, and staff costs needed to conduct the exam should be reasonable. The highest score (the most cost-effective exam) for this criterion is if there are no hardware, software or staff costs, and if the time needed to prepare and conduct each exam is linear to the number of student groups and the number of exam assignments. The lowest cost (the least cost-effective exam) is if the exam is individual.

Individualism. It should be assured that the individual students, who prepare and take part in the exam, achieve a good outcome of the efforts. In addition, it should be possible to grade each student individually in a precise and fair manner. The lowest score for this criterion is if one or more students are able to "hide" in a large group of students. The highest score is obtained if each student demonstrates knowledge of all the topics covered by the exam assignment, and if the exam is prepared and conducted individually.

Fraud safety. It is possible for the evaluators to prevent or to detect that students are cheating in solving the exam assignment. The lowest score for this criterion is if the students are allowed to take the exam home, if people from outside the exam group make contributions, or if existing program parts — beyond standard libraries— are reused in the solution. The highest score is if the exam is conducted in a closed room with constant supervision and with no possibility of communication.

Feedback. The students should get detailed feedback from the evaluators. Capable students should be told what they did well and what could be improved. Students that fail the exam should be told accurately what they need to improve on to pass the exam. The lowest score for this criterion is if the evaluators do not provide any feedback. The highest score is obtained if detailed, written feedback is given on all of the central exam topics to each student individually.

Note that some of these criteria are relevant for most exams, such as cost-effectiveness and fraud safety. Other criteria are more specific to programming exams (e.g., realism and construction).

3   Programming Exams

This section describes the final programming exams used or considered at the Department of Computer Science, Aalborg University. After having defined and discussed these different exams, we characterize each of them according to the criteria discussed in the previous section.

Programming exams can be characterized according to the following (almost) orthogonal dimensions:

- Oral or written
- Paper/blackboard, pencil/chalk, or computer supported
- The time period used for the exam activity
- The number of students involved in a single exam activity

Individual, oral programming exams using chalk and blackboard are widely used at Danish universities. For an oral exam, 10 to 15 topics are posted in advanced. At the exam, each student is randomly assigned a topic and without further preparation has to discuss the topic and to provide small examples. An oral exam typically lasts 20 to 30 minutes and is primarily useful to test a random sample of the students' conceptual programming knowledge. The exam is not useful for testing concrete programming skills (the craftsman skills). This form of exam is called an *oral exam* in the following.

Individual, written programming exams, which are based on paper and pencil exercises, are also in widespread use. Such exams typically last two to six hours and they are carried out under supervision in a room where students cannot communicate. This form of exam is called a *pencil-based written exam.*

Individual written exams based on the use of a computer rather than paper and pencil are also common. The duration of these exams is typically the same as for the pencil-based written exams. This form of exam is called a *computer-based written exam.*

Problem-based learning, or PBL, is becoming increasingly popular in teaching and education [Kjærsdam and Enemark, 1994]. PBL emphasizes development of analytic, methodical and transferable skills. The main idea behind PBL is use of different methods and strategies to reach the needed knowledge. The success of the outcome depends on the experiences of the problem solver(s). At Aalborg University, PBL is the dominating and the most important teaching activity.

At the Department of Computer Science, PBL is practiced in groups of up to seven students, who hand in a project report at the end of a semester. The project report is discussed at an oral group exam with individual grading. Many programming activities are evaluated via project reports and the subsequent oral group exams. This form of exam is called a *project exam* in the following.

4   Discussion of Exams

The overall goal of a programming exam is to ensure that the students can construct a running program of a non-trivial size. This includes arguments for the pros and cons of the overall program design and explaining all details of how the program is implemented.

In general, a written exam is almost always more comprehensive than an oral exam. In addition, a written exam is better suited to test the concrete programming skills than an oral exam. Computer-based written exams are more realistic than both pencil-based written and oral exams. In the every day programming situation, at least a computer, an editor and a compiler are used.

At the Computer Science Department at Aalborg University we have refrained from using computer-based written exams due to the practical difficulties. In order to run such exams we must provide in the magnitude of 100 computers with identical software installed. Alternatively, we may have to deal with the students' own computers. In addition, we must deal with other important issues such as communication with the outside world, which software to allow, and hardware breakdowns.

The project exam has a number of positive and negative aspects. At the positive end, it is possible to address large scale and real-world programming challenges in such exams. At the negative end, it is difficult to make sure that all students in the group have a minimal set of programming skills. The main reasons are that (1) the groups have up to seven students, (2) programming skills are often only a subset of the exam criteria, and (3) the evaluators (project advisor and censor) may not always have the necessary background to carry out an examination of all aspects of the project.

Table 1 below summarizes the characteristics of each programming exam form according to the criteria introduced previously. In the table, each programming exam is given the grade high, medium or low for each criterion. Because we have no experience with computer-based written exams we have merged the two written exams (pencil-based written and computer-based written) into a single column labeled Written. The column labeled MIP will be introduced and discussed in the next section.

The oral exam scores low on realism because it is typically only small program fragments that the students can discuss. The written exam gets the grade medium because the students have longer time to address bigger and more realistic examples compared to the oral exam. The project exam has a high degree of realism because there is an entire semester to work on a real-world problem.

Due to the fact that actual running programs are constructed only in a few cases at both the oral and written exams, these exams get the score low with respect to construction. The project exam gets the score high because the basis for the exam is a running non-trivial program constructed by the students.

Table 1. Characteristic of Exam Forms according to Criteria

	Oral	Written	Project	MIP
Realism	Low	Medium	High	High
Construction	Low	Low	High	High
Preparation	High	High	Low	Medium
Comprehensiveness	Low	Medium	Medium	High
Cost-effectiveness	High	Low	Low	Medium
Individualism	High	High	Low	Medium
Fraud safety	High	High	Medium	Low
Feedback	Low	Low	Medium	Medium

The students are familiar with both oral and written exams from other courses. Therefore, the students know in details how the exam is conducted. Further, students can rehearse the actual exam because it is fairly short. Of these reasons, the oral and written exams are graded high with respect to preparation. The project exam is graded low because it is used less frequently and, therefore, the students are not as familiar with this exam form. In addition, a project exam is longer, which makes rehearsal unrealistic.

The project exam gets the score medium for comprehensiveness because programming is typically only one of many topics involved in the exam. The written programming exam gets the grade medium because it is typically of considerable length at 2 to 6 hours. The oral exam is graded low because it is only possible to cover a few randomly selected central topics from the course syllabus in 20 to 30 minutes.

With respect to cost-effectiveness, the oral exam receives the grade high. Typically only 20 minutes per student are used. Further, preparation for the evaluators is fairly simple. The written exam is labor intensive both in constructing the exam set and grading all solutions. For the written exam, the quality assurance of the exam assignment is particularly labor intensive. The project exam is also labor intensive, and therefore, receives the score low with respect to cost-effectiveness. Compared to the written exam there is less preparation for the evaluators because the basis for the project exam is a report that is well known to these. However, a project exam typically takes 40 to 50 minutes per student to conduct.

The oral and written exams receive the grade high for the individualism criterion because the oral exam is taken individually and the written exam assignment is solved individually. The project exam receives the grade low because there are up to seven students per group.

The oral and written exams are very fraud safe because the exam assignment is not known in advance and the exam is taken in a room under supervision. The project exam gets the grade medium because the main problem discussed in the projects is typically quite unique and it can be hard to find material, e.g., on the Internet that can be used directly in the project report handed in.

With respect to feedback to the students both the oral and written exams get the grade low because there is limited time to provide feedback to the students. The project exam gets a medium grade because the evaluators can have a longer discussion with the students than it is possible at the written and oral exams.

5 The MIP Concept

This section first describes the background and outset for designing the MIP exam and the constraints related to other exam activities at Aalborg University. Next, the MIP concept itself is explained in details. Finally, a variant of the MIP exam is discussed.

5.1 Background

At the Department of Computer Science, PBL is practiced in self-selected groups of up to seven students with larger groups at the earlier semesters of study and with smaller groups at the later semesters. The groups can change each semester. The students spend approximately half of the study time on courses; the other half is spent on project work. At the end of a semester, each project group hands in a project report that documents its work.

Many programming activities are evaluated naturally through project exams. As a positive aspect of project exams, it is possible to address large scale and real-world programming challenges. However, a negative aspect is that it is often difficult to make sure that all the students in a group have obtained a minimal set of programming skills. The other exam forms introduced previously are not attractive. Stated briefly, oral exams are non-comprehensive and non-constructive. Pencil-based written exams are too far away from the students' everyday programming situation. Computer-based written exams are unrealistic due to the practical circumstances, and the project exam is too coarse-grained and uneven. This analysis leads us to look for a new cost-effective exam form targeted at a fair and fine-grained evaluation of each student's programming skills.

5.2 Concept

The MIP exam is based on a medium-size programming project in combination with a final oral group exam. It has the following characteristics:

- The assignment is a medium scale and (fairly) realistic programming exercise.
- The time spent on the problem solving is a few days, typically 48 hours.
- The MIP exam is a take-home assignment. The student's solutions have to fulfill certain requirements, but the assignment also has certain degrees of freedom. In this way, the better students can make advanced or elegant solutions, and thereby, they also see the assignment as a challenge.
- Between two and four students work together. In our setup, this is typically half of a project group.

- There are no restrictions on the use of computers. It is also allowed to look for outside inspiration, for instance on the Internet. However, any outside help and inspiration must be stated very explicitly in the documentation and in the resulting program. If the students do not comply with this rule, the work will be seen as the result of cheating, and they will need to face the consequences according to Aalborg University fraud rules.
- The program, the program design, and programming skills are the topics discussed at the exam. This is seen in contrast to the many other topics typically discussed in a project exam.
- The exam is group based, but the grade is individual.
- The outcome of the oral exam is a pass/no-pass grade.

The program that is handed in by a group of students is evaluated against requirements, which are known by the students in advance. A short demonstration of the program as well as the program itself is used as the basis for an oral group exam where each student individually is asked questions about the program. The students have to demonstrate that they have actually taken part in the programming exercise. It is not enough to be able to explain why the program is written in a certain way. It is expected that the individual students are able to discuss alternative solutions to the chosen approach together with possible consequences. The individual grade pass/no pass can be based on the oral exam alone, or it can be based on a combination of the program quality and the overall oral impression. The evaluators may have to revert to the oral exam form in order to ensure an appropriate level of understanding by the student. When the group exam has finished and the grades have been given to each individual, the evaluators give oral feedback on the program. This feedback tells the students which parts of the program could be improved and where the program demonstrates good programming skills.

To ensure that the program demonstrated at the oral exam is identical with the program submitted in advance, the students hand in a disk with the completed program along with a short design document and other necessary documentation such as status information and print-outs. At the exam, the group is asked to compile and to demonstrate the program, either on their personal computer or from the disk handed in by the group. The latter approach prevents the students from improving on their program after the submission date.

5.3 Variant

The first year introductory C programming course uses a slightly modified version of the MIP exam. Here, the students know the MIP assignment a few weeks before the submission date, and the program has to be handed in well in advance of the oral group examination. In addition, the students use the exercise hours for the last 2 to 3 lectures in the course to get started with the MIP assignment. During these exercises hours, the lecturer and the teaching assistants guide and discuss the assignment with the students. However, the amount of work involved is still expected to be a couple of days. We find that these are minor changes to the MIP concept and will discuss both variants as a single exam form in the following.

6   Experience

The MIP concept has been used since 1997 on the third semester in the OOP course using Java. In addition, the MIP exam is used at the second semester C programming course. The experience we report on in this section is based on four instances of the OOP course and three instances of the C programming course. This corresponds to 110 Java MIP programs and approximately 200 MIP programs written in C. In this section, we discuss the MIP exam in relation to the most relevant criteria for a programming exam introduced earlier in this chapter.

6.1   Individualism

One of the initial goals of the MIP exam was to ensure a fine grained, individual examination of the students' programming skills. The project exam covers the aspects of analysis, design (including design of a graphical user interface), programming and test. However, we could not in all cases guarantee that the individual students in a project group were examined thoroughly in the programming details. A problem based programming project is a joint effort by all participants, where division of labor among the students is encouraged. As such, it would harm and seriously affect the project work if we split the project group during the project exam.

The introduction of the MIP exam has clearly improved our confidence about the programming skills of individual students. Of the 110 students who passed the project exam in autumn 2003, 29 failed the MIP exam. In 2004 the numbers were 61 and 8, respectively. These numbers indicate that some students manage to pass a project exam about software construction without a solid programming background. Such students may, for instance, have been able to analyze the initial problem, or to design the program's user interface without being able to implement the program.

We find that the main reason students pass the project exam, but fail the MIP exam is that the individual contributions are fairly easy to reveal during the MIP examination. Students who have not been actively involved in the program development have a hard time justifying and explaining the code in detail. Experience from project work shows that the project groups tend to divide a problem into smaller tasks, e.g., analysis, and then split the group to allow one or maybe a few students to work on this particular problem and sometimes only obtaining superficial knowledge of the other topics. This experience is the main reason for limiting the groups to four students. Limiting the group size makes it easier for the evaluators at the oral exam to reveal if a student has or has not been active in MIP. One of the main purposes of introducing MIP was to ensure that all the students have a minimum level of programming skills, and not just the few who have a keen interest or previous experience.

6.2   Realism and Comprehensiveness

Adding realism relative to the traditional pencil-based written exam was another motivation behind our introduction of the MIP exam. Often, the students are asked to make very specific contributions in a pencil-based written exam. For example, filling in the blanks of an already existing program is a typical task. In the scope of the OOP course, it has in MIP been possible to address issues such as coding style, test methodology and documentation. In the C course, an aspect such as organization of the program in several source files and the use of header files has been part of the requirements to a good solution. We feel that none of these issues are possible to be tested in a pencil-based written exam since the issues are related to "best practice". It is worth pointing out that the time scale (we use 48 hours) sets a limit to the obtained realism. Many aspects of large scale program development are still out of reach. These include proper testing, debugging, and graphical user interfaces. Despite these limitations, we find that MIP has been successful in achieving a more realistic, and hopefully more fun, programming situation during the exam period.

In addition, we found that it is possible to design the MIP exam with the aim of covering almost all the central aspects of the associated programming course, depending on the formulation of the programming assignment. This is due to the way the oral exams are conducted. Basically, the evaluators ask a specific question to one student at a time. If the student cannot answer, the evaluators will ask another student in the group. In this fashion, many central aspects can be covered fairly quickly.

6.3   Cost Effectiveness

From a teacher's perspective, the main challenge with MIP is to come up with an appropriate assignment, allowing the students to fulfill the basic requirements set for the exam, but also allowing them to be creative. In our opinion, MIP does, not require as many resources as a pencil-based written exam. Teaching a course for the average class size of ca. 100 students means receiving 25 to 33 programs to read and comment, but of course, all the received programs will (try to) solve the same problem and are, therefore, often similar in structure. The oral exam spans 4 to 5 days, as each group exam takes 30 to 50 minutes, depending on the size of the group.

The cost-effectiveness on the teachers' part has been a design parameter of the MIP exam form. Individual MIP exams were ruled out due to a massive need for teacher as well as censor evaluation hours. By forming groups of up to four students, the number of teacher evaluation hours is reduced by a factor two or three. However, this organization prompted the need for an oral exam, during which the program submitted by the group is discussed individually with each of the students. This adds to the number of teacher evaluation hours, but in our experience, the oral exam contributes positively in several other respects. First, it is possible to reveal fraud during the oral exam (see below). Second, the oral exam gives a fair amount of feedback to the students since they receive comments and advice to their program both in design and implementation, making the exam part of the learning process. Hereby, participation in the oral exam helps the students understand possible problems or shortcomings in the submitted program. It would be more costly to deliver such feedback in a written form, either on a group basis, or to individual students.

6.4 Fraud Safety

Some students may be tempted to get outside help for programming the solution to the MIP assignment, for instance from fellow students, friends, family or the Internet. The MIP exam of the C programming course has been oriented towards simple games (such as hang man, master mind, wheel of fortune), where solutions already exist on the Internet. As part of the MIP rules, we require that any outside help has to be pointed out very explicitly in the program and the supporting documentation. If fraud is revealed either before or during the exam, the students risk severe punishment. Regrettably, we have had an unfortunate incident where two students were expelled for half a year due to fraud. As mentioned above, we hypothesize that most instances of undeclared, outside inspiration can be revealed during the oral exam. It seems to be difficult for many students to explain, to defend, or even to provide rationales for programs they have not written entirely themselves. In case the evaluators become suspicious of dishonesty during the discussion and questioning of the MIP program, some more general questions covering aspects of the course syllabus often reveal that the students do not understand enough to actually be able to contribute to the presented solutions.

7   MIP Compared to Other Exam Forms

Based on the discussion in the previous section, we can now return to Table 1 and discuss the last column labeled MIP that characterizes the MIP exam according to our criteria. The MIP exam is graded high with respect to realism. It is a much more realistic programming assignment compared to both the oral and the written exam. The realism in the project exam is higher than in the MIP exam, however. Using only three different grades we will argue that the MIP exam should be given the top grade. With respect to construction the MIP exam is also given a high grade. The students must construct a running program and give a demonstration of this program at the exam.

This is basically the same as for the project exam, except that the program typically is smaller for the MIP exams. The MIP exam is graded medium with respect to preparation. This is due to the fact that the MIP takes 48 hours. This makes it too time consuming for the students to try out an entire MIP assignment from a previous year. This is possible with both the oral and written exams. The MIP exam is graded higher than the project exam with respect to preparation because the focus of the MIP exam is narrower than the project exam. With respect to comprehensiveness, the MIP exam is graded high.

We find that working with a programming language for 48 hours followed by an oral examination makes it possible for the evaluators to make students work with most, if not all, of the central topics in a programming course syllabus.

The MIP exam is again graded higher than the project exam due to the narrow focus of the MIP exam. With respect to cost effectiveness, we find that the MIP exam is not as cost effective as an oral exam. However the MIP exam is more cost-effective than the pencil-based written exam because we find it is faster to build and quality assure a MIP exam than a pencil-based written exam. In addition, correcting pencil-based written exams is slower than correcting MIP exams because MIP exams are conducted with up to four students at a time whereas a pencil-based written exam is individual. The four students per exam is also the reason why the MIP exam is graded lower than the written exam with respect to the individualism criterion. The MIP exam is graded higher than the project exam because there are fewer students in a MIP group than in a project group.

The main drawback of the MIP exam is with respect to the criterion fraud safety. The MIP exam is a take-home assignment, which makes it possible to get outside help. This means that the MIP exam cannot prevent fraud. In this respect, the MIP exam is different from the oral and written exams that are conducted under constant supervision. Instead, fraud has to be detected for the MIP exam. This is made possible because the students have to defend their program at an oral exam after they have handed in the program. However, with the relative, concrete MIP assignments we have used, it is not possible to reveal all types of outside help. This is because of the many Internet resources and the good refactoring capabilities in modern integrated development environments. With these reasons, we have given the MIP exam the grade low with respect to fraud safety because it does not prevent fraud, but has to rely on fraud detection. However, we do not find that this invalidates the use of MIP exams all together since most (if not all) take-home assignments have this weakness.

The amount of feedback that evaluators can provide to the students via a MIP exam is larger than that given at an oral or a written exam. However, individual feedback on all the major topics in the course syllabus is not possible so the MIP exam is graded medium with respect to feedback.

8 Related Work

Fraud is a growing concern when students work on programming assignments, and there have been a number of approaches to minimizing the risk of fraud. [Daly and Horgan, 2005] describe a technique to analyze how students plagiarize programs in an introductory course at a setting similar to ours. The technique involved introducing a watermark on the individual student's program and then monitoring the watermark during submission of the programming assignment. This made it possible to distinguish between the supplier and the recipient of the code. One of the surprising results of this work is that dishonest students and honest students performed more or less the same in the exams. However, if the dishonest students are classified as supplier or recipient of watermarked code, the recipients performed noticeably worse than the suppliers in the exam. This confirms our own MIP experience with students who have "borrowed" code from elsewhere or have been passive during the process. Basically, they have a difficult time defending and explaining the code.

Various examination systems are being developed and tested at different universities. One such system (AES) is described by [Jonsson et al., 2005]. The overall idea of the examination method is based on a pedagogical view in programming courses. The basic criteria for AES are individual grading, efficient and useful feedback, and authenticity of the examination form. With AES, all the students and the examining teachers are connected to the same system. The exam itself, the communication and the grading is supported by this system. This enables the students to gain rapid responses from the examiners, including grades when leaving the exam. Grades are based on the number of correct solutions and the amount of time taken to solve the exercises, which is based on given deadlines. The success of using AES was evaluated by students filling in questionnaires after the exam. In general, the students liked this set-up, and they were happy with the teacher "response-time" and "approval-time" in the online setting. One drawback of this approach is the need for examiners to be online during the exam. Jonsson et. al. do not mention this, although the class sizes were rather large. One of our aims with MIP is to reduce the necessary teacher time during exams.

[Jacobson, 2000] describes an examination system where programming competency is assessed using on-computer tests or "lab exams" instead of graded programming assignments and coding at exams. One of the goals of introducing lab exams was to make cheating less tempting. Comparing lab exams to MIP exams one aspect is very different, namely that several lab exams are given during the course, whereas MIP is a final exam. The lab exams described by Jacobson are given at certain intervals to test the students' current programming abilities, dependent on the progress of the course. Another difference is that in the lab exams the students do not write a complete program, but fill in "missing functions" in an existing program, hopefully making the program run correctly. The students are allowed to use on-line help during the exam. In case a student fails the lab exam, it has to be re-taken and passed. A number of initiatives are taken to prevent cheating during the exam, including using special, test-taking accounts. Apart from the cheating aspect, lab exams are also claimed to introduce other benefits. Since the lab exams are aimed at measuring basic programming competency, there is no need for a fine-grained grading system. This compares well with our experience with MIP exams, where the grades are limited to pass/no-pass. However, according to Jacobson the drawback of the lab-exams is that since students only fill in program snippets in the exam, they are never tested in the skill of writing an entire program. In MIP, this is exactly what is tested.

The MIP exam is a new approach in evaluating the programming skills of students. This topic is well described in the computer science literature. [Lane and VanLehn, 2005] describe how to asses a student's ability to solve a programming exercise correctly the first time by introducing an intension-based scoring where a program is semi-automatically graded each time the student compiles the program. In this way, it is possible to examine the process that leads up the final program and grade incomplete (non-running) solutions to exercises. In contrast, the MIP exam only looks at the final program and is graded manually. Further, in the MIP exam it is a requirement that the program is runnable and demonstrable to pass the exam.

[Ellsworth et al., 2004] describe a quiz verification system called Quiver that can be used to automatically grade solutions to programming exercises. The grading is based on correctness of the programs, which is determined by JUnit test cases. The system can easily be extended with new quizzes and supports multiple object-oriented programming languages. Compared to the MIP exam, the exercises used in the Quiver system are much smaller and only the input and output of programs are examined (via JUnit test cases). The MIP exam emphasizes both the correctness and the internal structure of the program.

[East and Schafer, 2005] look at how to provide efficient feedback to students on their programming assignments. This is done in face-to-face meetings with each student twice per semester. They show that this gives a huge improvement in the students learning and that the students are very satisfied with this type of feedback. Compared to the MIP exam, the individual feedback of East and Schafer is much more detailed. However, it is also more time-consuming to provide.

In the previous chapter of this book Malmi and Korhonen describe two CS courses that use the constructivist learning paradigm. At an abstract level there is a clear overlap between the criteria in this current chapter and the didactic goals in the previous chapter. Both (a) strive to assess students in a broad selection of the core topics covered in a course, (b) make the students work on realistic problems, (c) make the students argue for their design choices, (d) make the students collaborate in small groups, and (e) make it efficient to assess a large number of students. However, in the previous chapter the focus is more on individual exercises with immediate feedback, e.g., in the *lecture and algorithm simulation exercises*. In the current chapter, we focus solely on final exams. At a more concrete level Malmi and Korhonen describe how a compulsory design project is solved in groups of 2 to 3 students, where the task is to design a solution for a realistic nontrivial problem. In another course, groups of 2 to 3 students carry out small-scale experimental research projects to acquire practical experience in addition to the theoretical courses. Malmi and Korhonen mention that some of the group work is peer reviewed and given feedback. Their general observation about collaboration is that working in small groups motivates the students to discuss solutions and to learn from each other. This is similar to our experiences with MIP. Another quite surprising observation by Malmi and Korhonen is that collaboration seems to reduce plagiarism.

9   Conclusion

In this chapter, we have introduced and discussed Mini Project Programming (MIP) exams. We have introduced a number of programming exam criteria, and we have characterized different final programming exams relative to these. At Aalborg University, problem-based learning (PBL) and project work is the most important - and the most valued - teaching activity, also in the area of programming. MIP exams were introduced as a consequence of the lack of individualism in ordinary PBL-based project exams, especially in relation to ensure a sufficient level of programming skills of all participating students. Due to concerns of realism and emphasis on the constructive aspects of programming, we did not want to revert to traditional oral or written programming exams. Based on cost-effectiveness considerations, we find it unrealistic to arrange exams where each student individually turns in a non-trivial program for evaluation.

We find that MIP exam assignments easily can be designed to cover most parts of the constructive aspects of a programming course curriculum. As opposed to traditional written and oral exams, a MIP exam is a fair and realistic programming challenge, quite similar to (small) real-world programming tasks. Due to the group-based organization of the programming assignment, it is possible to evaluate the programs with reasonable teacher resources. The MIP exam, however, adds a considerable amount of hours to the teachers' total work load. But, we find that the oral exam part is necessary to ensure and to justify the individual grading, to detect fraud, and to provide for realistic and necessary feedback to the students. We conclude that the MIP exam form balances the criteria for final programming exams as discussed in this chapter.

Part V

Appendix

References

Abelson et al., 1985. Abelson, H., Sussman, G.J., Sussman, J.: Structure and Interpretation of Computer Programs. MIT Press, Cambridge (1985)

ACM-Forum, 2002. ACM-Forum, Hello World gets mixed greetings. Communication of the ACM, 45(2), 11–17 (2002)

Adams, 2002. Adams, R.: The colossal cave adventure (2002) (March 23, 2007), http://www.rickadams.org/adventure

Aharoni, 2000. Aharoni, D.: Cogito, ergo sum! Cognitive processes of students dealing with data structures. In: Proceedings of the thirty-first SIGCSE technical symposium on Computer science education, Austin, Texas, United States, pp. 26–30 (2000)

Alford, 2003. Alford, K.L.: Video faqs - instruction-on-demand. In: Proceedings of the thirthy-third frontiers in education conference, Boulder, Colorado, United States (2003)

Alphonce and Ventura, 2002. Alphonce, C., Ventura, P.: Object orientation in CS1-CS2 by design. In: ITiCSE 2002: Proceedings of the 7th annual conference on Innovation and technology in computer science education, Aarhus, Denmark, pp. 70–74 (2002)

Andrianoff and Levine, 2002. Andrianoff, S., Levine, D.: Role playing in an object-oriented world. In: Proceedings SIGCSE 2002, Kovington, Kentucky, United States (2002)

Ant, 2005. Ant, Apache ant. (2005) (December 2006), http://jakarta.apache.org/ant/

Arendale, 1997. Arendale, D.: Supplemental instruction (SI): Review of Research Concerning the Effectiveness of SI from the University of Missouri-Kansas City and Other Institutions from across the United States. In: Proceedings of the seventeenth and eighteenth Annual Institutes for Learning Assistance Professionals, Tucson, Arizona, United States, pp. 1–25 (1996, 1997)

Arnow et al., 2004. Arnow, D.M., Dexter, S., Weiss, G.: Introduction to Programming Using Java: An Object-Oriented Approach. Addison-Wesley Longman, Boston (2004)

Asklund et al., 2004. Asklund, U., Bendix, L., Ekman, T.: Software configuration management practices for extreme programming teams. In: Proceedings of the 11th Nordic Workshop on Programming and Software Development Tools and Techniques - NWPER 2004, Turku, Finland (2004)

Astrachan et al., 2005. Astrachan, O., Bruce, K., Koffman, E., Kölling, M., Reges, S.: Resolved: objects early has failed. In: Proceedings of the thirty-sixth SIGCSE technical symposium on Computer science education, St. Louis, Missouri, United States, pp. 451–452 (2005)

Astrachan and Reed, 1995. Astrachan, O., Reed, D.: AAA and CS1: the applied apprenticeship approach to CS1. In: Proceedings of the twenty-sixth SIGCSE technical symposium on Computer science education, Nashville, Tennessee, United States, pp. 1–5 (1995)

Astrachan et al., 1997. Astrachan, O., Smith, R., Wilkes, J.: Application-based modules using apprentice learning for cs 2. In: Proceedings of the twenty-eighth SIGCSE technical symposium on Computer science education, San Jose, California, United States, pp. 233–237 (1997)

246

Babich, 1986. Babich, W.A.: Software configuration management: coordination for team productivity. Addison-Wesley Longman, Boston (1986)

Bacvanski and Börstler, 1997. Bacvanski, V., Börstler, J.: Doing your first OO project - OO education issues in industry and academia. In: Addendum to the 1997 ACM SIGPLAN conference on Object-oriented programming, systems, languages, and applications, Atlanta, Georgia, United States (1997)

Bailie et al., 2003. Bailie, F., Courtney, M., Murray, K., Schiaffino, R., Tuohy, S.: Objects first - does it work? Journal of Computing in Small Colleges 19(2), 303–305 (2003)

Barnes and Kölling, 2003. Barnes, D.J., Kölling, M.: Objects First with Java, A Practical Introduction Using BlueJ. Pearson Education, Essex, United Kingdom (2003)

Barnes and Kölling, 2005. Barnes, D.J., Kölling, M.: Objects First with Java - A Practical Introduction Using BlueJ, 2nd edn. Pearson Education, Harlow, United Kingdom (2005)

Barnes and Kölling, 2006. Barnes, D.J., Kölling, M.: Objects First with Java - A Practical Introduction Using BlueJ, 3rd edn. Pearson Education, Harlow, United Kingdom (2006)

Bass et al., 2003. Bass, L., Clements, P., Kazman, R.: Software Architecture in Practice, 2nd edn. Addison-Wesley, Boston (2003)

BeanShell, 2003. BeanShell, BeanShell - lightweight scripting for Java (June 2003), http://www.beanshell.org/

Beck, 1999a. Beck, K.: Embracing change with extreme programming. IEEE Computer 32(10), 70–77 (1999a)

Beck, 1999b. Beck, K.: Extreme Programming Explained: Embrace Change. Addison-Wesley Professional, Reading (1999b)

Beck, 2002. Beck, K.: Test Driven Development: By Example. Addison-Wesley Longman, Boston (2002)

Beck, 2003. Beck, K.: Test-Driven Development By Example. Addison-Wesley Professional, Boston (2003)

Beck and Andres, 2004. Beck, K., Andres, C.: Extreme Programming Explained: Embrace Change, 2nd edn. Addison-Wesley Professional, Boston (2004)

Beck and Cunningham, 1989. Beck, K., Cunningham, W.: A laboratory for object-oriented thinking. In: Proceedings of the 1989 OOPSLA conference, New Orleans, Louisiana United States (1989)

Beck and Gamma, 2005. Beck, K., Gamma, E.: Test infected: Programmers love writing tests (2005) (December 2007), http://members.pingnet.ch/gamma/junit.htm

Beck and Gamma, 2007. Beck, K., Gamma, E.: Junit cookbook (March 14, 2007), http://junit.sourceforge.net/doc/cookbook/cookbook.htm

Becker-Pechau et al., 2003. Becker-Pechau, P., Breitling, H., Lippert, M., Schmolitzky, A.: Teaching team work: An extreme week for first-year programmers. In: Marchesi, M., Succi, G. (eds.) XP 2003. LNCS, vol. 2675, pp. 386–393. Springer, Heidelberg (2003)

Beedle et al., 2000. Beedle, M., Devos, M., Sharon, Y., Schwaber, K., Sutherland, J.: Scrum: A pattern language for hyperproductive software development. In: Harrison, N., Foote, B., Rohnert, H. (eds.) Pattern Languages of Program Design 4, pp. 637–652. Addison Wesley, Reading (2000)

Beekman, 2005. Beekman, G.: Computer Confluence - exploring tomorrow's technology, 6th edn. Prentice Hall, Upper Saddle River (2005)

Bell and Scott, 1987. Bell, D., Scott, P.: A first course in programming. SIGCSE Bulletin (Association for Computing Machinery, Special Interest Group on Computer Science Education) 19(2), 48–50 (1987)

Bellin and Simone, 1997. Bellin, D., Simone, S.S.: The CRC Card Book. Addison-Wesley, Reading (1997)

Ben-Ari, 1998. Ben-Ari, M.: Constructivism in computer science education. In: Proceedings of the twenty-ninth SIGCSE technical symposium on Computer science education, Atlanta, Georgia, United States, pp. 257–261 (1998)

Bennedsen and Caspersen, 2003. Bennedsen, J., Caspersen, M.: Rationale for the design of a web-based programming course for adults. In: Proceedings for the International Conference on Open and Online Learning (ICOOL 2003), University of Mauritius, Mauritius (2003)

Bereiter, 2002. Bereiter, C.: Education and Mind in the Knowledge Age. Lawrence Erlbaum, Mahwah (2002)

Bereiter and Scardamalia, 2003. Bereiter, C., Scardamalia, M.: Learning to work creatively with knowledge. In: Corte, E.D., Verschaffel, L.N.E., van Merriënboer, J. (eds.) Powerful Learning Environments: Unravelling Basic Components and Dimensions, pp. 55–68. Pergamon Press, Oxford (2003)

Bergin, 2000a. Bergin, J.: Fourteen pedagogical patterns for teaching computer science. In: Paper presented at the Proceedings of the Fifth European Conference on Pattern Languages of Programs (EuroPLop 2000), Irsee, Germany (2000a)

Bergin, 2000b. Bergin, J.: Why procedural is the wrong first paradigm if OOP is the goal (2000b) (May 2007),
http://csis.pace.edu/~bergin/papers/Whynotproceduralfirst.html

Bergin et al., 2004. Bergin, J., Caristi, J., Dubinsky, Y., Hazzan, O., Williams, L.: Teaching software development methods: the case of extreme programming. In: Proceedings of the Thirty-Fifth SIGCSE Technical Symposium on Computer Science Education, Norfolk, Verginia, United States, pp. 448–449 (2004)

Berkeley, 2007. Berkeley, Uc berkeley webcasts (February 17, 2007),
http://webcast.berkeley.edu/courses

Berliner, 1990. Berliner, B.: CVS II: Parallelizing software development. In: Proceedings of the USENIX Winter 1990 Technical Conference, Washington, District of Columbia, United States, pp. 341–352 (1990)

Biggs, 2003. Biggs, J.: Teaching for quality learning at University, 2nd edn. The Society for research into Higher Education Open University Press, London, United Kingdom (2003)

Bjørner and Jones, 1978. Bjørner, D., Jones, C. (eds.): The Vienna Development Method: The Meta-Language. Springer, Berlin (1978)

Blackwell, 2001. Blackwell, A.: See what you need: Helping end-users to build abstractions. Journal of Visual Languages and Computing 12, 475–499 (2001)

Blackwell, 2002. Blackwell, A.: What is programming? In: Proceedings of the fourteenth psycology of programming workshop, Brunel University, London, United Kingdom, pp. 204–218 (2002)

Bloom, 1956. Bloom, B.: Taxonomy of Educational Objectives, Handbook 1: Cognitive Domain. Pearson Longman, New York (1956)

BlueJ, 2007. BlueJ, BlueJ - the interactive Java environment (March 23, 2007)
http://www.bluej.org

Börstler, 2004. Börstler, J.: Object-oriented analysis and design through scenario role-play. Technical Report UMINF-04.04, Dept. of Computing Science, Umeå University, Sweden (2004)

Börstler, 2005. Börstler, J.: Improving crc-card role-play with role-play diagrams. In: OOPSLA 2005 Addendum to the Proceedings (Educators Symposium), San Diego, California, United States (2005)

Börstler et al., 2002. Börstler, J., Johansson, T., Nordström, M.: Introducing OO concepts with CRC cards and BlueJ - a case study. In: Proceedings of the thirty-second Frontiers in Education Conference, Boston, Massachusetts, United States (2002)

Börstler and Schulte, 2005. Börstler, J., Schulte, C.: Teaching object oriented modelling with crc-cards and roleplaying games. In: Proceedings WCCE 2005, Cape Town, South Africa (2005)

Börstler and Sharp, 2003. Börstler, J., Sharp, H.: Special issue on learning and teaching object technology. Computer Science Education 13(4) (2003)

Boyle, 2003. Boyle, T.: Design principles for authoring dynamic, reusable learning objects. Australian Journal of Educational Technology 19(1), 46–58 (2003)

Brightman, 1998. Brightman, H.: On learning styles. technical report (1998) (March 22, 2007), http://www.gsu.edu/~dschjb/masterteacher.html

Bruce et al., 2005. Bruce, K., Cutler, R., Cross, J., Grissom, S., Klee, K., Rodger, S., Trees, F., Utting, I., Yellin, F.: ACM Java task force (2005) (December 2007), http://jtf.acm.org/

Bruce, 2005. Bruce, K.B.: Controversy on how to teach CS1: A discussion on the SIGCSE-members mailing list. SIGCSE Bulletin (Association for Computing Machinery, Special Interest Group on Computer Science Education) 37(2), 111–117 (2005)

Campione et al., 2000. Campione, M., Walrath, K., Huml, A.: The Java(TM) Tutorial: A Short Course on the Basics, 3rd edn. Addison-Wesley Professional, Upper Saddle River (2000)

Capron and Johnson, 2002. Capron, H., Johnson, J.: Computers - tools for an information age, 7th edn. Prentice Hall, Upper Saddle River (2002)

Carter et al., 1985. Carter, H., Mace, A., White, J.M.: The Discovery of the Tomb of Tutankhamen. Dover Publications, New York (1985)

Caspersen and Christensen, 2000. Caspersen, M.E., Christensen, H.B.: Here, there and everywhere - on the recurring use of turtle graphics in CS1. In: ACSE 2000: Proceedings of the Australasian conference on Computing education, Melbourne, Australia, pp. 34–40 (2000)

Caspersen and Kölling, 2006. Caspersen, M.E., Kölling, M.: A novice's process of object-oriented programming. In: Companion To the twenty-first ACM SIGPLAN Conference on Object Oriented Programming Systems Languages and Applications (OOPSLA 2006), Portland, Oregon, United States, pp. 892–900 (2006)

Chen et al., 2005. Chen, Y., Dios, R., Mili, A., Wu, L., Wang, K.: An empirical study of programming language trends. IEEE Software 22(3), 72–78 (2005)

chromatic, 2003. chromatic: Extreme Programming Pocket Guide. O'Reilly Media, Inc., Sebastopol (2003)

Clancey, 2004. Clancey, M.: Misconceptions and attitudes that infer with learning to program. In: Petre, S.F.M. (ed.) Computer Science Education Research, pp. 85–100. Taylor & Francis, Lisse, The Netherlands (2004)

Cooper et al., 2000. Cooper, S., Dann, W., Pausch, R.: Alice: A 3-d tool for introductory programming concepts. Journal of Computing in Small Colleges 15(5), 107–116 (2000)

Cooper et al., 2003. Cooper, S., Dann, W., Pausch, R.: Teaching objects first in introductory computer science (2003)

Cunningham, 1996. Cunningham, W.: EPISODES: a pattern language of competitive development. In: Vlissides, J., Coplien, J., Kerth, N. (eds.) Pattern Languages of Program Design 2, pp. 371–388. Addison-Wesley Longman, Reading (1996)

Daly and Horgan, 2005. Daly, C., Horgan, J.: Patterns of plagiarism. In: Proceedings of the thirty-sixth SIGCSE technical symposium on Computer science education, St. Louis, Missouri United States, pp. 383–387 (2005)

De Gallow, 2007. De Gallow: What is problem-based learning? (March 19, 2007), http://www.pbl.uci.edu/whatispbl.html

de Raadt et al., 2004. de Raadt, M., Watson, R., Toleman, M.: Introductory programming: What's happening today and will there be any students to teach tomorrow? In: Proceedings of the Sixth Australasian Computing Education Conference, Dunedin, New Zealand, pp. 277–282 (2004)

Decker and Hirshfield, 1993. Decker, R., Hirshfield, S.: Top-down teaching: object-oriented programming in CS1. In: Proceedings of the twenty-fourth SIGCSE technical symposium on Computer science education, Indianapolis, Indiana, United States, pp. 270–273 (1993)

Denning, 2004. Denning, P.: Role playing in an object-oriented world. In: Proceedings of the Thirty-Fifth SIGCSE Technical Symposium on Computer Science Education, Norfolk, Verginia, United States (2004)

Dijkstra, 1989. Dijkstra, E.: On the cruelty of really teaching computing science. Communication of the ACM 32(12), 1398–1404 (1989)

Dijkstra, 1969. Dijkstra, E.W.: Notes on structured programming. Technical Report EWD 249, Technoligical University Eindhoven, Eindhoven, the Nederlands (1969)

diSessa and Abelson, 1981. diSessa, A.A., Abelson, H.: Turtle Geometry: the computer as a medium for exploring mathematics. MIT Press, Cambridge (1981)

DrJava, 2003. DrJava: DrJava. (June 2003) http://drjava.sourceforge.net/

du Boulay, 1989. du Boulay, B.: Some difficulties of learning to program. In: Soloway, E., Spohrer, J.C. (eds.) Studying the novice programmer, pp. 57–73. Lawrence Erlbaum, Hillsdale (1989)

East and Schafer, 2005. East, J.P., Schafer, J.B.: In-person grading: an evaluative experiment. In: Proceedings of the thirthy-sixth SIGCSE technical symposium on Computer science education, St. Louis, Missouri United States, pp. 378–382 (2005)

Eclipse, 2007. Eclipse, The eclipse Java development tools subproject (March 14, 2007), http://www.eclipse.org

Eliasson et al., 2006a. Eliasson, J., Kallin Westin, L., Nordström, M.: Investigating students' confidence in programming and problem solving. In: Thirty-sixth ASEE/IEEE Frontiers in Education Conference (FIE 2006), San Diego, California, United States (2006)

Eliasson et al., 2006b. Eliasson, J., Kallin Westin, L., Nordström, M.: Investigating students' change of confidence during CS1 - four case studies. Technical report, Department of Computer Science, UmeåUniversity (2006b)

Ellis et al., 1998. Ellis, A., Carswell, L., Bernat, A., Deveaux, D., Frison, P., Meisalo, V., Meyer, J., Nulden, U., Rugelj, J., Tarhio, J.: Resources, tools, and techniques for problem based learning in computing. In: Working Group reports of the 3rd annual SIGCSE/SIGCUE ITiCSE conference on Integrating technology into computer science education, Dublin, Ireland, pp. 46–50 (1998)

Ellsworth et al., 2004. Ellsworth, C.C., James, B., Fenwick, J., Kurtz, B.L.: The Quiver system. In: Proceedings of the thirty-fifth SIGCSE technical symposium on Computer science education, Norfolk, Virginia, United States, pp. 205–209 (2004)

Engel and Roberts, 2001. Engel, G., Roberts, E.: Computing curricula 2001 computer science, final report (2001) (March 10, 2006),
http://www.computer.org/portal/cms_docs_ieeecs/ieeecs/education/cc2001/cc2

Evans and Patterson, 1985. Evans, H., Patterson, W.: Implementing ada as the primary programming language. In: Proceedings of the sixteenth SIGCSE technical symposium on Computer science education, New Orleans, Louisiana, United States, pp. 255–265 (1985)

ExtremeHour, 2007. ExtremeHour: Extremehour (March 14, 2007),
http://c2.com/cgi/wiki?ExtremeHour

Fekete et al., 1998. Fekete, A., Greening, T., Kingston, J.: Conveying technical content in a curriculum using problem-based learning. In: Proceedings of the third Australasian conference on Computer science education, Brisbane, Australia, pp. 198–202 (1998)

Felleisen et al., 2001. Felleisen, M., Findler, R., Flatt, M., Krishnamurthi, S.: The structure and interpretation of the computer science curriculum. Journal of Functional Programming 14(4), 365–378 (2001)

Fincher, 1999. Fincher, S.: What are we doing when we teach programming? In: Proceedings of the twnety-nineth Frontiers in Education conference, San Juan Puerto Rico, pp. 12a4–1 – 12a4–5 (1999)

Fitzgerald and Larsen, 1998. Fitzgerald, F., Larsen, P.: Modelling Systems - Practical Tools and Techniques in Software Development. Cambridge University Press, Cambridge (1998)

Fjuk et al., 2004. Fjuk, A., Berge, O., Bennedsen, J., Caspersen, M.E.: Learning object-orientation through ict-mediated apprenticeship. In: ICALT 2004: Proceedings of the IEEE International Conference on Advanced Learning Technologies (ICALT 2004), Joensuu, Finland, pp. 380–384 (2004)

Fleury, 2000. Fleury, A.E.: Programming in Java: student-constructed rules. In: Proceedings of the Thirty-First SIGCSE Technical Symposium on Computer Science Education, Austin, Texas, United States, pp. 197–201 (2000)

Foote and Yoder, 2000. Foote, B., Yoder, J.W.: Big ball of mud. In: Harrison, N., Foote, B., Rohnert, H. (eds.) Pattern Languages of Program Design 4, pp. 654–692. Addison-Wesley, Reading (2000)

Forte and Guzdial, 2005. Forte, A., Guzdial, M.: Motivation and nonmajors in computer science: Identifying discrete audiences for introductory courses. IEEE Transactions on Education 48(2), 248–253 (2005)

Fowler and Beck, 1999. Fowler, M., Beck, K.: Refactoring: improving the design of existing code. Addison-Wesley Longman, Boston (1999)

Fowler and Scott, 2000. Fowler, M., Scott, K.: UML distilled: a brief guide to the standard object modeling language, 2nd edn. Addison-Wesley Longman, Boston (2000)

Freeman, 2005. Freeman, S.: How mock objects happened (2005) (December 2007),
http://www.mockobjects.com

Gamma et al., 1994. Gamma, E., Helm, R., Johnson, R., Vlissides, J.: Design Patterns: Elements of Reuseable Object-Oriented Software. Addison-Wesley, Reading (1994)

Gantenbein, 1989. Gantenbein, R.E.: Programming as process: A novel approach to teaching programming. In: Proceedings of the twentieth SIGCSE technical symposium on Computer science education, Louisville, Kentucky, United States, pp. 22–26 (1989)

Grand, 1998. Grand, M.: Patterns in Java, vol. 1. Wiley, New York (1998)

Greening et al., 1997. Greening, T., Kay, J., Kingston, J., Crawford, K.: Results of a pbl trial in first-year computer science. In: Second Australasian Conference of Computer Science Education, Melbourne, Australia, pp. 201–206 (1997)

Gries, 1974. Gries, D.: What should we teach in an introductory programming course? In: Proceedings of the Fourth SIGCSE Technical Symposium on Computer Science Education, Detroit, Michigan United States, pp. 81–89 (1974)

Gries et al., 2002. Gries, D., Gries, P., Hall, P.: ProgramLive: Master JAVA programming in a dynamic, self-paced learning environment. Wiley, New York (2002)

Guzdial, 1995. Guzdial, M.: Centralized mindset: A student problem with object-oriented programming. In: Proceedings of the twenty-sixth SIGCSE technical symposium on Computer science education (1995)

Hafler, 1998. Hafler, J.: Case writing: case writers perspectives. In: Boud, D., Feletti, G. (eds.) The Challenge of Problem-Based Learning, 2nd edn., pp. 151–159. Kogan Page, London (1998)

Hagan and Markham, 2000. Hagan, D., Markham, S.: Teaching Java with the BlueJ environment. In: Paper presented at the Australian Society for Computers in Learning in Tertiary Education (ASCILITE 2000), Coffs Harbour, Australia. (2000)

Hansen et al., 1999. Hansen, M., Kristensen, J., Rischel, H.: A theory-based introductory programming course. In: Proceedings of the twenty-nineth Frontiers in Education conference, San Juan, Puerto Rico, pp. 11b4–25 – 11b4–30 (1999)

Hansen and Rischel, 1999. Hansen, M., Rischel, H.: Introduction to Programming using SML. Addison Wesley Longman, Harlow (1999)

Hedin et al., 2003a. Hedin, G., Bendix, L., Magnusson, B.: Coaching coaches. In: Marchesi, M., Succi, G. (eds.) Proceedings of fourth International Conference on Extreme Programming and Agile Processes in Software Engineering, Genova, Italy, pp. 154–160 (2003a)

Hedin et al., 2003b. Hedin, G., Bendix, L., Magnusson, B.: Introducing software engineering by means of extreme programming. In: Proceedings of the twenty-fifth International Conference on Software Engineering, Portland, Oregon, United States, pp. 586–593 (2003b)

Hedin et al., 2005. Hedin, G., Bendix, L., Magnusson, B.: Teaching extreme programming to large groups of students. Journal of Systems & Software 74(2), 133–146 (2005)

Helenius and Tengstrand, 2005. Helenius, O., Tengstrand, A.: Nybörjarstudenter och matematik. matematikundervisningen under första året på tekniska och naturvetenskapliga utbildningar. Technical Report Högskoleverkets rapportserie 2005:36 R, Högskoleverket (2005)

Henze et al., 1999. Henze, N., Nejdl, W., Wolpers, M.: Modeling constructivist teaching functionality and structure in the kbs hyperbook system. In: CSCL 1999: Proceedings of the 1999 conference on Computer support for collaborative learning, Palo Alto, California, p. 28. International Society of the Learning Sciences (1999)

Hilburn, 1993. Hilburn, T.B.: A top-down approach to teaching an introductory computer science course. In: Proceedings of the twenty-fourth SIGCSE technical symposium on Computer science education, Indianapolis, Indiana, United States, pp. 58–62 (1993)

Högskoleverket, 1999. Högskoleverket: Räcker Kunskaperna i Matematik? Högskoleverket, Stockholm, Sweden (in Swedish, 1999)

Holland et al., 1997. Holland, S., Griffiths, R., Woodman, M.: Avoiding object misconceptions. In: Proceedings of the twenty-eighth SIGCSE technical symposium on Computer science education, San Jose, California, United States, pp. 131–134 (1997)

Horstmann, 2001. Horstmann, C.S.: Big Java: Programming and Practice. John Wiley & Sons, Inc., New York (2001)

Hosch and Niño, 2002. Hosch, F., Niño, J.: An Introduction to Programming and Object Oriented Design Using Java. John Wiley & Sons, Inc., New York (2002)

Hu, 2005. Hu, C.: Dataless object considered harmful. Communications of the ACM 48(2), 99–101 (2005)

Hughes, 1989. Hughes, J.: Why functional programming matters. Computer Journal 32(2), 98–107 (1989)

Hutchins, 1995. Hutchins, E.: Cognition in the Wild. The MIT Press, Cambridge (1995)

Hyland and Clynch, 2002. Hyland, E., Clynch, G.: Initial experiences gained and initiatives employed in the teaching of Java programming in the institute of technology tallaght. In: PPPJ 2002/IRE 2002: Proceedings of the inaugural conference on the Principles and Practice of programming, 2002 and Proceedings of the second workshop on Intermediate representation engineering for virtual machines, 2002, Dublin, Ireland, pp. 101–106. National University of Ireland (2002)

Hyvönen and Malmi, 1993. Hyvönen, J., Malmi, L.: Trakla - a system for teaching algorithms using email and a graphical editor. In: Proceedings of the HYPERMEDIA conference, pp. 141–147. Vaasa Institute of Technology, Finland (1993)

IBM Rational Rose, 2003. IBM Rational Rose, Visual modelling with Rational Rose (June 2003), http://www.rational.com/products/rose/index.jsp

Ingalls et al., 1997. Ingalls, D., Kaehler, T., Maloney, J., Wallace, S., Kay, A.: Back to the future: the story of squeak, a practical smalltalk written in itself. In: Proceedings of the twelfth ACM SIGPLAN OOPSLA conference, Atlanta, Georgia (1997)

Inkpen et al., 1994. Inkpen, K., Upitis, R., Klawe, M., Lawry, J., Anderson, A., Ndunda, M., Sedighian, K., Leroux, S., Hsu, D.: we have never forgetful flowers in our garden: girls responses to electronic games. Journal of Computers in Math and Science Teaching 13, 383–403 (1994)

Jackson et al., 1997. Jackson, U., Manaris, B., McCauley, R.: Strategies for effective integration of software engineering concepts and techniques into the undergraduate computer science curriculum. In: Proceedings of the twenty-eighth SIGCSE technical symposium on Computer science education, San Jose, California, United States, pp. 360–364 (1997)

Jacobson et al., 1997. Jacobson, I., Griss, M., Jonsson, P.: Software Reuse: Architecture Process and Organization for Business Success. ACM Press, New York (1997)

Jacobson, 2000. Jacobson, N.: Using on-computer exams to ensure beginning students' programming competency. SIGCSE Bulletin (Association for Computing Machinery, Special Interest Group on Computer Science Education) 32(4), 53–56 (2000)

JBuilder, 2003. JBuilder, Borland software corporation - JBuilder (June 2003), http://www.borland.com/jbuilder/

Jeffries et al., 2000. Jeffries, R.E., Anderson, A., Hendrickson, C.: Extreme Programming Installed. Addison-Wesley Longman, Boston (2000)

Jenkins, 2002. Jenkins, T.: On the difficulty of learning to program. In: Proceedings of the 3rd Annual LTSN-ICS conference, Loughborough University, Leicestershire, United Kingdom, pp. 53–58 (2002)

Jenkins and Davy, 2000. Jenkins, T., Davy, J.: Dealing with diversity in introductory programming. In: LTSN-ICS Conference on the Teaching of Computing, Edinburgh, UK (2000)

JHotDraw, 2005. JHotDraw, Jhotdraw (December 2005), http://jhotdraw.sourceforge.net/

Jones, 1990. Jones, C.: Systematic Software Development Using VDM, 2nd edn. Prentice-Hall, New York (1990)

Jones et al., 2003. Jones, R., Boyle, T., Pickard, P.: Objectworld: Helping novice programmers to succeed through a graphical objects-first approach. In: Proceedings of 4th Annual LTSN-ICS Conference, NUI Galwa, pp. 111–114 (2003)

Jonsson et al., 2005. Jonsson, T., Loghmani, P., Nadjm-Tehrani, S.: Evaluation of an authentic examination system (AES) for programming courses (August 12, 2005), http://www.hgur.se/activities/projects/financed_projects/i-j/jonsson_torbjorn_00_slutrapport.pdf

JUnit, 2002. JUnit: Testing resources for extreme programming (September 2002), http://www.junit.org

JUnit, 2005. JUnit: Junit (2005), http://www.junit.org

JUnit, 2007. JUnit: Testing resources for extreme programming (March 23, 2007), http://www.junit.org

Kaiser, 2001. Kaiser, W.: Become a programming picasso with jhotdraw (2001)(December 2007), http://www.javaworld.com/javaworld/jw-02-2001/jw-0216-jhotdraw.html

Kallin Westin and Nordström, 2001. Kallin Westin, L., Nordström, M.: Vad ska vi kunna det här för - kommer det på tentan? In: Lärarens liv - Vision och verklighet, Proceedings of Universitetspedagogisk konferens in Umeå, Umeå, Sweden, pp. 141–156 (2001)

Kallin Westin and Nordström, 2003. Kallin Westin, L., Nordström, M.: Supplemental instruction (si) - applied on the course object-oriented programming methodology. Technical Report UMINF 03.01, Department of Computer Science, Umeå University, Umeå, Sweden (2003)

Kallin Westin and Nordström, 2004. Kallin Westin, L., Nordström, M.: Teaching OO concepts - a new approach. In: Proceedings of the thirty-fourth Frontiers in Education Conference, Savannah, Georgia, United States (2004)

Karlsson, 1995. Karlsson, E.-A.: Software Reuse – A Holistic Approach. John Wiley & Sons, Inc., New York (1995)

Kay et al., 2000a. Kay, J., Barg, M., Fekete, A., Greening, T., Hollands, O., Kingston, J., Crawford, K.: Problem-based learning for foundation computer science courses. Computer Science Education 10(2), 109–128 (2000a)

Kay et al., 2000b. Kay, J., Barg, M., Fekete, A., Greening, T., Hollands, O., Kingston, J.H., Crawford, K.: Problem-based learning for foundation computer science courses. Computer Science Education 10(2), 1209–1218 (2000)

Keedy and Rosenberg, 1989. Keedy, J., Rosenberg, J.: Support for objects in the monads architecture. In: Proceedings of the Third International Workshop on Persistent Object Systems, Newcastle, New South Wales, Australia, pp. 392–405 (1989)

Keefe and Dick, 2004. Keefe, K., Dick, M.: Using extreme programming in a capstone project. In: Proceedings of the sixth conference on Australasian computing education, Dunedin, New Zealand, pp. 151–160 (2004)

Kinnunen, 2004. Kinnunen, P.: Interaction among university students in a PBL-group. PhD thesis, Helsinki University of Technology, Helsinki, Finland (2004)

Kinnunen and Malmi, 2002. Kinnunen, P., Malmi, L.: Problem based learning in introductory programming - does it scale up? In: Proceedings of Second Finnish/Baltic Sea Conference of Computer Science Education, Koli, Finland, pp. 38–42 (2002) Report A-2002-7

Kitchenham and Pfleeger, 1996. Kitchenham, B., Pfleeger, S.L.: Software quality: The elusive target. IEEE Software 13(1), 12–21 (1996)

Kjærsdam and Enemark, 1994. Kjærsdam, F., Enemark, S.: The Aalborg Experiment – Project Innovation in University Education. Aalborg University Press, Aalborg, Denmark (1994)

Knudsen and Madsen, 1988. Knudsen, J.L., Madsen, O.L.: Teaching object-oriented programming is more than teaching object-oriented programming languages. In: Gjessing, S., Nygaard, K. (eds.) ECOOP 1988. LNCS, vol. 322, pp. 21–40. Springer, Heidelberg (1988)

Knudsen and Madsen, 1996. Knudsen, J.L., Madsen, O.L.: Using object-orientation as a common basis for system development education. SIGPLAN Notices 31(12), 52–62 (1996)

Koffman and Wolz, 1999. Koffman, E., Wolz, U.: CS1 using Java language features gently. In: Proceedings of the fourth SIGCSE/SIGCUE Conference on Innovations and Technology in Computer Science Education, Cracow, Poland, pp. 40–43 (1999)

Kolb, 1984. Kolb, D.A.: Experiential Learning: Experience as the Source of Learning and Development. Prentice-Hall, Englewood Cliffs (1984)

Kölling, 1999a. Kölling, M.: The problem of teaching object-oriented programming, part 2: Environments. Journal of Object-Oriented Programming 11(9), 6–12 (1999)

Kölling, 1999b. Kölling, M.: Teaching object orientation with the blue environment. Journal of Object-Oriented Programming 12(2), 14–23 (1999b)

Kölling, 2003. Kölling, M.: The curse of hello world. In: Invited lecture at Workshop on Learning and Teaching Object-orientation - Scandinavian Perspectives, Oslo, Norway (2003)

Kölling and Barnes, 2004. Kölling, M., Barnes, D.J.: Enhancing apprentice-based learning of Java. In: Proceedings of the thirty-fifth SIGCSE technical symposium on Computer science education, Norfolk, Virginia, United States, pp. 286–290 (2004)

Kölling and Patterson, 2004. Kölling, M., Patterson, A.: Going interactive: Combining ad-hoc and regression testing. In: Eckstein, J., Baumeister, H. (eds.) XP 2004. LNCS, vol. 3092, pp. 270–273. Springer, Heidelberg (2004)

Kölling et al., 2003. Kölling, M., Quig, B., Patterson, A., Rosenberg, J.: The BlueJ system and its pedagogy. Journal of Computer Science Education 13(4), 249–268 (2003)

Kölling and Rosenberg, 2001. Kölling, M., Rosenberg, J.: Guidelines for teaching object orientation with Java. In: Proceedings of the 6th conference on Information Technology in Computer Science Education (ITiCSE 2001), Canterbury, England, pp. 33–36 (2001)

Korhonen and Malmi, 2000. Korhonen, A., Malmi, L.: Algorithm simulation with automatic assessment. In: Proceedings of the fifth annual SIGCSE/SIGCUE ITiCSE conference on Innovation and technology in computer science education, Helsinki, Finland, pp. 160–163 (2000)

Korhonen and Malmi, 2002. Korhonen, A., Malmi, L.: Internet-based training of data structures and algorithms at university education. In: Bobpry, J., Eteläpelto, A. (eds.) Collaboration and Learning in Virtual Environments, pp. 137–146. University of Jyväskylä, Finland (2002)

Korhonen et al., 2003. Korhonen, A., Malmi, L., Silvasti, P., Nikander, J., Tenhunen, P., Mård, P., Salonen, H., Karavirta, V.: TRAKLA2. computer program (2003) (December 2007), http://www.cs.hut.fi/Research/TRAKLA2/

Kristensen et al., 2001. Kristensen, J., Hansen, M., Rischel, H.: Teaching object-oriented programming on top of functional programming. In: Proceedings of the thirthy-first Frontiers in Education Conference, Reno, Navada, United States, pp. 15–20 (2001)

Kumar, 2003. Kumar, A.N.: The effect of closed labs in computer science i: an assessment. Journal of Computing in Small Colleges 18(5), 40–48 (2003)

Lambrix and Kamkar, 1998. Lambrix, P., Kamkar, M.: Computer science as an integrated part of engineering education. In: Third ACM SIGCSE/SIGCUE Conference on Integrating Technology into Computer Science Education, Dublin, Ireland, pp. 153–156 (1998)

Lane and VanLehn, 2005. Lane, H.C., Van Lehn, K.: Intention-based scoring: an approach to measuring success at solving the composition problem. In: Proceedings of the thirty-sixth SIGCSE technical symposium on Computer science education, St. Louis, Missouri United States, pp. 373–377 (2005)

Lappo, 2002. Lappo, P.: No pain, no XP: Observations on teaching and mentoring extreme programming to university students. In: Proceedings of the Third International Conference on extreme Programming and Agile Processes in Software Engineering, Alghero, Sardinia, Italy, pp. 35–38 (2002)

Lauvås, 1996. Lauvås, P.: Studenterevalueringer som hjælpemiddel til forbedring af undervisningen. In: Jacobsen, Wied, R. (eds.) Kursusevaluering, pp. 47–60. Evalueringscenteret, København, Denmark (1996)

Lauvås, P., 2003. Lauvås, P.: Formativ og summativ vurdering: Mappevinden blæser i nord - men i hvilken retning (in Danish) (March 14, 2003), http://www.ipn.dk/log/upload/ipn/nr12-2003.pdf

Lave and Wenger, 1991. Lave, J., Wenger, E.: Situated Learning: Legitimate Peripheral Participation. Cambridge University Press, Cambridge (1991)

Levy et al., 2003. Levy, R.B.B., Ben-Ari, M., Uronen, P.A.: The jeliot 2000 program animation system. Computers & Education 1, 1–15 (2003)

Lewis, 2000. Lewis, J.: Myths about object-orientation and its pedagogy. In: Proceedings of the thirty-first SIGCSE technical symposium on Computer science education, Austin, Texas, United States, pp. 245–249 (2000)

Linn and Clancy, 1992. Linn, M.C., Clancy, M.J.: The case for case studies of programming problems. Communications of the ACM 35(3), 121–132 (1992)

Lister, 2004. Lister, R., et al.: A multi-national study of reading and tracing skills in novice programmers. SIGCSE Bulletin (Association for Computing Machinery, Special Interest Group on Computer Science Education) 36(4), 119–150 (2004)

Ma et al., 1996. Ma, W.H., Lee, Y.J., Du, D.H.C., McCahill: Video-based hypermedia for education-on-demand. In: Proceedings of the Fourth ACM International Conference on Multimedia, Boston, Massachusetts, United States, pp. 449–450 (1996)

Madden and Chambers, 2002. Madden, M., Chambers, D.: Evaluation of student attitudes to learning the Java language. In: Proceedings of the inaugural conference on the Principles and Practice of programming, Dublin, Ireland (2002)

Madsen et al., 1993. Madsen, O.L., Møller-Pedersen, B., Nygaard, K.: Object-oriented programming in the BETA programming language. ACM Press/Addison-Wesley Publishing Co., New York (1993)

Malmi et al., 2005. Malmi, L., Karavirta, V., Korhonen, A., Nikander, J.: Experiences on automatically assessed algorithm simulation exercises with different resubmission policies. Journal of Educational Resources in Computing 5(3): article no 7 (2005)

Malmi et al., 2004. Malmi, L., Karavirta, V., Korhonen, A., Nikander, J., Seppälä, O., Silvasti, P.: Visual algorithm simulation exercise system with automatic assessment: TRAKLA2. Informatics in Education 3(2), 267–288 (2004)

Malmi et al., 2002. Malmi, L., Korhonen, A., Saikkonen, R.: Experiences in automatic assessment on mass courses and issues for designing virtual courses. In: Proceedings of the seventh annual conference on Innovation and technology in computer science education, Aarhus, Denmark, pp. 55–59 (2002)

McCartney et al., 2005. McCartney, R., Mostrom, J., Sanders, K., Seppala, O.: Take note: The effectiveness of novice programmers annotations on examinations. Informatics in Education 4(1), 69–86 (2005)

McCracken et al., 2001. McCracken, M., Almstrum, V., Diaz, D., Guzdial, M., Hagan, D., Kolikant, Y.B.-D., Laxer, C., Thomas, L., Utting, I., Wilusz, T.: A multi-national, multi-institutional study of assessment of programming skills of first-year cs students. In: ITiCSE-WGR 2001: Working group reports from ITiCSE on Innovation and technology in computer science education, Canterbury, UK, pp. 125–180 (2001)

Mcgettrick et al., 2005. Mcgettrick, A., Boyle, R., Ibbett, R., Lloyd, J., Lovegrove, G., Mander, K.: Grand challenges in computing: Education—a summary. The Computer Journal 48(1), 42–48 (2005)

Meyer, 1992. Meyer, B.: Applying design by contract. Computer Journal 25(10), 40–51 (1992)

Meyer, 1997. Meyer, B.: Object-oriented software construction, 2nd edn. Prentice-Hall, Inc., Upper Saddle River (1997)

Millwood, 1996. Millwood, R.: Building learning for the future from lessons in the past. In: Beyond the Classroom (colloquium organized by the Humanities Computing Unit, University of Oxford), Oxford, United Kingdom (1996), (December 2007), http://www.hcu.ox.ac.uk/beyond/classroom/richard.html

Milner et al., 1997. Milner, R., Tofte, M., Harper, R., MacQueen, D.: The Definition of Standard ML (Revised). MIT Press, Cambridge (1997)

MIT, 2006. MIT: Structure and interpretation of computer programs, video lectures (2006) (February 17, 2007), http://www.swiss.ai.mit.edu/classes/6.001/abelson-sussman-lectures

Mugridge et al., 2003. Mugridge, R., MacDonald, B., Roop, P.S., Tempero, E.D.: Five challenges in teaching XP. In: Marchesi, M., Succi, G. (eds.) Proceedings of fourth International Conference on Extreme Programming and Agile Processes in Software Engineering, Genova, Italy, pp. 386–393 (2003)

Müller and Tichy, 2001. Müller, M.M., Tichy, W.F.: Case study: extreme programming in a university environment. In: Proceedings of the twenty-third International Conference on Software Engineering, Toronto, Ontario, Canada, pp. 537–544 (2001)

Myers and McCaulley, 1985. Myers, I., McCaulley, M.: Manual: A Guide to the Development and Use of the Myers-Briggs Type Indicator. Consulting Psychologist Press, Mountain View, California (1985)

Nielsen and Kvale, 1997. Nielsen, K., Kvale, S.: Current issues of apprenticeship. Nordisk Pedagogik 17, 130–139 (1997)

Noll, 2002. Noll, J.: Some observations of extreme programming for student projects. In: position paper at the first Workshop on Empirical Evaluation of Agile Processes, Chicago, Illinois, United States (2002)

Nordström, 2007. Nordström, M.: PigLatinJava - troubleshooting examples. Technical Report UMINF-07.26, Department of Computer Science, UmeåUniversity (2007)

Nordström and Kallin Westin, 2006. Nordström, M., Kallin Westin, L.: Si - small scale advantages. Technical Report UMINF 2006-23, Dept. of Computing Science, Umeå University, Sweden (2006)

Norman and Spohrer, 1996. Norman, D., Spohrer, J.: Learner-centered education. Communications of the ACM 39(4), 24–27 (1996)

Novak and Cañas, 2006. Novak, J., Cañas, A.: The theory underlying concept maps and how to construct them. Technical Report IHMC CmapTools 2006-01, Florida Institute for Human and Machine Cognition, Pensacola, Florida, United States (2006)

Nuutila and Törmä, 2004. Nuutila, E., Törmä, S.: Text graphs: Accurate concept mapping with well-defined meaning. In: Concept Maps: Theory, Methodology, Technology. Proceedings of the First International Conference on Concept Mapping, Pamplona, Spain, pp. 477–485 (2004)

Nuutila et al., 2005. Nuutila, E., Törmä, S., Malmi, L.: Pbl and computer programming - the seven steps method with adaptations. Computer Science Education 15(2), 123–142 (2005)

Oldham, 2005. Oldham, J.D.: What happens after python in CS1? Journal of Computing in Small Colleges 20(6), 7–13 (2005)

OMG., 2003. OMG, UML 2.0 superstructure specification. Object Management Group (2003)

Papert, 1980. Papert, S.: Mindstorms: children, computers, and powerful ideas. Basic Books, Inc., New York (1980)

Patterson et al., 2003. Patterson, A., Kölling, M., Rosenberg, J.: Introducing unit testing with BlueJ. In: Proceedings of the eighth annual conference on Innovation and technology in computer science education, Thessaloniki, Greece, pp. 11–15 (2003)

Pattis, 1993. Pattis, R.E.: The procedures early approach in CS1: a heresy. In: Proceedings of the twenty-fourth SIGCSE technical symposium on Computer science education, Indianapolis, Indiana, United States, pp. 122–126 (1993)

Phillips, 2000. Phillips, D.: Constructivism in Education. Opinions and Second Opinions on Controversial Issues. The University of Chicago Press, Chicago, Illinois, United States (2000)

Ragonis and Ben-Ari, 2005. Ragonis, N., Ben-Ari, M.: On understanding the statics and dynamics of object-oriented programs. In: Proceedings SIGCSE 2005, St. Louis, Missouri, United States. (2005)

Reek, 1995. Reek, M.M.: A top-down approach to teaching programming. In: Proceedings of the twenty-sixth SIGCSE technical symposium on Computer science education, Nashville, Tennessee, United States, pp. 6–9 (1995)

Reges, 2000. Reges, S.: Conservatively radical Java in CS1. In: Proceedings of the thirty-first SIGCSE technical symposium on Computer science education, Austin, Texas, United States, pp. 85–89 (2000)

Roberts et al., 2006. Roberts, E., Bruce, K., Cutler, R., Cross, J., Grissom, S., Klee, K., Rodger, S., Trees, F., Utting, I., Yellin, F.: The ACM Java task force version 1.0 (2006) (March 22, 2007), http://jtf.acm.org/

Robins et al., 2003. Robins, A., Rountree, J., Rountree, N.: Learning and teaching programming: A review and discussion. Journal of Computer Science Education 13(2), 449–450 (2003)

Rosenberg and Kölling, 1997. Rosenberg, J., Kölling, M.: Testing object-oriented programs: Making it simple. In: Proceedings of the Twenty-Eighth SIGCSE Technical Symposium on Computer Science Education, San Jose, California, United States, pp. 77–81 (1997)

Ruefli and Leibrock, 1999. Ruefli, T., Leibrock, L.: Teaching information technology to mba students (1999) (March 14, 2007),
http://www.utexas.edu/cc/newsletter/may99/mba.html

Rumbaugh et al., 2004. Rumbaugh, J., Jacobson, I., Booch, G.: Unified Modeling Language Reference Manual, 2nd edn. Pearson Higher Education, London (2004)

Schmidt, 1983. Schmidt, H.: Problem-based learning: Rational and description. Medical Education 17, 11–16 (1983)

Schmolitzky, 2004. Schmolitzky, A.: objects first, interfaces next or interfaces before inheritance. In: OOPSLA 2004: Companion to the nineteenth annual ACM SIGPLAN conference on Object-oriented programming systems, languages, and applications, Vancouver, British Columbia, Canada, pp. 64–67 (2004)

Shaffer, 1986. Shaffer, D.: The use of logo in an introductory computer science course. SIGCSE Bulletin (Association for Computing Machinery, Special Interest Group on Computer Science Education) 18(4), 28–31 (1986)

Shukla and Williams, 2002. Shukla, A., Williams, L.: Adapting extreme programming for a core software engineering course. In: Proceedings of the fifteenth Conference on Software Engineering Education and Training, Covington, Kentucky, United States, pp. 184–191 (2002)

Sicilia, 2006. Sicilia, M.: Strategies for teaching object-oriented concepts with Java. Computer Science Education 16(1), 1–18 (2006)

SIGCSE-members, 2005. SIGCSE-members, Archives of SIGCSE-members acm.org. (2005) (March 22, 2006),
http://listserv.acm.org/archives/sigcse-members.html

Simon, 1969. Simon, H.: The Sciences of the Artificial. The MIT Press, Cambridge (1969)

Smith et al., 1999. Smith, T., Ruocco, A., Jansen, B.: Digital video in education. In: Proceedings of the Thirtieth SIGCSE Technical Symposium on Computer Science Education, New Orleans, Louisiana, United States, pp. 122–126 (1999)

Snyder, 2004. Snyder, L.: Fluency with Information Technology - Skills, Concepts and Capabilities. Pearson Education, Upper Saddle River (2004)

Soloway, 1986. Soloway, E.: Learning to program = learning to construct mechanisms and explanations.. Communications of the ACM 29(9), 850–858 (1986)

Soloway and Spohrer, 1988. Soloway, E., Spohrer, J.C.: Studying the Novice Programmer. Lawrence Erlbaum Associates, Inc., Mahwah (1988)

Spohrer and Soloway, 1986a. Spohrer, J., Soloway, E.: Analyzing the high-frequency bugs in novice programs. In: Soloway, E., Iyengar, S. (eds.) Empirical studies of programmers, pp. 230–251. Ablex Publishing Corporation, Washington, District of Columbia, United States (1986)

Spohrer and Soloway, 1986b. Spohrer, J.C., Soloway, E.: Novice mistakes: Are the folk wisdoms correct? Communications of the ACM 29(7), 624–632 (1986b)

Steimann et al., 2003. Steimann, F., Gößner, J., Mück, T.A.: Filleting XP for educational purposes. In: Marchesi, M., Succi, G. (eds.) Proceedings of fourth International Conference on Extreme Programming and Agile Processes in Software Engineering, Genova, Italy, pp. 386–393 (2003)

Stephenson and West, 1998. Stephenson, C., West, T.: Language choice and key concepts in introductory computer science courses. Journal of Research in Computing Education 31(1), 89–95 (1998)

Tewari and Gitlin, 1994. Tewari, R., Gitlin, D.: On object-oriented libraries in the undergraduate curriculum: importance and effectiveness. In: Proceedings of the twenty-fifth SIGCSE symposium on Computer science education, Phoenix, Arizona, United States, pp. 319–323 (1994)

The RAISE language group, 1992. The RAISE language group. The RAISE Specification Language. Prentice-Hall, New York (1992)

Thimbleby, 1999. Thimbleby, H.: A critique of Java. Software - Practice and Experience 29(5), 457–478 (1999)

Thompson, 1996. Thompson, S.: HASKELL The craft of Functional programming. Addison-Wesley, Harlow (1996)

Turk, 1997. Turk, M.: Introducing object-orientation to experienced procedural programmers. In: Proceedings of the Second Australasian Conference of Computer Science Education, Melbourne, Australia (1997)

Ungar and Smith, 1987. Ungar, D., Smith, R.: Self: The power of simplicity. In: OOPSLA 1987 Proceedings, Orlando, Florida, United States, pp. 227–241 (1987)

Wake, 2001. Wake, W.: Extreme programming explored. Addison-Wesley Longman, Boston (2001)

Wegner et al., 1996. Wegner, P., Roberts, E., Rada, R., Tucker, A.B.: Strategic directions in computer science education. ACM Computing Survay 28(4), 836–845 (1996)

West, 2004. West, D.: Object Thinking. Microsoft Press, Redmond (2004)

Westfall, 2001. Westfall, R.: Hello, world considered harmful. Communications of the ACM 44(10), 129–130 (2001)

Wilson, 2001. Wilson, D.: Teaching XP: a case study. In: Proceedings of XP Universe 2001, Raleigh, North Carolina, United States (2001)

Woods et al., 1996. Woods, D., Hall, F., Eyes, C., Hrymak, A., Duncan-Hewitt, W.: Tutored versus tutorless groups in problem-based learning. American Journal of Pharmaceutical Education 60, 231–238 (1996)

Zull, 2002. Zull, J.: The Art of Changing the Brain: Enriching Teaching by Exploring the Biology of Learning. Stylus Publishing, Sterling, Virginia (2002)

Author Index

Lecture Notes in Computer Science

Sublibrary 2: Programming and Software Engineering

Vol. 4634: H. Riis Nielson, G. Filé (Eds.), Static Analysis. XI, 469 pages. 2007.

Vol. 4620: A. Rashid, M. Aksit (Eds.), Transactions on Aspect-Oriented Software Development III. IX, 201 pages. 2007.

Vol. 4615: R. de Lemos, C. Gacek, A. Romanovsky (Eds.), Architecting Dependable Systems IV. XIV, 435 pages. 2007.

Vol. 4610: B. Xiao, L.T. Yang, J. Ma, C. Muller-Schloer, Y. Hua (Eds.), Autonomic and Trusted Computing. XVIII, 571 pages. 2007.

Vol. 4609: E. Ernst (Ed.), ECOOP 2007 – Object-Oriented Programming. XIII, 625 pages. 2007.

Vol. 4608: H.W. Schmidt, I. Crnković, G.T. Heineman, J.A. Stafford (Eds.), Component-Based Software Engineering. XII, 283 pages. 2007.

Vol. 4591: J. Davies, J. Gibbons (Eds.), Integrated Formal Methods. IX, 660 pages. 2007.

Vol. 4589: J. Münch, P. Abrahamsson (Eds.), Product-Focused Software Process Improvement. XII, 414 pages. 2007.

Vol. 4574: J. Derrick, J. Vain (Eds.), Formal Techniques for Networked and Distributed Systems – FORTE 2007. XI, 375 pages. 2007.

Vol. 4556: C. Stephanidis (Ed.), Universal Access in Human-Computer Interaction, Part III. XXII, 1020 pages. 2007.

Vol. 4555: C. Stephanidis (Ed.), Universal Access in Human-Computer Interaction, Part II. XXII, 1066 pages. 2007.

Vol. 4554: C. Stephanidis (Ed.), Universal Acess in Human Computer Interaction, Part I. XXII, 1054 pages. 2007.

Vol. 4553: J.A. Jacko (Ed.), Human-Computer Interaction, Part IV. XXIV, 1225 pages. 2007.

Vol. 4552: J.A. Jacko (Ed.), Human-Computer Interaction, Part III. XXI, 1038 pages. 2007.

Vol. 4551: J.A. Jacko (Ed.), Human-Computer Interaction, Part II. XXIII, 1253 pages. 2007.

Vol. 4550: J.A. Jacko (Ed.), Human-Computer Interaction, Part I. XXIII, 1240 pages. 2007.

Vol. 4542: P. Sawyer, B. Paech, P. Heymans (Eds.), Requirements Engineering: Foundation for Software Quality. IX, 384 pages. 2007.

Vol. 4536: G. Concas, E. Damiani, M. Scotto, G. Succi (Eds.), Agile Processes in Software Engineering and Extreme Programming. XV, 276 pages. 2007.

Vol. 4530: D.H. Akehurst, R. Vogel, R.F. Paige (Eds.), Model Driven Architecture - Foundations and Applications. X, 219 pages. 2007.

Vol. 4523: Y.-H. Lee, H.-N. Kim, J. Kim, Y.W. Park, L.T. Yang, S.W. Kim (Eds.), Embedded Software and Systems. XIX, 829 pages. 2007.

Vol. 4498: N. Abdennahder, F. Kordon (Eds.), Reliable Software Technologies - Ada-Europe 2007. XII, 247 pages. 2007.

Vol. 4486: M. Bernardo, J. Hillston (Eds.), Formal Methods for Performance Evaluation. VII, 469 pages. 2007.

Vol. 4470: Q. Wang, D. Pfahl, D.M. Raffo (Eds.), Software Process Dynamics and Agility. XI, 346 pages. 2007.

Vol. 4468: M.M. Bonsangue, E.B. Johnsen (Eds.), Formal Methods for Open Object-Based Distributed Systems. X, 317 pages. 2007.

Vol. 4467: A.L. Murphy, J. Vitek (Eds.), Coordination Models and Languages. X, 325 pages. 2007.

Vol. 4454: Y. Gurevich, B. Meyer (Eds.), Tests and Proofs. IX, 217 pages. 2007.

Vol. 4444: T. Reps, M. Sagiv, J. Bauer (Eds.), Program Analysis and Compilation, Theory and Practice. X, 361 pages. 2007.

Vol. 4440: B. Liblit, Cooperative Bug Isolation. XV, 101 pages. 2007.

Vol. 4408: R. Choren, A. Garcia, H. Giese, H.-f. Leung, C. Lucena, A. Romanovsky (Eds.), Software Engineering for Multi-Agent Systems V. XII, 233 pages. 2007.

Vol. 4406: W. De Meuter (Ed.), Advances in Smalltalk. VII, 157 pages. 2007.

Vol. 4405: L. Padgham, F. Zambonelli (Eds.), Agent-Oriented Software Engineering VII. XII, 225 pages. 2007.

Vol. 4401: N. Guelfi, D. Buchs (Eds.), Rapid Integration of Software Engineering Techniques. IX, 177 pages. 2007.

Vol. 4385: K. Coninx, K. Luyten, K.A. Schneider (Eds.), Task Models and Diagrams for Users Interface Design. XI, 355 pages. 2007.

Vol. 4383: E. Bin, A. Ziv, S. Ur (Eds.), Hardware and Software, Verification and Testing. XII, 235 pages. 2007.

Vol. 4379: M. Südholt, C. Consel (Eds.), Object-Oriented Technology. VIII, 157 pages. 2007.

Vol. 4364: T. Kühne (Ed.), Models in Software Engineering. XI, 332 pages. 2007.

Vol. 4355: J. Julliand, O. Kouchnarenko (Eds.), B 2007: Formal Specification and Development in B. XIII, 293 pages. 2006.

Vol. 4354: M. Hanus (Ed.), Practical Aspects of Declarative Languages. X, 335 pages. 2006.

Vol. 4350: M. Clavel, F. Durán, S. Eker, P. Lincoln, N. Martí-Oliet, J. Meseguer, C. Talcott, All About Maude - A High-Performance Logical Framework. XXII, 797 pages. 2007.

Vol. 4348: S. Tucker Taft, R.A. Duff, R.L. Brukardt, E. Plödereder, P. Leroy, Ada 2005 Reference Manual. XXII, 765 pages. 2006.

Vol. 4346: L. Brim, B.R. Haverkort, M. Leucker, J. van de Pol (Eds.), Formal Methods: Applications and Technology. X, 363 pages. 2007.

Vol. 4344: V. Gruhn, F. Oquendo (Eds.), Software Architecture. X, 245 pages. 2006.

Vol. 4340: R. Prodan, T. Fahringer, Grid Computing. XXIII, 317 pages. 2007.

Vol. 4336: V.R. Basili, H.D. Rombach, K. Schneider, B. Kitchenham, D. Pfahl, R.W. Selby (Eds.), Empirical Software Engineering Issues. XVII, 193 pages. 2007.